IMAGES
of America

RUSTON

I0807685

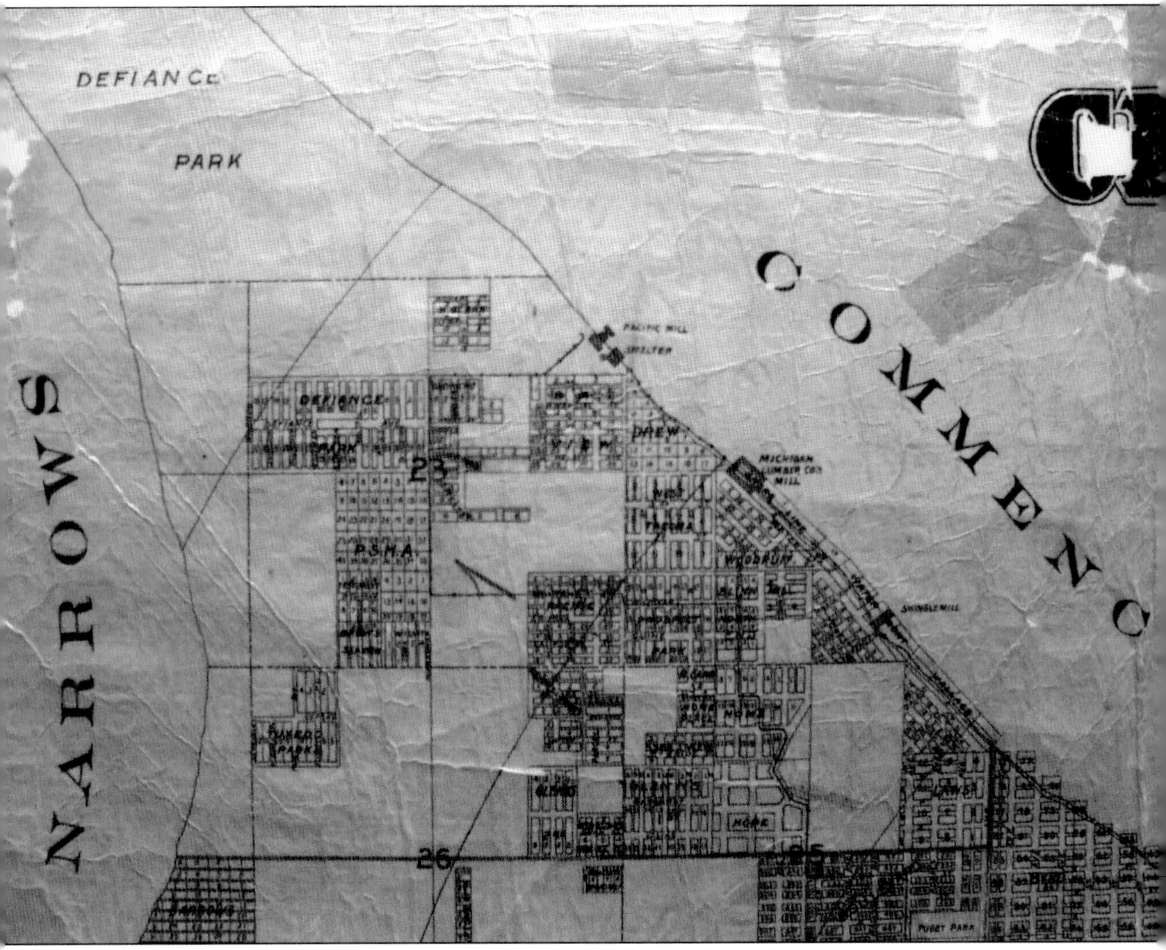

This 1880s map of Commencement Bay shows just how isolated the early smelting operation was from the larger city of Tacoma. Most of the area had not even been assigned parcels or platted. There was only limited access by rail or water. The smelter complex laid the seed for the town of Ruston, which incorporated in 1906. (Courtesy of Tacoma Public Library.)

On the Cover: This 1931 photograph captures the community sentiment heralded in local newspapers of the time, when industrial might was glorified, and young boys dreamed of even bigger conquests. Both Ruston and Tacoma took pride in having one of the world's tallest smokestacks, part of the growing smelting operations of the Guggenheim empire's American Smelting and Refining Company (ASARCO) Tacoma Plant. (Courtesy of Tacoma Public Library.)

IMAGES
of America

RUSTON

Karen Pickett

ARCADIA
PUBLISHING

ISBN 978-0-7385-7574-2

Published by Arcadia Publishing
Charleston, South Carolina

Printed in the United States of America

Library of Congress Control Number: 2011924616

For all general information, please contact Arcadia Publishing:
Telephone 843-853-2070
Fax 843-853-0044
E-mail sales@arcadiapublishing.com
For customer service and orders:
Toll-Free 1-888-313-2665

Visit us on the Internet at www.arcadiapublishing.com

To the blue-collar families who were not afraid of speaking their minds and who would make any sacrifice to build this town

Contents

Acknowledgments

First and foremost, let me acknowledge the many contributions from Ruston residents who give to our community every day and gave so generously to make this book a reality. Mayor Bruce Hopkins and clerk Myriah Mesa allowed easy access to town archives. Numerous neighbors shared their pictures. And a special thanks goes to Don and Beth Torbet, for their collection of decades of photographs, news clippings, and memories that they so graciously donated to this effort.

I also wish to thank my University of Washington Tacoma professors, who fueled my love of history and gave me the chance to write about Ruston before it was cool. My deepest gratitude goes to Mike Allen, patriot and rodeo historian extraordinaire; Michael Sullivan, lover of buildings and times past and one of the best storytellers of all time; and Michael Kucher, whose environmental history class awakened the dream.

I want to acknowledge the influence of Tom Aldrich, my mentor at ASARCO. His love for the people of ASARCO profoundly influenced my career and deepened my understanding of their impact on Ruston. Tom taught me integrity, honesty, and commitment and gave me confidence to pursue my heart. Finally, I need to thank my family for their patience as I've devoted myself to this project. They are my world.

This endeavor confirms the treasures we have in the Northwest Room at the Tacoma Public Library and the Washington State Historical Society archives, housed in Tacoma. I offer my humble thanks to the courteous and knowledgeable staff who helped me research and shared their stories of Ruston.

Unless otherwise noted, the images shared here appear courtesy of the Tacoma Public Library (TPL), the Washington State Historical Society (WSHS), the Town of Ruston archives (TR), and the author's personal collection (KP).

Introduction

Images capture a moment in time—sometimes caught with a camera, some only in memory. Shared images build a community. Stories and photographs give glimpses of another time and connect generations. When a community has experienced upheaval as tremendous as that seen by this little town of 750 residents, such images are easily lost or fragmented. So it is in Ruston, Washington. There is little evidence left of Ruston's past: buildings are demolished, housing is new, and local culture has changed dramatically.

Just as individual families share their heritage, communities too share memories and a history. Generations build one upon the other, connecting the past to the future in faces and images. Sandwiched between an old, dark tunnel and Point Defiance Park, Ruston stands in many ways as one of the last vestiges of small-town America, despite its dramatic changes. Community connections still run strong in this five-block-by-five-block town, but the link to the past dims as the area transitions from company town to upper-class enclave. The hope is for this book to build connections both in the here and now and to the past.

Once an isolated encampment near Point Defiance Park, Ruston's first buildings were part of a large industrial complex used to smelt ore. Raw dirt, containing lead and copper, was brought by rail and ship, melted in huge furnaces, and the purified metal was poured off and shipped out for use in wire, bullets, or for other everyday conveniences. Housing and shops soon grew to support the hardworking men. In time, families moved in, a schoolhouse was built, and a community was born.

After a couple of decades of operation, it was clear that Tacoma would soon control utilities vital to smelter operations, like electrical power. Owner and manager W.R. Rust knew that business concerns would be heard more clearly by a small, loyal municipality than by the larger city. Rust organized meetings, had smelter lawyers draw up the necessary papers to incorporate as a separate town, and took the issue to the voters. After a successful election, residents named their new town Ruston in his honor when they officially incorporated on October 22, 1906.

There was a thriving hotel business in Ruston by 1910. The census from that year shows six addresses had over 10 people listed as boarders. Another seven houses had at least five roomers. These in-house communities were often comprised of immigrants of the same origin. The area around North Forty-ninth and Baltimore Streets had 17 homes with boarders, all born in Austria, Sweden, or Norway. Most spoke Slovenian or Croatian, with only one or two in the group who could speak English. Almost everyone worked at the smelter. The only exception was a boardinghouse with 17 Japanese immigrants who worked at a local sawmill.

In 1910, North Fifty-first Street had at least two major hotels located at the bottom of the hill near the smelter gates. In one hotel was a mixture of boarders who were primarily born in Midwestern states and worked at a variety of local businesses. The other had 18 residents from Hungary who spoke Romanian. The area north of Fifty-first Street appears to have been the upper-class neighborhood, with single-family homes that had few extra occupants.

Up the hill from the hotels, a commercial district took shape around the intersection of North Fifty-first and Pearl Streets. These stores were in addition to commercial businesses located next to the first school on the 5200 block of North Shirley Street. Most residents lived, worked, and played within the five-block-by-five-block square town limits. Travel to Tacoma was only available by rail, boat, or "an ill-kept wagon road." To help keep the population entertained, the building that is now Coles Tavern on North Fifty-first Street began a vaudeville theater with a stage lit by kerosene lamps. The neighboring structure, now an antique mall, was a drugstore, complete with a soda fountain, for many years. A grocery store operated across the street in the building that is now the Antique Sandwich Company.

One

Community Birthed

Ruston's legacy comes from the Industrial Revolution, born of man's pride in taming the Earth and using its riches to enhance his own life. The need for metal was great during the industrial expansion of the late 19th century. For that metal to be useful, it first had to be mined and purified. By this time, the ancient craft of melting ore to remove the impurities had taken on gigantic proportions with huge industrial complexes called smelters.

During Tacoma's boom years of the 1880s, several local businessmen formed the Tacoma Milling & Smelting Company and began the process of building a lead smelter. The group elected wealthy St. Paul native Dennis Ryan as president, and construction began. The first 50 employees fired up the furnace in 1880 and began melting metal ores that were easily shipped by water and rail to the fledging camp on Ruston's shore. Lumber was scavenged from driftwood as much as possible, and the shoreline began to expand as the smelting by-product, slag, was poured into the bay.

Ruston's tiny shoreline housed many businesses by the turn of the century. Besides the smelter, a lumber mill continued to operate to the north and a brickyard to the south. On the far side of the brickyard, just outside of town, early insurance maps show a Japanese housing facility, perhaps to lodge mill employees. The former military reservation at Point Defiance had been opened to the community for use as a park at the northern edge of town, creating a new destination point and bringing visitors via rail, and later trolley car lines, down Pearl Street.

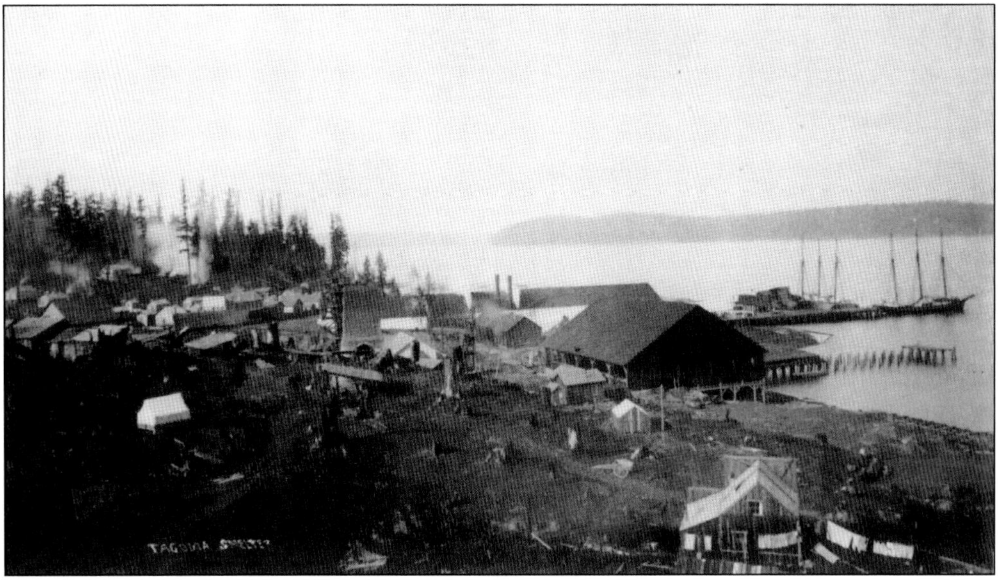

This 1888 image is the earliest known photograph of the smelter, still under construction. The first stack is half built, but docks are already in place. A map from this era notes the buildings on the far hillside, and the logs visible in the water beyond the main building are part of Pacific Mill. The shadow of Vashon Island lies in the distance, looking much the same as today. (WSHS.)

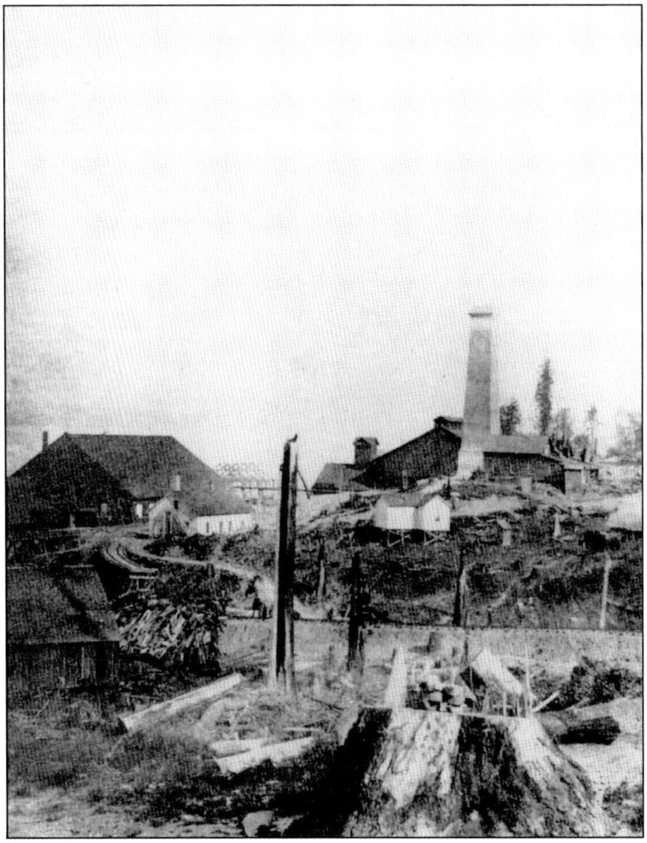

From 1889, this grainy image shows the just-completed smelter complex with a short stack, surrounded by large buildings used to process lead ore. Old-growth timber had clearly been harvested in the area and was probably used to construct smelter buildings. To the left is a rail line used to ship in ore and carry out the finished product. (TPL.)

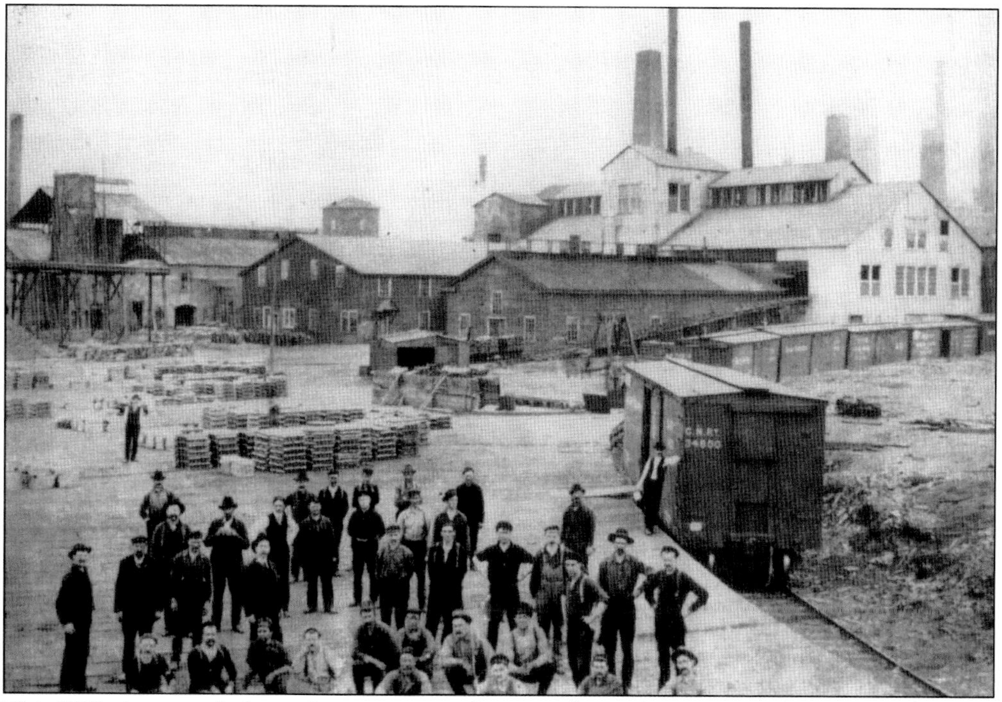

This 1910 photograph shows the growing smelter complex with various stacks, an active rail line with material ready to ship, and men to carry out the work. The smelter was once a source of community pride and good wages for men emigrating from Europe. Those wages paid passage for family members to eventually settle in Ruston. (TPL.)

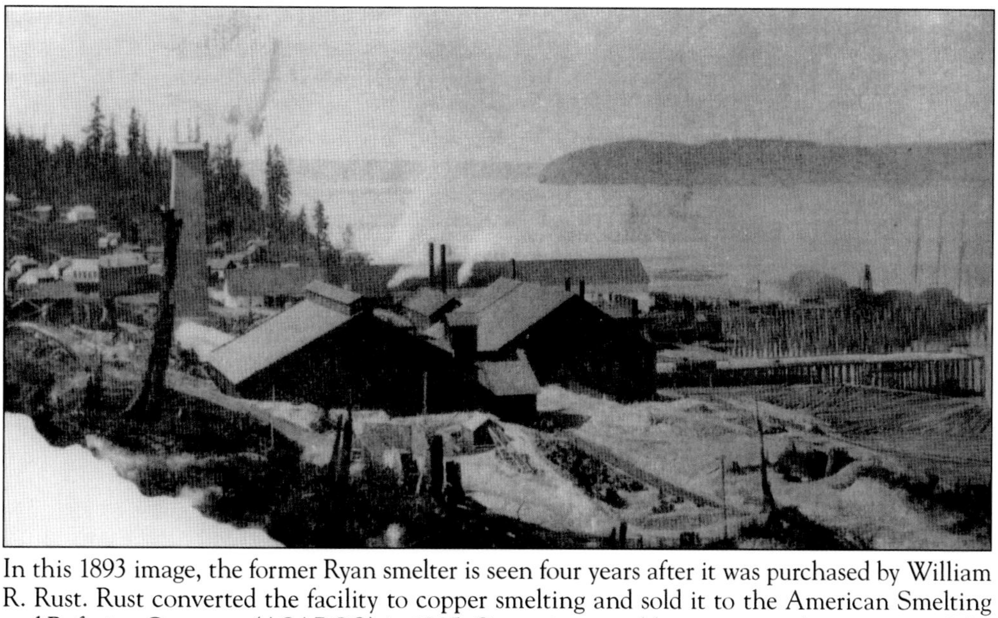

In this 1893 image, the former Ryan smelter is seen four years after it was purchased by William R. Rust. Rust converted the facility to copper smelting and sold it to the American Smelting and Refining Company (ASARCO) in 1905. Operations would soon grow to become one of the leading producers of copper in the world. (TPL.)

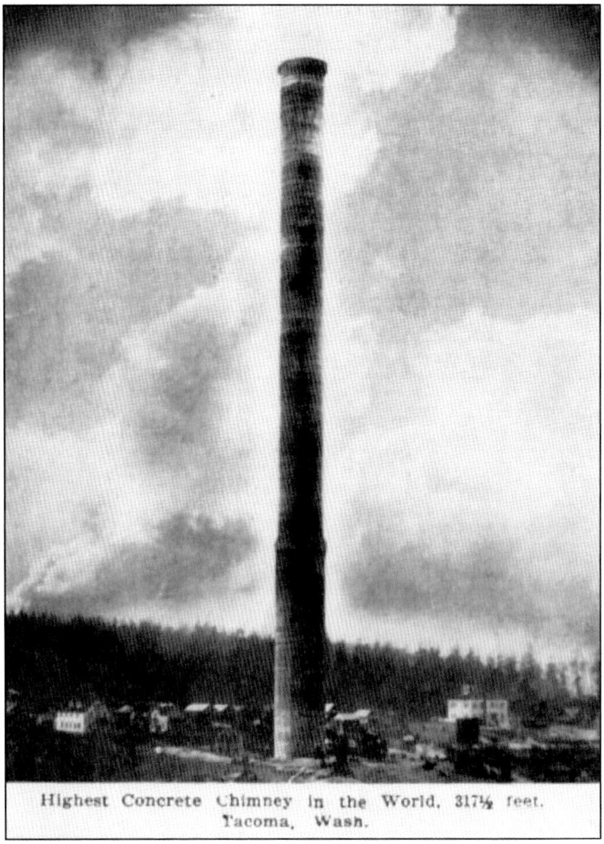

This 1906 photograph shows the main concrete smelter stack (completed the previous year), the largest in the world at 317.5 feet. Bragging rights were hard to hold during this era of worldwide industrial expansion. Soon, another smelter built a taller stack, only to be outdone a few years later, in 1917, by an even taller stack in Ruston. (TPL.)

Only a small percentage of purified ore could be skimmed from each molten batch of ore. The remaining fiery mass of slag was poured into the adjacent bay, extending the shoreline to house expanding operations. In this 1909-era photograph, railcars of slag were dumped by hand. Pictured are, from left to right, M. Motorman, helper ? Dunbar, ? Pero, and ? Lyons. (TR.)

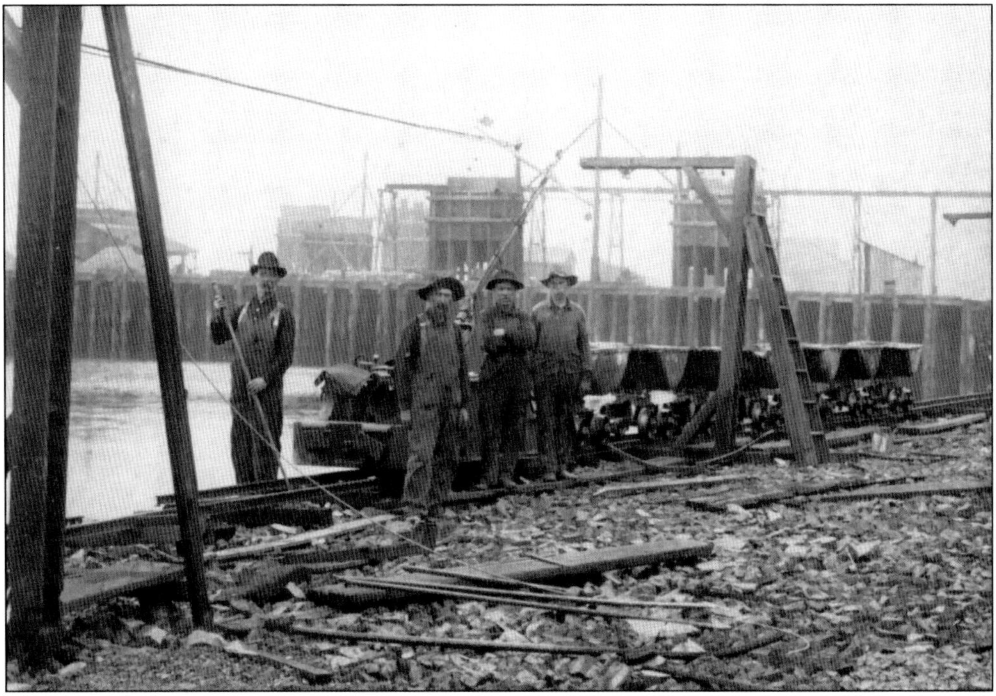

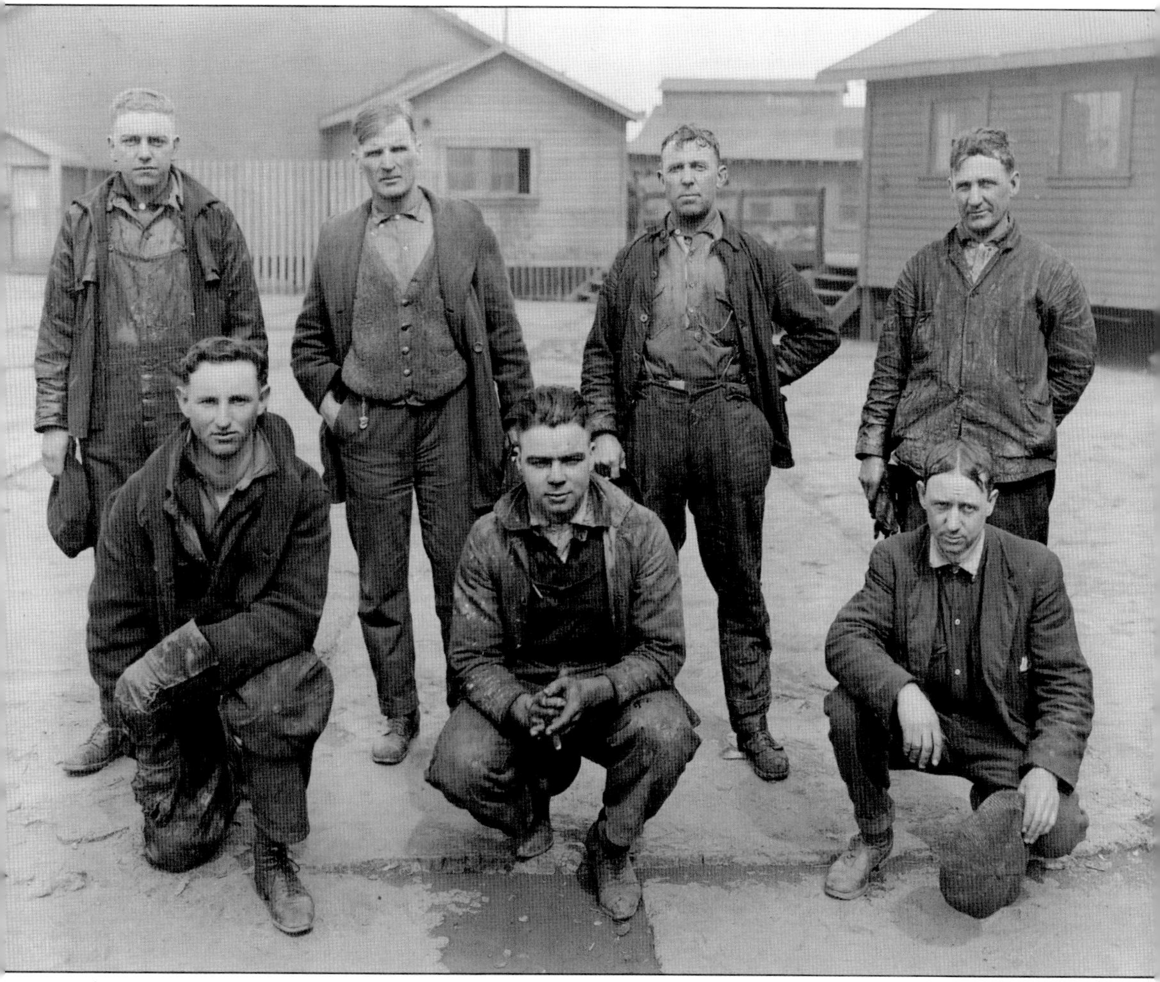

This arresting 1906 photograph of an unnamed smelter crew typifies the men of the time. There are clear differences in demeanor and dress—from the absence of work gloves to smiles—and a wide age range indicates an interesting crew. These men may have lived in the many hotels and boardinghouses just outside the smelter gates. As the town incorporated this same year, men like these would have voted in that first Ruston election. The 1905 city directory lists the Bayview Boarding House at 5317 North Fifty-first Street at the bottom of the Fifty-first Street hill. The building was later known as the Bayview Hotel or Bayview Rooms. A 1923 news story notes local law enforcement's struggle battling bootlegging and booze at this location. The building was closed in the 1960s and demolished in the early 1970s. (WSHS.)

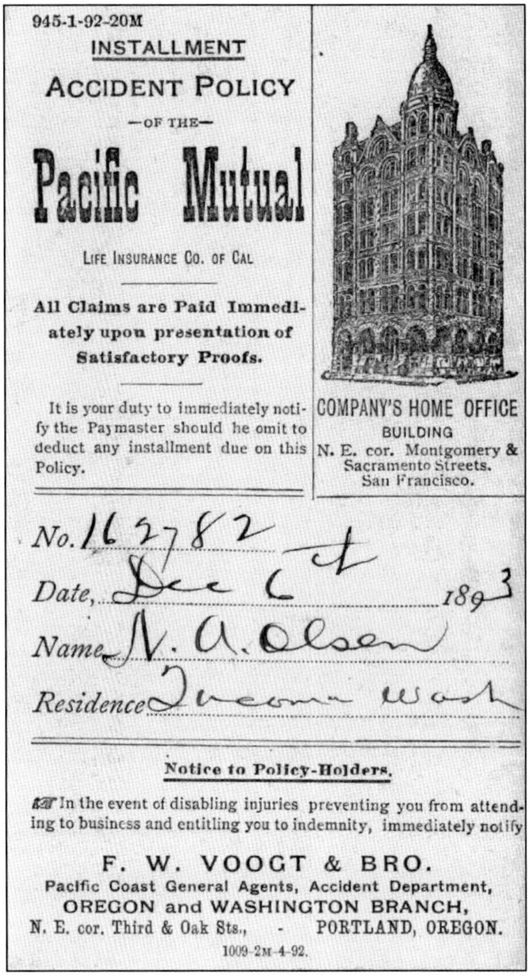

945-1-92-20M

INSTALLMENT

ACCIDENT POLICY

—OF THE—

Pacific Mutual

LIFE INSURANCE CO. OF CAL

All Claims are Paid Immediately upon presentation of Satisfactory Proofs.

It is your duty to immediately notify the Paymaster should he omit to deduct any installment due on this Policy.

COMPANY'S HOME OFFICE BUILDING
N. E. cor. Montgomery & Sacramento Streets.
San Francisco.

No. 162782

Date, Dec 6th 1893

Name N. A. Olson

Residence Tacoma Wash

Notice to Policy-Holders.

In the event of disabling injuries preventing you from attending to business and entitling you to indemnity, immediately notify

F. W. VOOGT & BRO.
Pacific Coast General Agents, Accident Department,
OREGON and WASHINGTON BRANCH,
N. E. cor. Third & Oak Sts., - PORTLAND, OREGON.

1009-2M-4-92.

This 1893 insurance policy provided payment if the employee were injured or disabled at work. It is interesting that insurance was available, even in high-risk jobs, long before safety laws came along in the 1920s. The policyholder was one of the Olson brothers; the Olsons were some of the first landowners in Ruston and opened one of the town's first stores. (TR.)

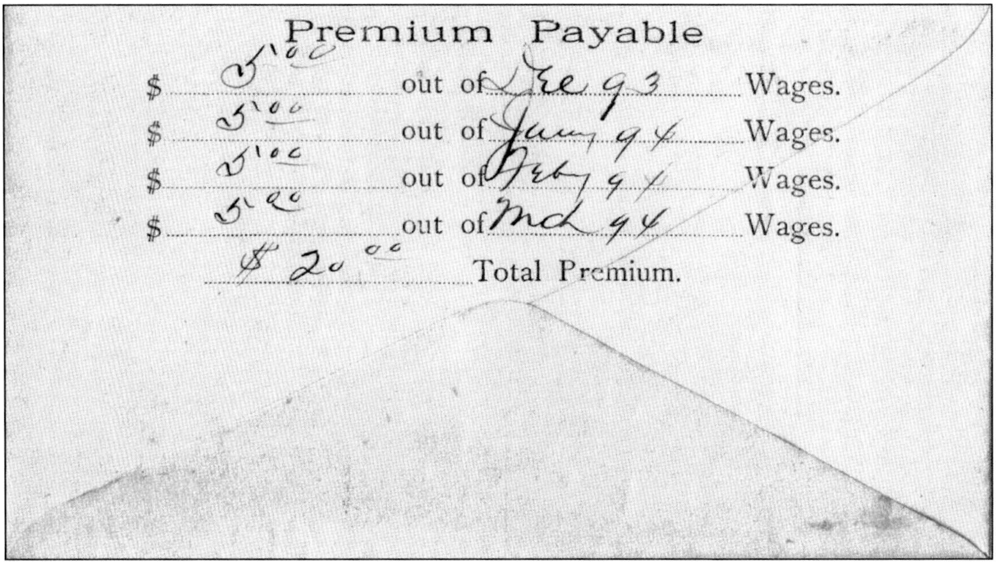

Premium Payable

$ 5.00 out of Dec 93 Wages.
$ 5.00 out of Jany 94 Wages.
$ 5.00 out of Feby 94 Wages.
$ 5.00 out of Mch 94 Wages.
$ 20.00 Total Premium.

The back of the envelope reveals the policy's cost. While $20 in 1893 may seem like a high price to pay for help in the event of injury, there was no assistance provided from the government or employer. The Olson name appear often in early town documents, such as the first council meeting minutes. Many of the children at the Ruston School in this era had this same name. (TR.)

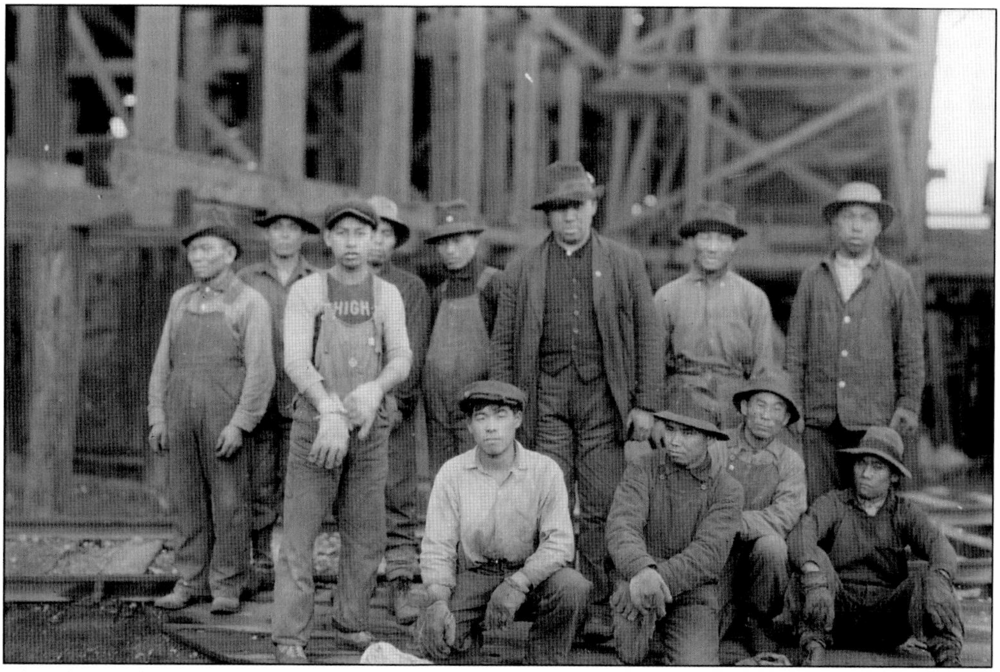

The above photograph was taken about 1906 and shows an all-Asian work crew. It appears segregation was enforced for this group, but a black man is pictured with the different work crew below. The 1910 census shows a local boardinghouse with 17 Japanese occupants who worked at a sawmill. Chinese immigrants did most of the work on the Nelson-Bennett tunnel that runs through the center of Ruston. This rail route has become one of the major West Coast lines. It is unclear if this crew above was related to any of the efforts to construct that tunnel. It is most likely that they worked at the smelter, because the image was taken at the same time that other crews were photographed. (Both, WSHS.)

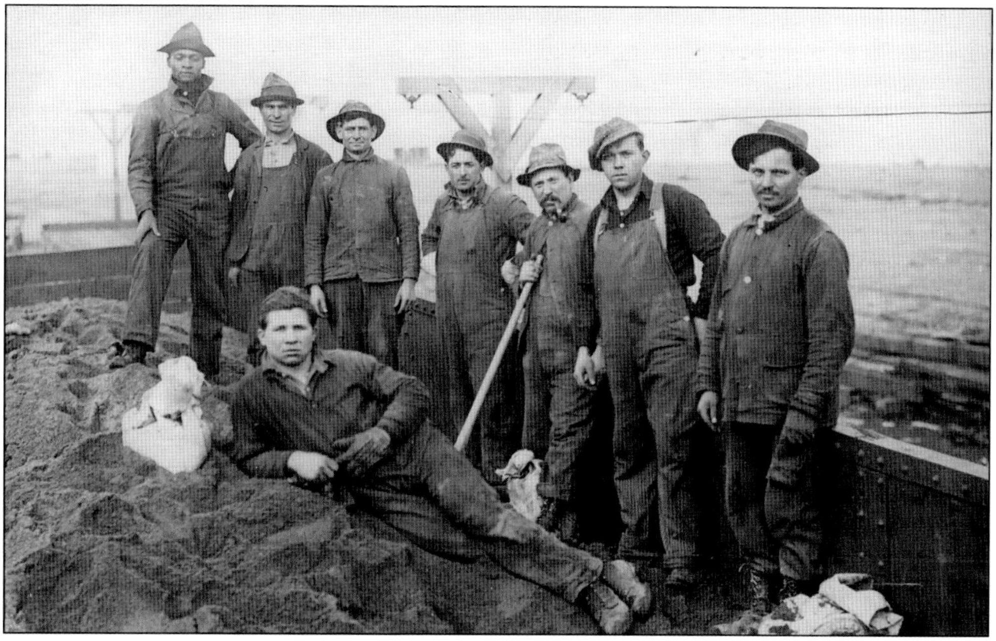

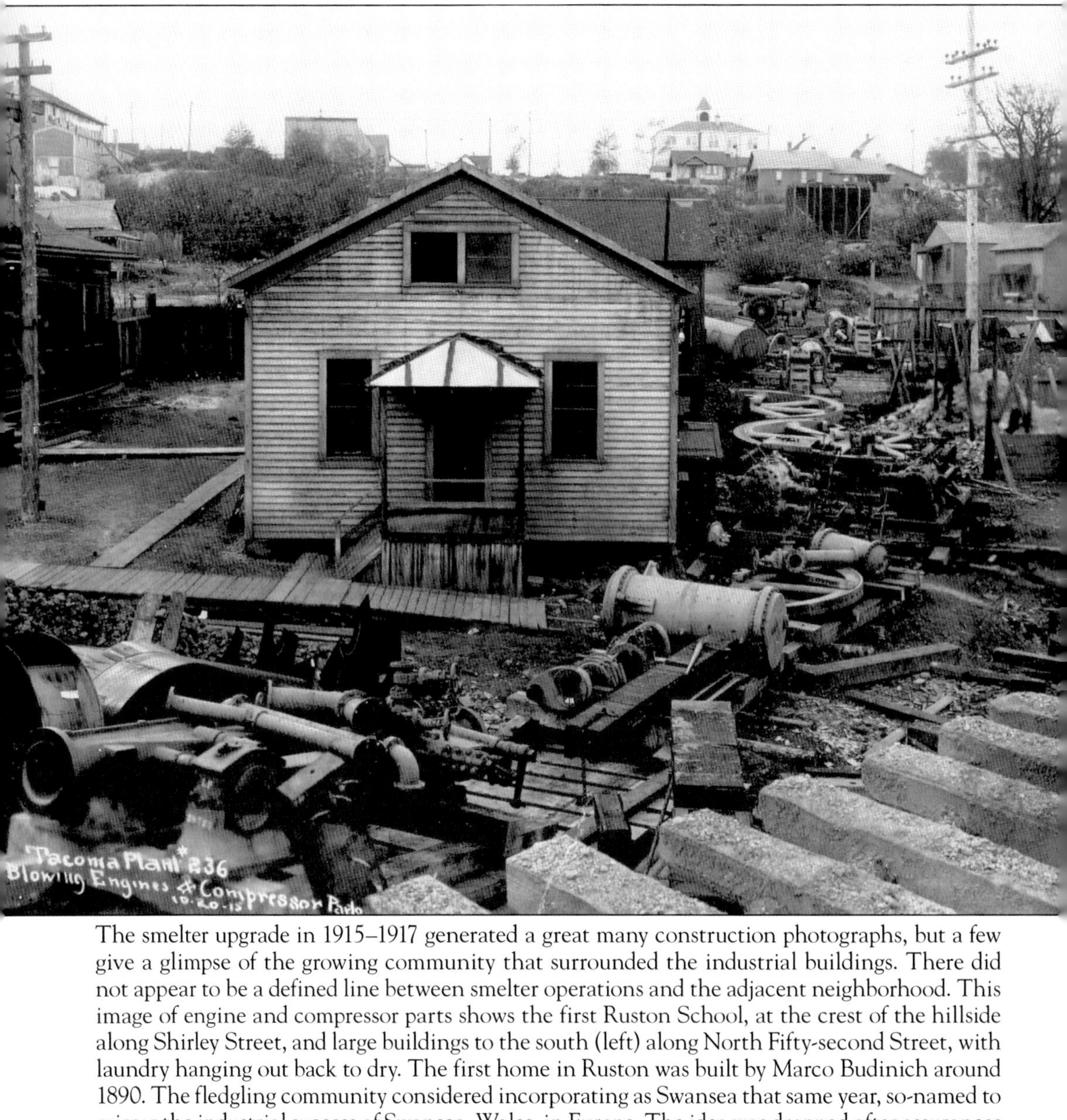

The smelter upgrade in 1915–1917 generated a great many construction photographs, but a few give a glimpse of the growing community that surrounded the industrial buildings. There did not appear to be a defined line between smelter operations and the adjacent neighborhood. This image of engine and compressor parts shows the first Ruston School, at the crest of the hillside along Shirley Street, and large buildings to the south (left) along North Fifty-second Street, with laundry hanging out back to dry. The first home in Ruston was built by Marco Budinich around 1890. The fledgling community considered incorporating as Swansea that same year, so-named to mirror the industrial success of Swansea, Wales, in Europe. The idea was dropped after assurances from the larger city of Tacoma to residents that the they would not be annexed. For the next decade, the area was known as Smelter or Smelterville. (KP.)

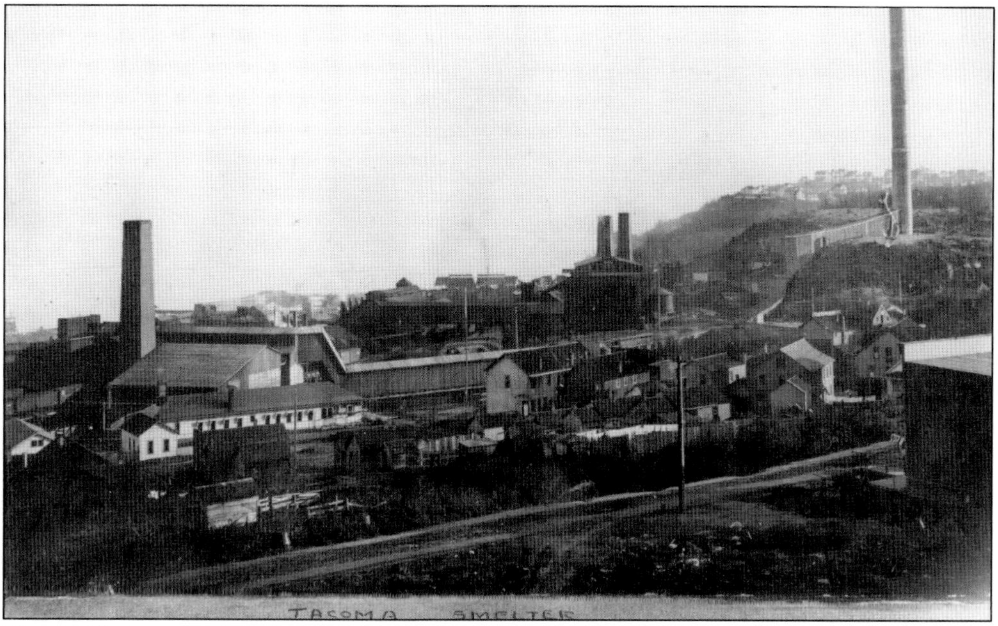

This 1905 photograph looks east over the ever-expanding smelter complex toward Tacoma. A well-developed neighborhood was already thriving on the bluff beyond North Orchard Street, outside of Ruston. The buildings in the front of what may be an early Bennett Street are residential in nature, with pens for livestock and laundry on the line. (TR.)

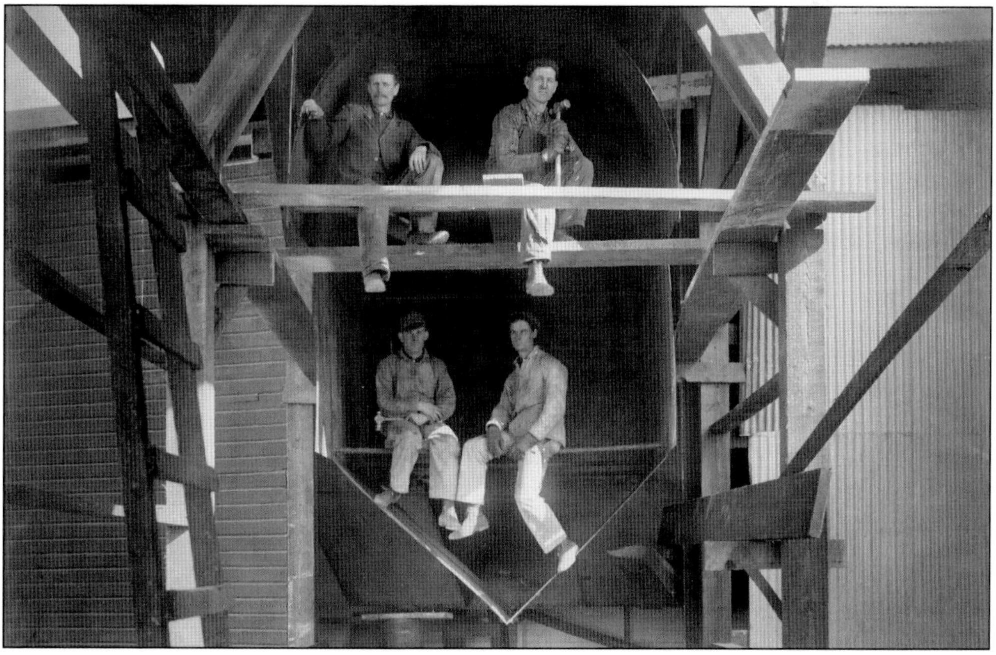

Leslie Tallman (second row, left) and Ed Austen (second row, right), one of Ruston's early mayors, are seen here with two unidentified men in 1902. Tallman was appointed as Ruston's marshal in 1907. He continued to work his day job at the smelter and provided law enforcement in his free time. One of his first duties was to notify residents to clear up their yards, "put rubbish in barrels, and have it hauled away." (WSHS.)

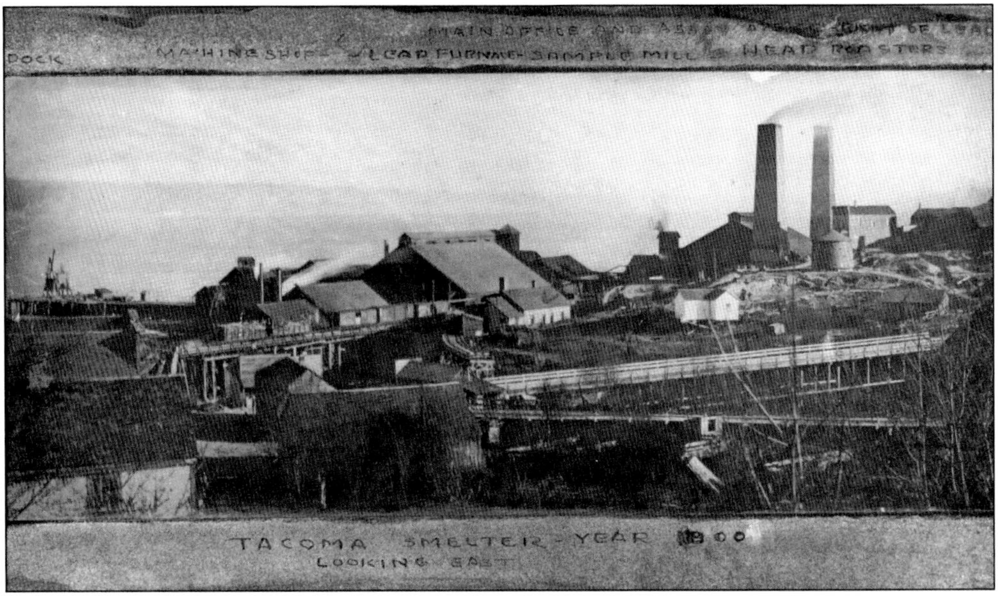

This 1900 photograph shows the view looking south towards Commencement Bay. The two raised bridges are likely North Baltimore Street and the bottom of North Fifty-first Street. Early town records indicate that Baltimore Street crossed a bridge before the roadway was filled. The connection between Baltimore Street and Gallagher Way was closed when remediation required removal of the old bridge timbers and other debris under the roadway in the early 2000s. (TR.)

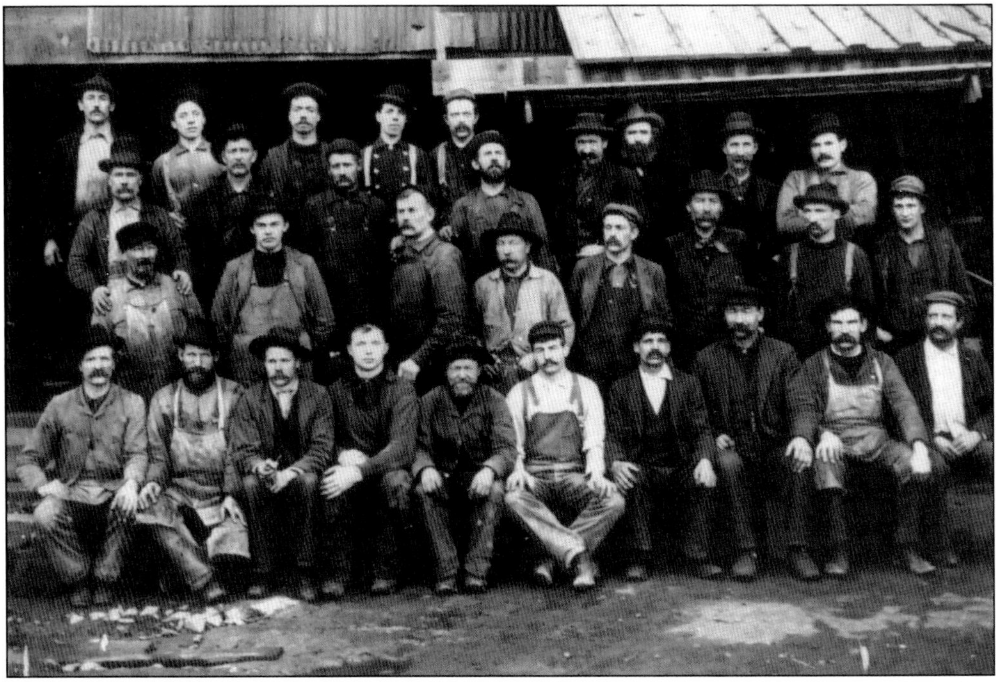

Early smelter employees are shown in 1910, in full work garb and complete with long moustaches or beards, hats, and black-stained hands on some. Although the names of these men may never be known, the industry they built was the foundation for the town of Ruston, which still manages to thrive more than a century later. (TPL.)

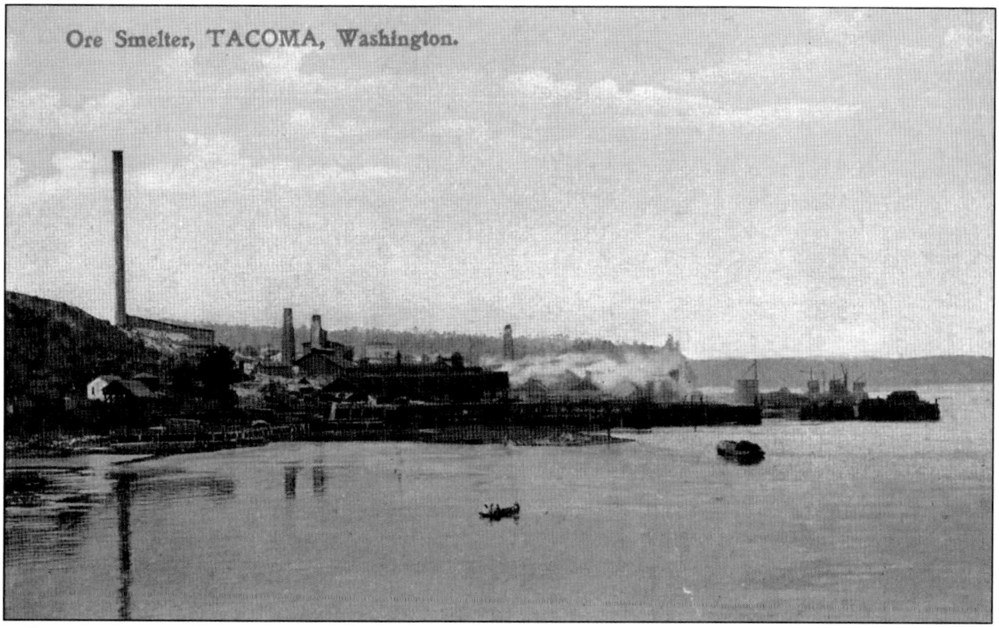

When compared to the current shoreline, this 1909 view of the former Ruston waterfront shows how much land was added over the next century by pouring slag into the bay. A rowboat in front stands in idyllic contrast to the smoky haze hanging over the smelter buildings, apparently escaping from the buildings themselves, as there is no smoke visible from the various stacks. (TPL.)

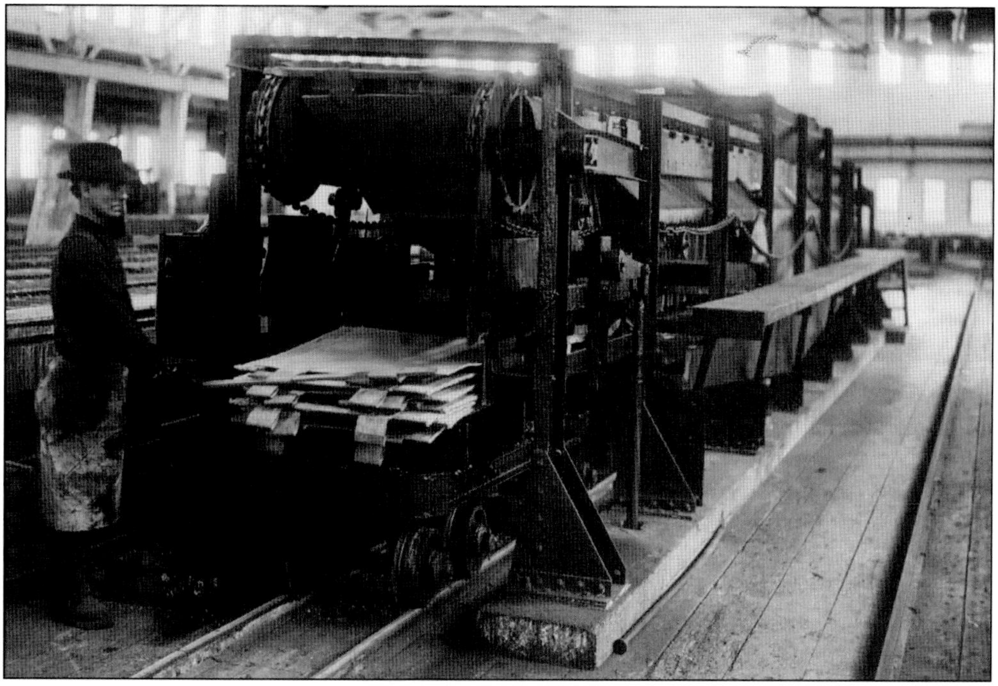

A rather stoic employee from the early 1900s was photographed working somewhere inside the smelter. Large copper plates seen inside the front railcar are hung in tanks (visible behind the man). The 99.99 percent pure copper, pure enough to be used for wire or other modern conveniences, will attach to the plate. The basic process for refining copper is much the same today. (KP.)

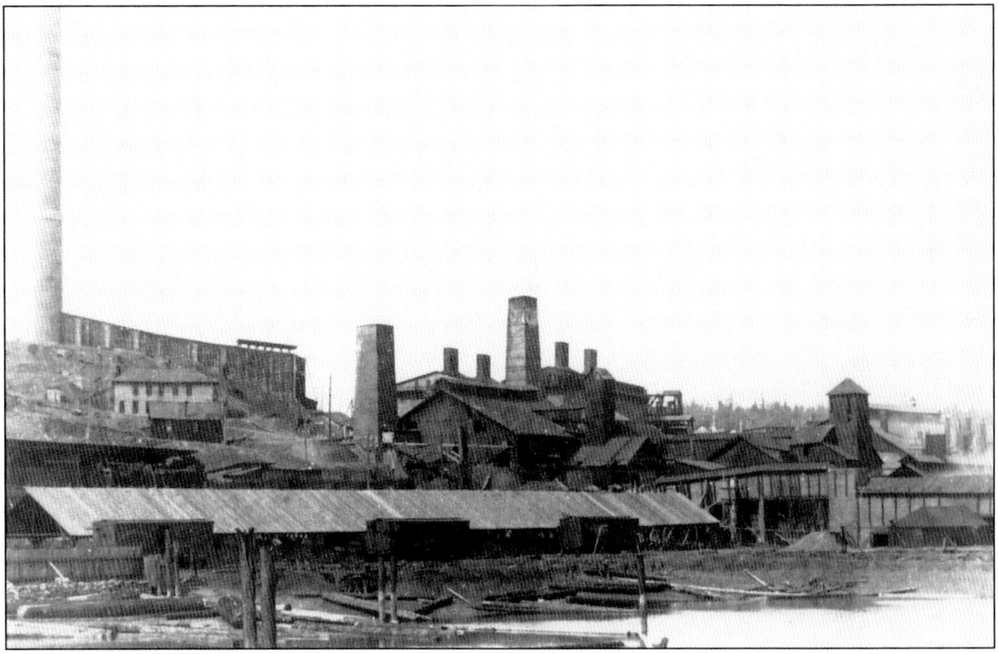

This 1905 image, taken from the water, shows clearly how the massive smelter buildings dwarf the smaller community on the hillside behind the smelter. The concrete chimney to the left in the photograph was completed the same year this photograph was taken. It appears to be low tide, and railcars are lined up along the water's edge. (TPL.)

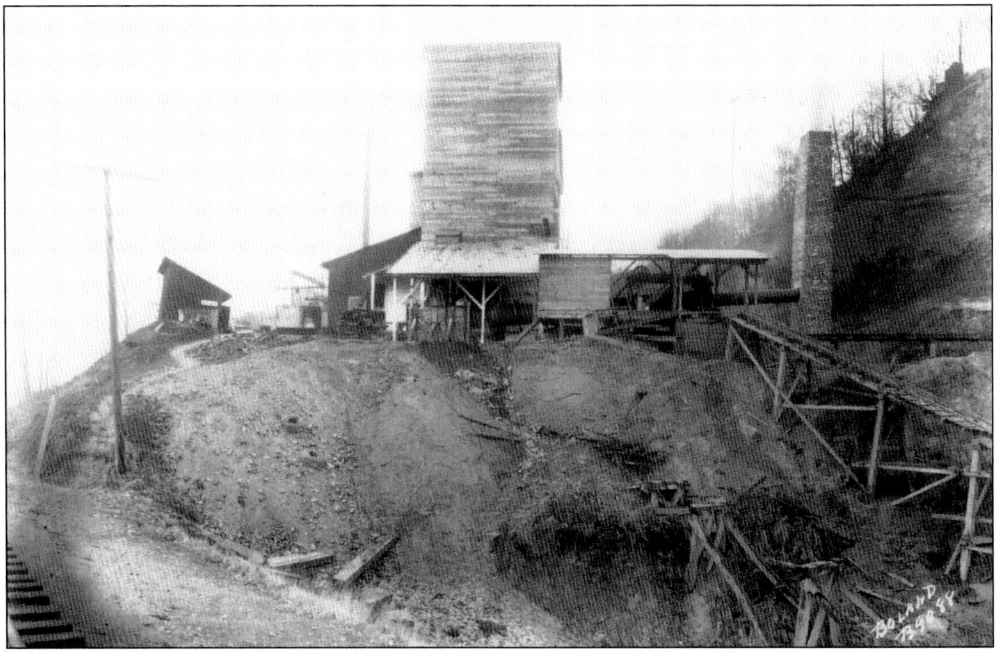

By 1923, the Tacoma Tile and Brick Company was ready to open south of the smelter. Using the abundant hillside clay, the operation took over in the same location as the Goss brickyard, which had been closed 10 years prior. Demand for bricks was growing at the time because there was no local source, and importing the heavy brick was expensive. The new brickyard employed about 40 people. (TPL.)

Two

EARLY RUSTON

Early census documents show that a thriving community was well established even before the town incorporated in 1906. By 1900, several homes are listed along Pearl Street. By 1910, most of the residences had at least one single man listed as a boarder or roomer. Many of the homes had extended families living together, with mothers-in-laws, aunts, cousins, and stepchildren listed at the same address in census documents.

The drive for independence for the tiny town took shape as the smelter changed hands around the turn of the century. Dennis Ryan, unable to make a profit, sold the lead-smelting company to William Ross Rust in the early 1890s. Rust converted the facility to a copper smelter, and business grew. The Guggenheim brothers bought the facility in 1905, adding it to their American Smelting and Refining Company.

At one early council meeting, 40 property owners presented a petition to the town and agreed to contribute $5 each for sewer-line construction. But nine others protested levying any taxes for sewers. The motion passed with only three votes from the five-member council. The town later passed an ordinance requiring homes to connect to the system, making it illegal to "maintain cesspools on the premises where sewers were accessible."

Two years after Ruston incorporated, the Tacoma newspaper ran a headline declaring, "Ruston More Than Doubles Population and Assessed Valuation in 18 Months." The town boasted 125 pupils in the Ruston School, a town hall with a jail cell in the basement, and a YMCA clubhouse, complete with gym, bowling alleys, pool tables, and reading rooms for the smelter men. Mayor Ed Austen had recently been replaced by Ed Daley.

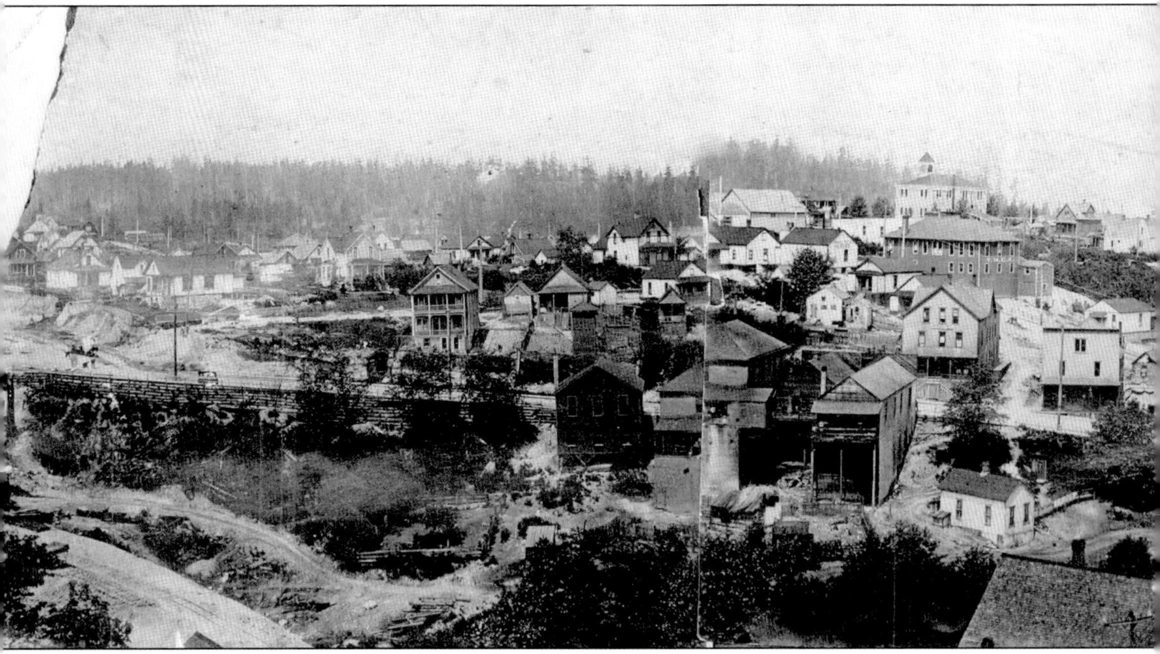

This panoramic view of Ruston in 1912 offers a rare glimpse of the growing community shortly after the first election in 1906 saw 121 voters register. Most of the American-born voters were from Ohio, with only one native to Washington, and 51 were of foreign birth. Of the voters, 64 worked at the smelter, with another 33 toiling in related fields. The room over Hank's Store, on North Fifty-first Street, was the official polling place. Voters listed boardinghouses as home,

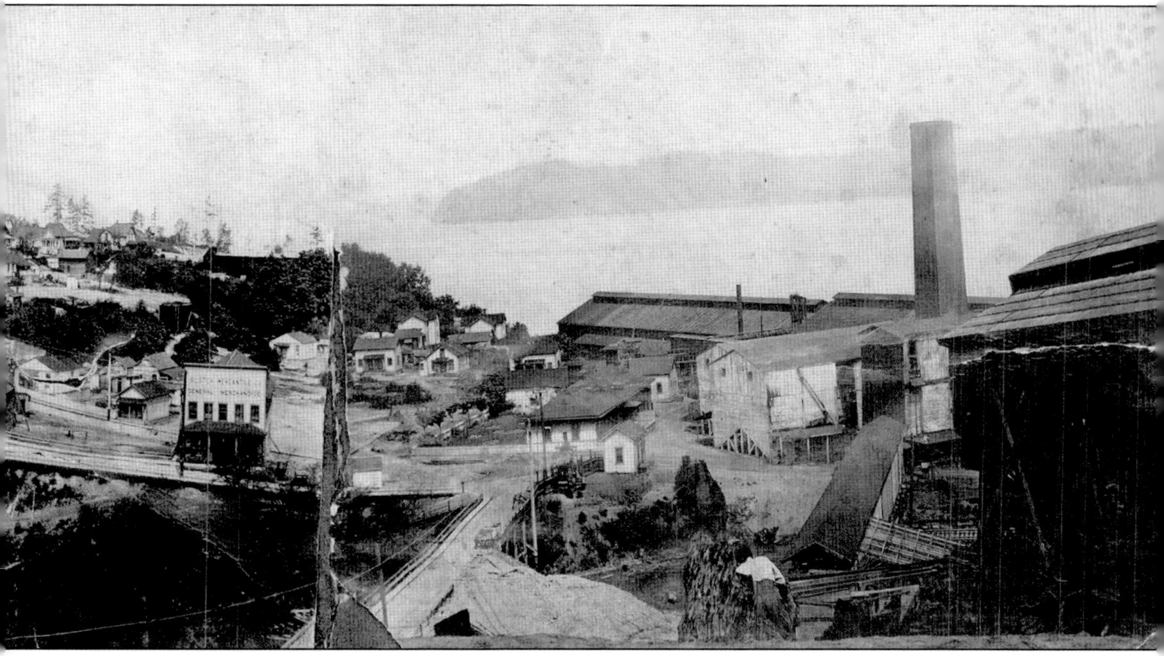

ranging from Smith's Store to Point Defiance Hotel. By spring of 1907, the first town hall was built at a cost of $1,762 on a lot donated by Rust. The first three business licenses to be issued were for saloons. The *Ruston Review* held the designation of official town newspaper, with a bill paid to the paper on December 31, 1906. (TR.)

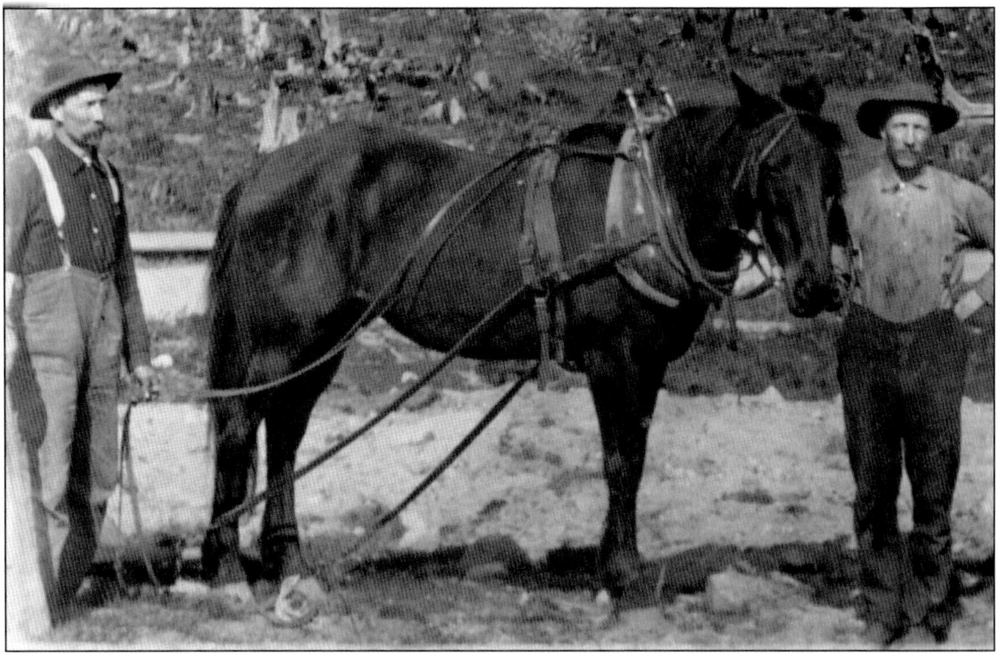

The England brothers were clearing land on Winnifred Street, near North Fifty-second Street, in 1909. A 1929 insurance map shows that Winnifred Street was designed with a spacious median in the middle from North Fifty-first to Fifty-fourth Streets, but it was named Market Street at the time. (TR.)

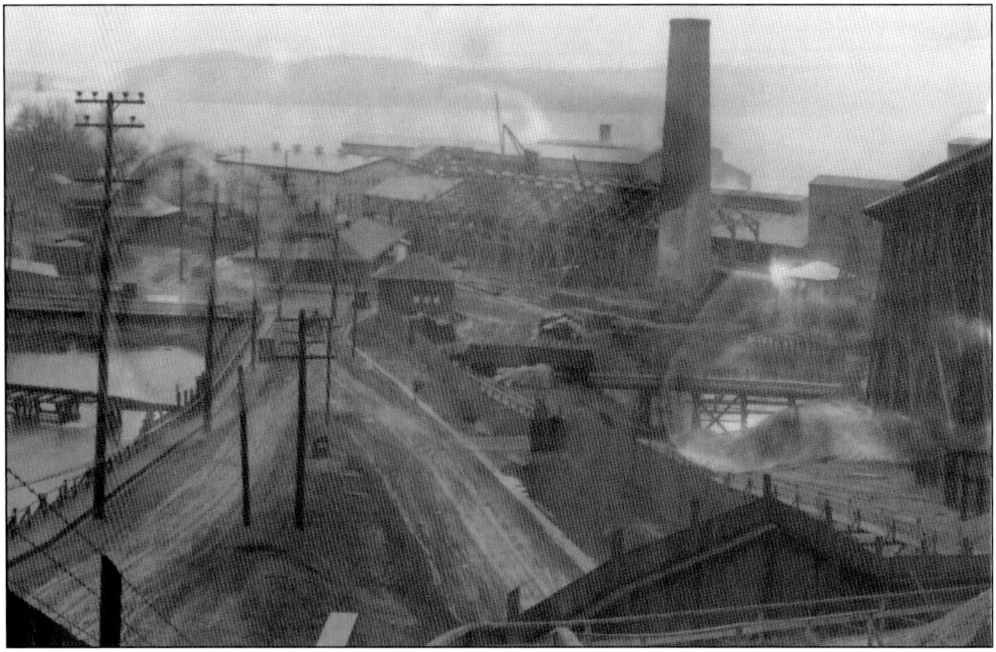

This undated shot shows the early connection between the now closed Baltimore Street and the road that would eventually become Gallagher Way. The connection next to the cooling pond looked very much the same until the road was closed in the early 2000s. Several early-model cars are visible on the muddy road. (KP.)

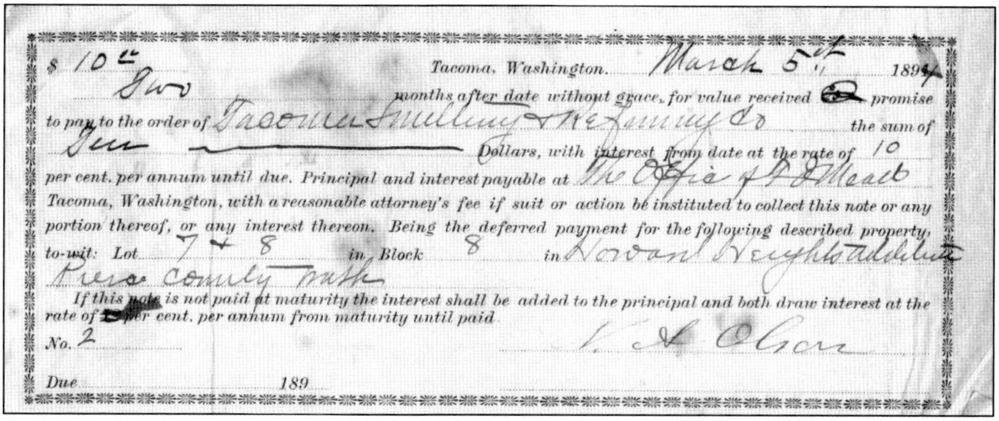

$ 10 00 Tacoma, Washington. March 5th 1893

Two months after date without grace, for value received I promise to pay to the order of Tacoma Smelting & Refining Co the sum of Ten Dollars, with interest from date at the rate of 10 per cent. per annum until due. Principal and interest payable at The Office of [illegible] Tacoma, Washington, with a reasonable attorney's fee if suit or action be instituted to collect this note or any portion thereof, or any interest thereon. Being the deferred payment for the following described property, to-wit: Lot 7 + 8 in Block 8 in Howard Heights Addition Pierce County Wash

If this note is not paid at maturity the interest shall be added to the principal and both draw interest at the rate of [illegible] per cent. per annum from maturity until paid

No. 2

N. A. Olson

Due 189

As denoted by this 1893 promissory note, Nils Olson purchased, from the smelter, two 25-foot lots in the newly formed Howard Heights Addition; the cost was $10. The Howard Heights Addition is located on the hillside and land just west of the smelter, including where the school building would eventually be built. (TR.)

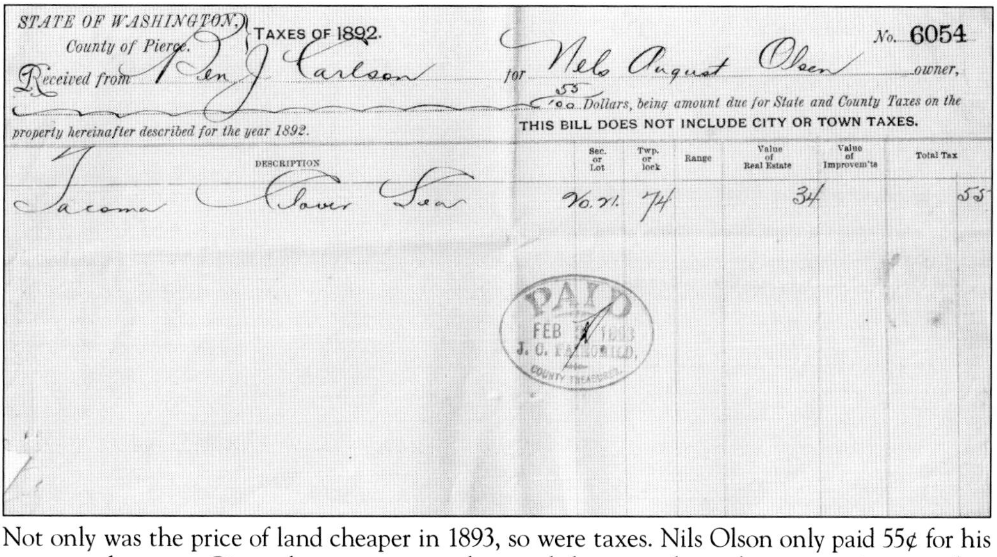

STATE OF WASHINGTON, County of Pierce. TAXES OF 1892. No. 6054

Received from Ben J Carlson for Nels August Olsen owner,

55/100 Dollars, being amount due for State and County Taxes on the property hereinafter described for the year 1892.

THIS BILL DOES NOT INCLUDE CITY OR TOWN TAXES.

DESCRIPTION	Sec. or Lot	Twp. or Block	Range	Value of Real Estate	Value of Improvem'ts	Total Tax
Tacoma Clover Lea	16.21.	74		34		55

Not only was the price of land cheaper in 1893, so were taxes. Nils Olson only paid 55¢ for his property that year. Given that wages were also much lower, perhaps the tax rate is not as low as it seems by modern standards. Property values in Ruston are now some of the highest in the county. (TR.)

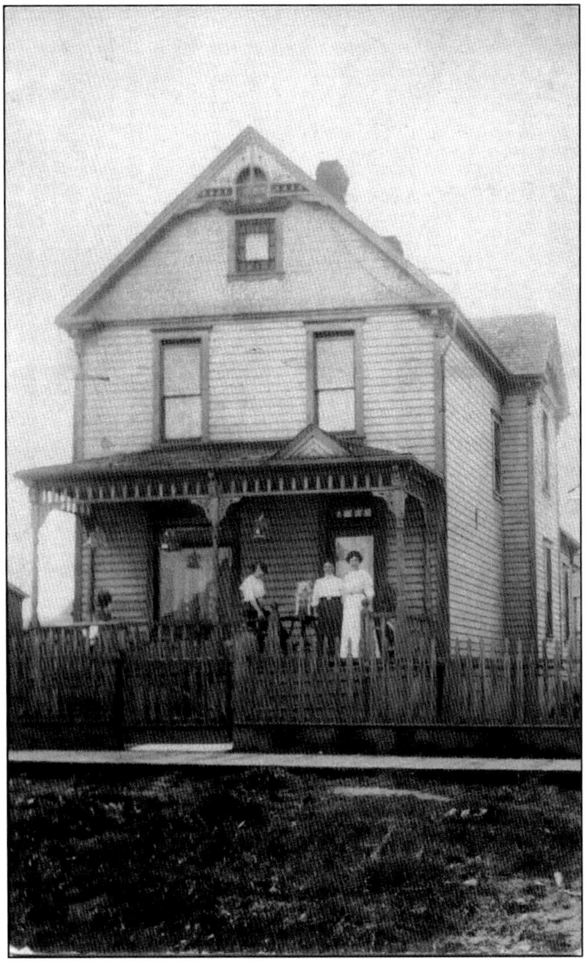

Mrs. Johnson, a young girl named Myrtle, and an unidentified woman, along with the family dog, are pictured in 1912, at their home at 5112 North Shirley Street. At the time this book was written, a house was no longer present at this address. (TR.)

Also from 1912, this image shows Bertha Boyd and two kittens nursing from Tutsy, the dog. The building across the street appears to be the first school. If so, this picture was taken somewhere on the 5200 block of North Shirley Street, looking east. (TR.)

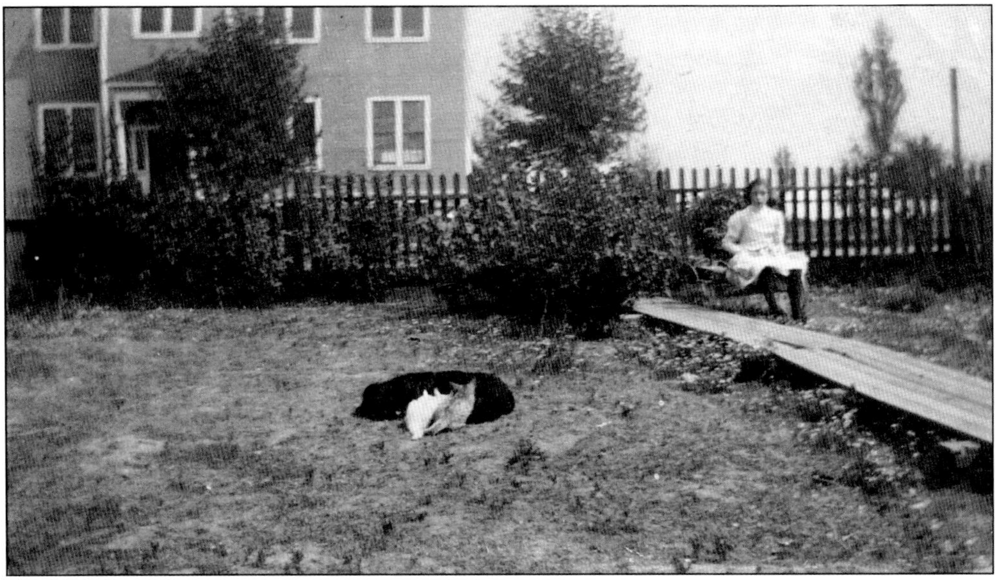

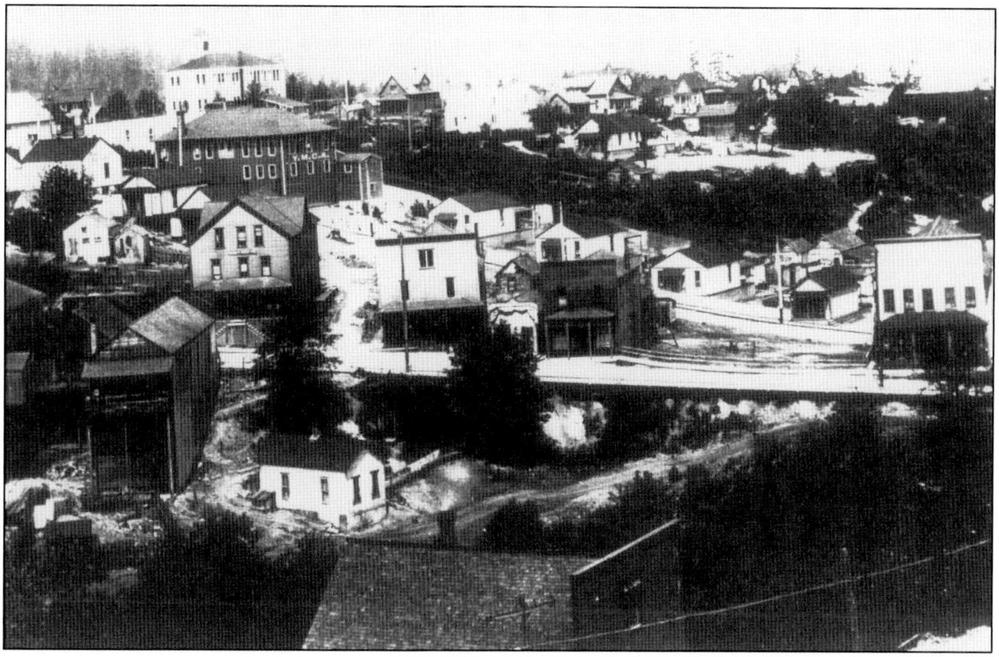

Old insurance maps show Ruston Town Hall on the west side of North Fifty-first Street, one of the buildings in the front left. The Ruston Tool House is listed at the location of the current town hall on Winnifred Street. A thriving community around the school flourishes on the hillside behind North Fifty-first Street in this 1912 photograph. (KP.)

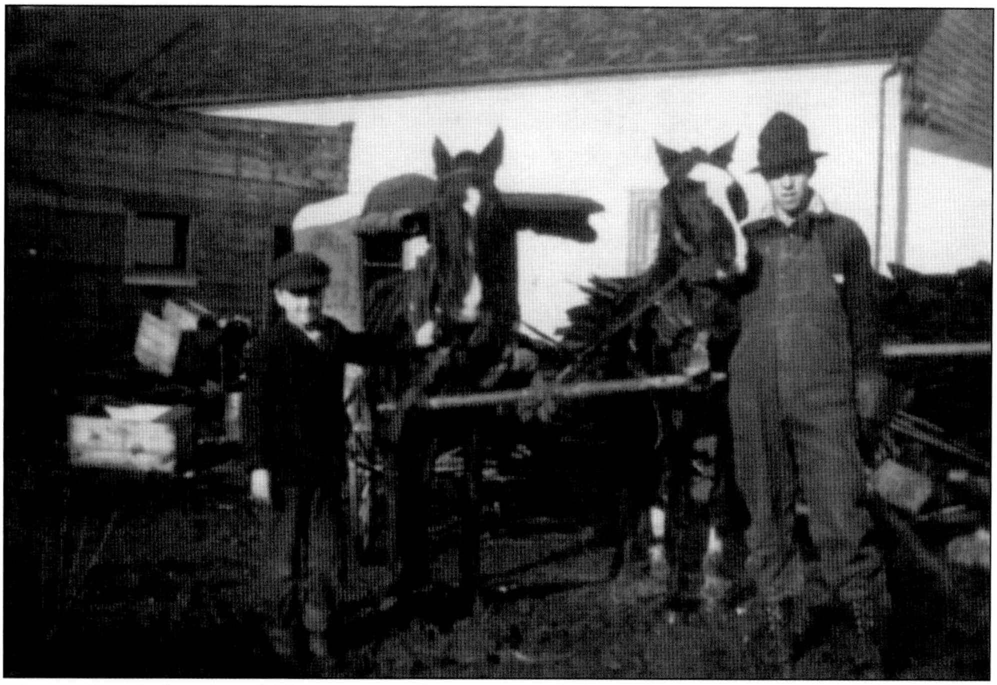

This undated photograph features Hershe Rummig (left) and Dick Matthews with their team and wagon from Wallace & Boyd Grocery, located on North Fifty-first and Pearl Streets, next to the former Shirley Drug Store. (TR.)

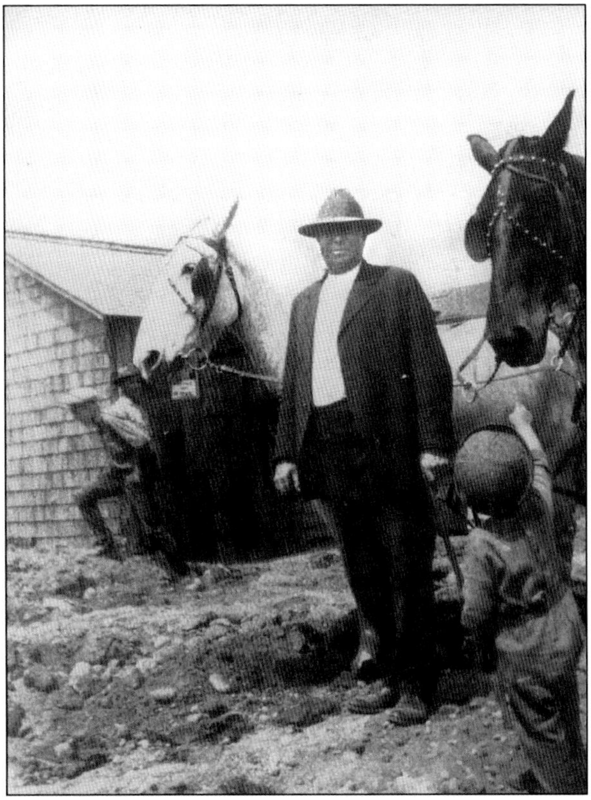

Ed Olson owned one of the first stores in Ruston, and brother Nils was an early landowner. Jack Olson and his team of horses are pictured in 1909 near the corner of North Fifty-second and Bennett Streets. As was common in those days, these men were likely part of an extended family of immigrants who all settled together in the area to build a new life. (TR.)

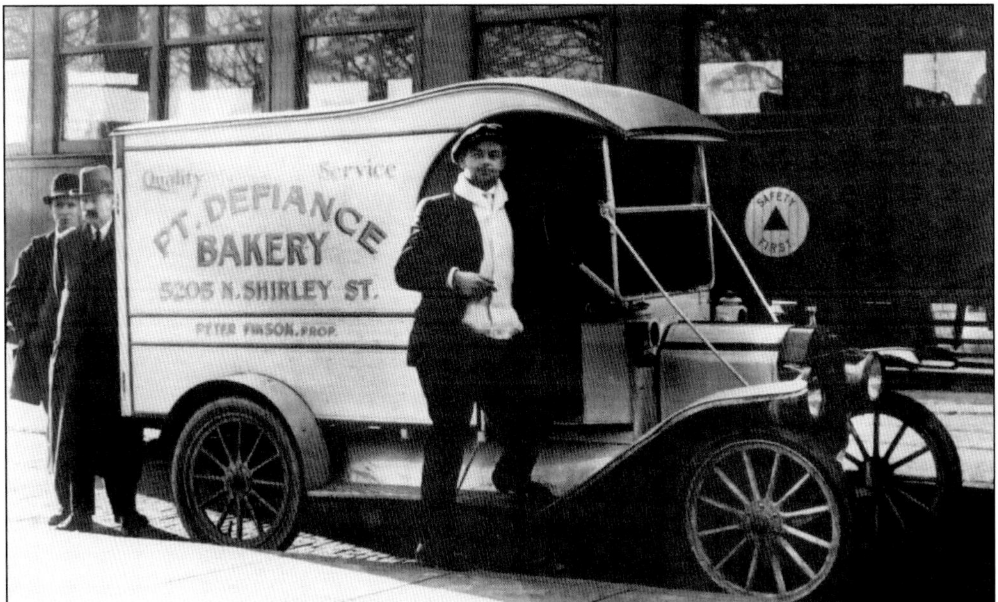

A bakery joined the Olson General Merchandise Store and the school on the 5200 block of North Shirley Street. The bakery apparently made deliveries in a handsome new truck. Although this photograph is not dated, the bakery was destroyed by fire in 1917. (TR.)

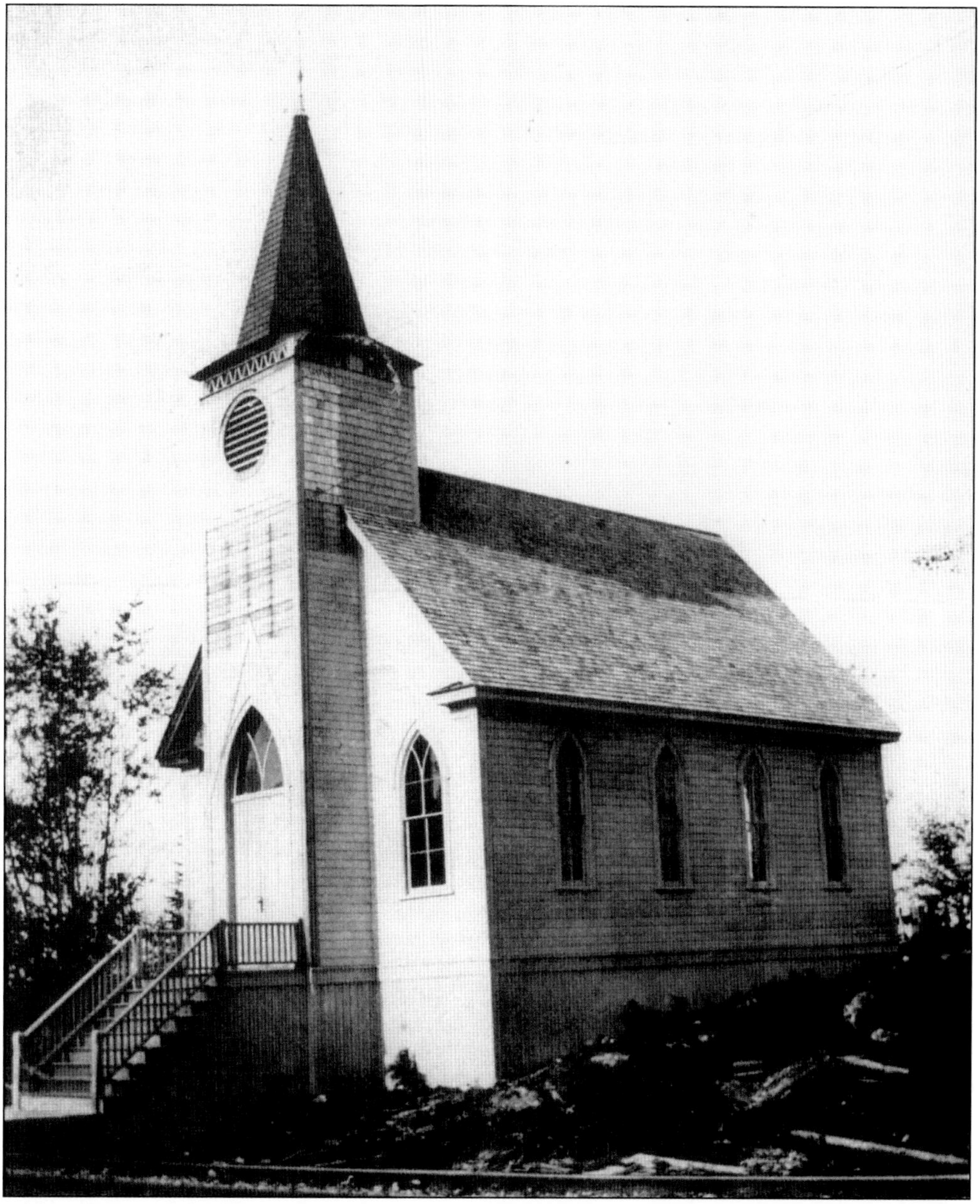

Although Ruston had far more taverns than churches, there were notable houses of worship in the tiny town. The Smelter Church was dedicated on March 9, 1902, the date of this photograph. Across town, the Unicorn Tavern endures as another long-standing Ruston icon. Known as "The Brick" for most of its years because of its brick construction, the business served as a watering hole for smelter workers. Just down the street, the Krillich Brothers Grocery operated for much of the century. George Krillich was the first in the family to arrive in Ruston in 1902. He set up a small grocery and eventually brought his wife and brothers from Croatia. He and his three brothers added a boardinghouse in 1912. When George died six years later, his family carried on the business. Each morning, smelter men would gather in the basement of the store to eat a meal and collect lunch before heading off to work. English and native Eastern European tongues were spoken. During the day, the local housewives would visit the grocery on the main floor. (TPL.)

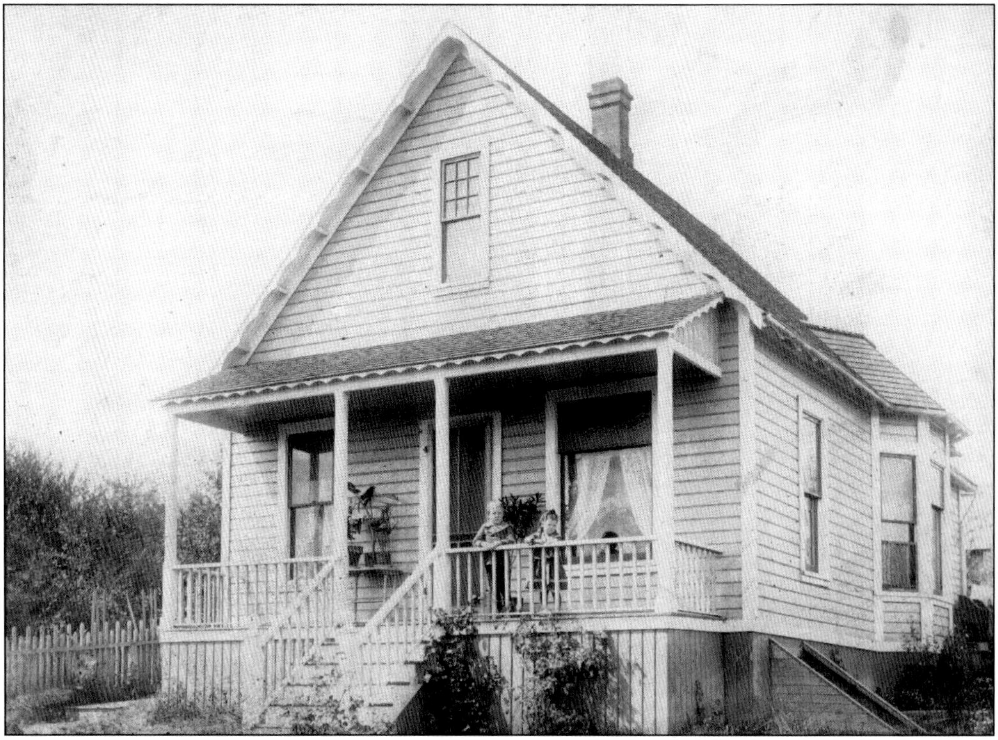

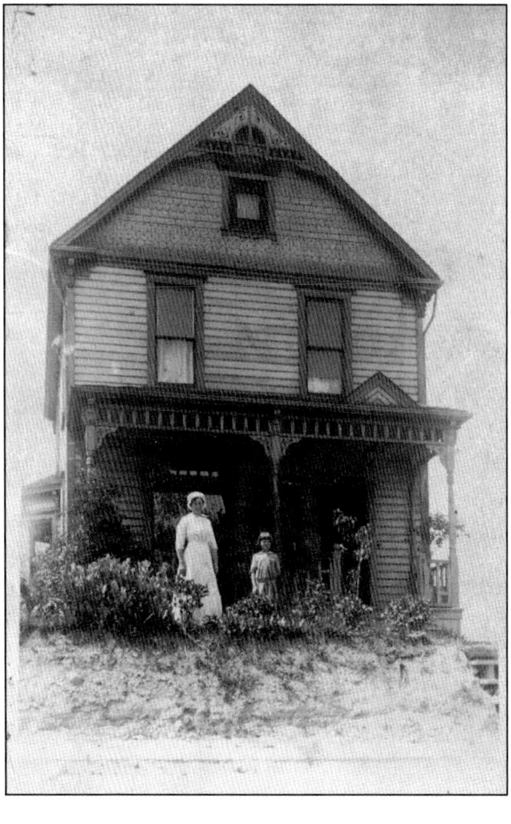

The summer of 1900 found young Lester R. and Agnes Vale posing on the front porch of their home at 5124 North Shirley Street (above). In 1913, Mrs. Johnson and an unidentified child are pictured at 5112 North Shirley Street (left). The new council was working to improve the town for families like these. It instructed the "chairman of the streets and alleys committee to notify Barney Rhodeseid that he must not tear boards off of the railing on Fifty-first Street for the purpose of getting to his chicken coop, but the council would allow him to put in a small gate which they think will be sufficient." Another new law stated, "It shall be unlawful for any cow, cattle, horse, mule, goat, sheep, [or] swine . . . to run at large between the hours of 8:00 a.m. and 5:00 p.m." (TR.)

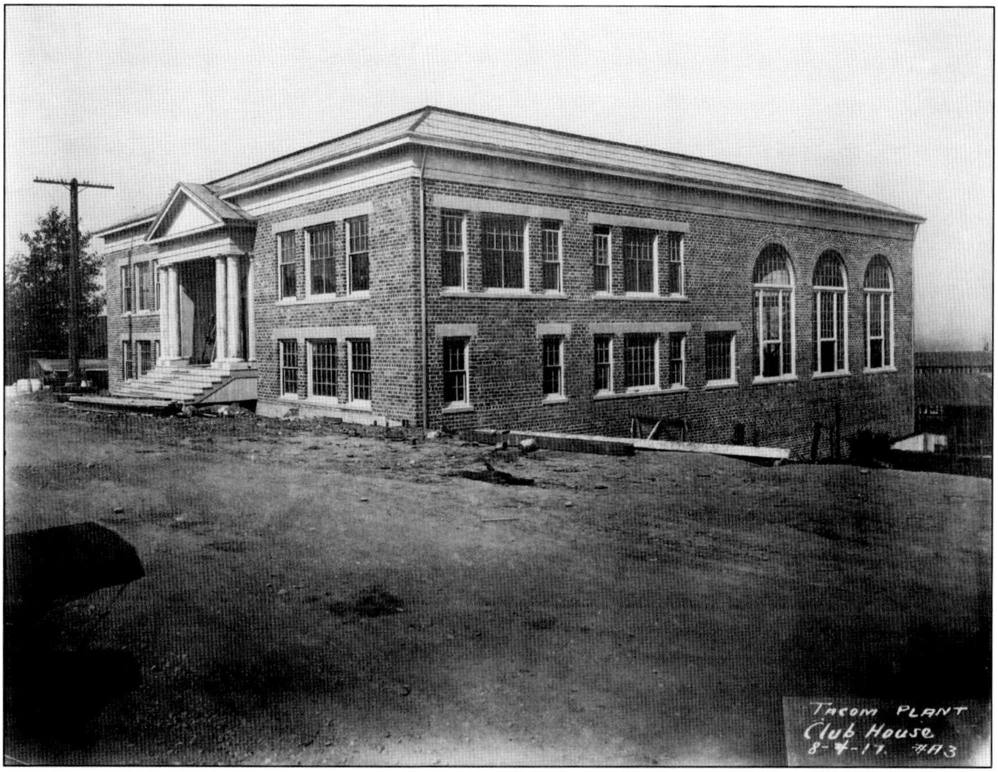

This 1917 photograph shows the employee clubhouse for smelter workers, located near North Fifty-second and Bennett Streets. Dances were held every weekend, and it was said that the clubhouse had enough space inside to hold baseball games when the weather was cold. On warmer days, the games moved outdoors, between the huge refinery buildings on the smelter grounds, just down the hill from the clubhouse. (WSHS.)

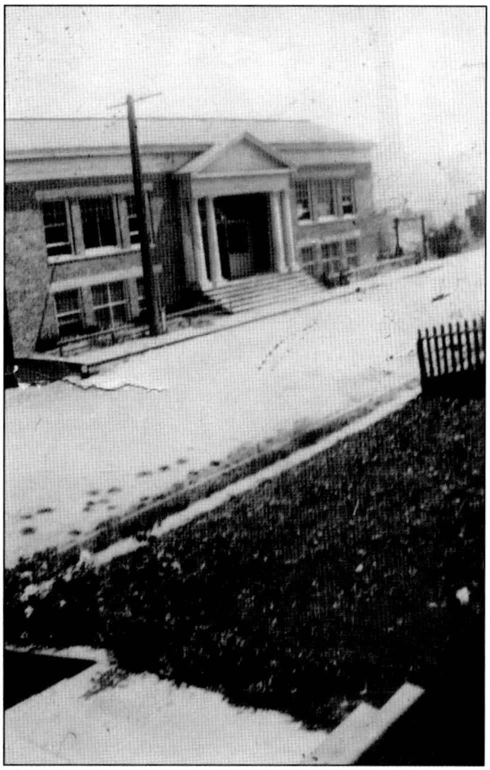

The Smelter Club served the employees and people of Ruston for several decades before being closed during World War II. Even when it was closed, local children were known to sneak inside to use the bowling lanes and pool tables. (TR.)

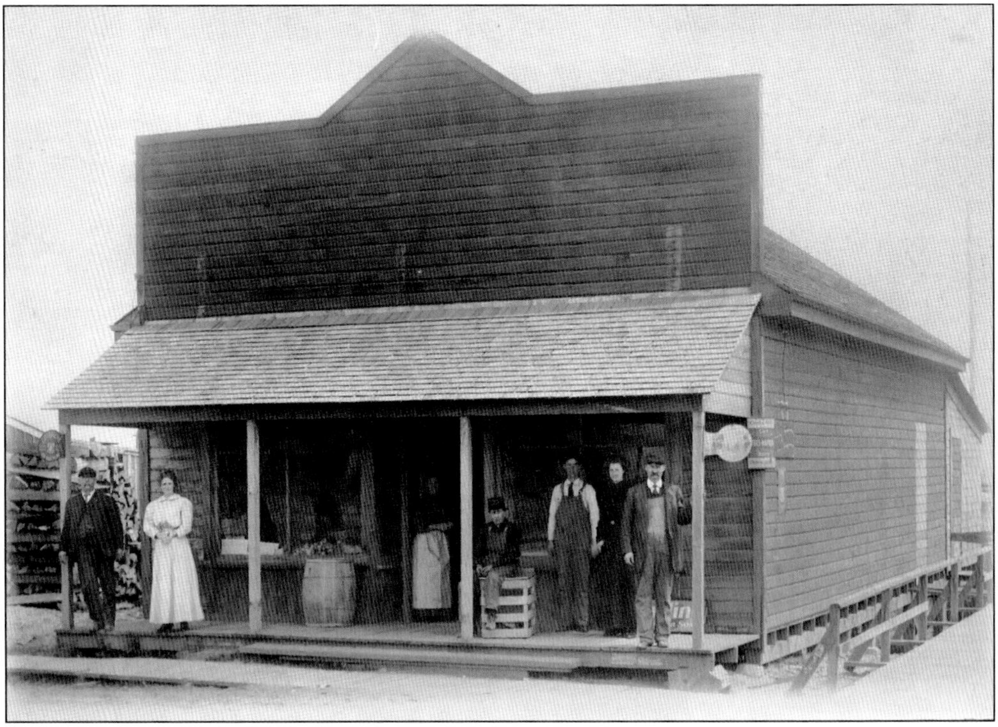

The prolific Olson brothers' early influence can be seen throughout Ruston's history. This 1906 picture shows Ed Olson's newly constructed store. The names written on the back of the photograph by an unknown hand list, right to left, Ed Olson, Harold ?, Lira Olson, Art ?, Edith Olson, and on the far left are Marshal Sam Boyd and Alice Boyd Wallace. (TR.)

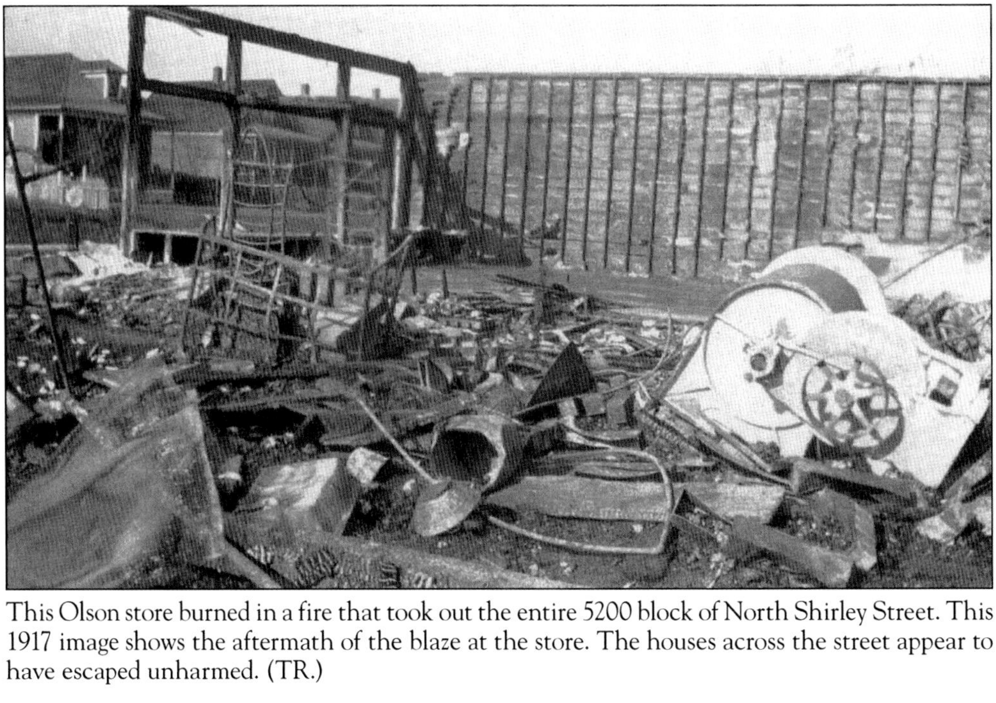

This Olson store burned in a fire that took out the entire 5200 block of North Shirley Street. This 1917 image shows the aftermath of the blaze at the store. The houses across the street appear to have escaped unharmed. (TR.)

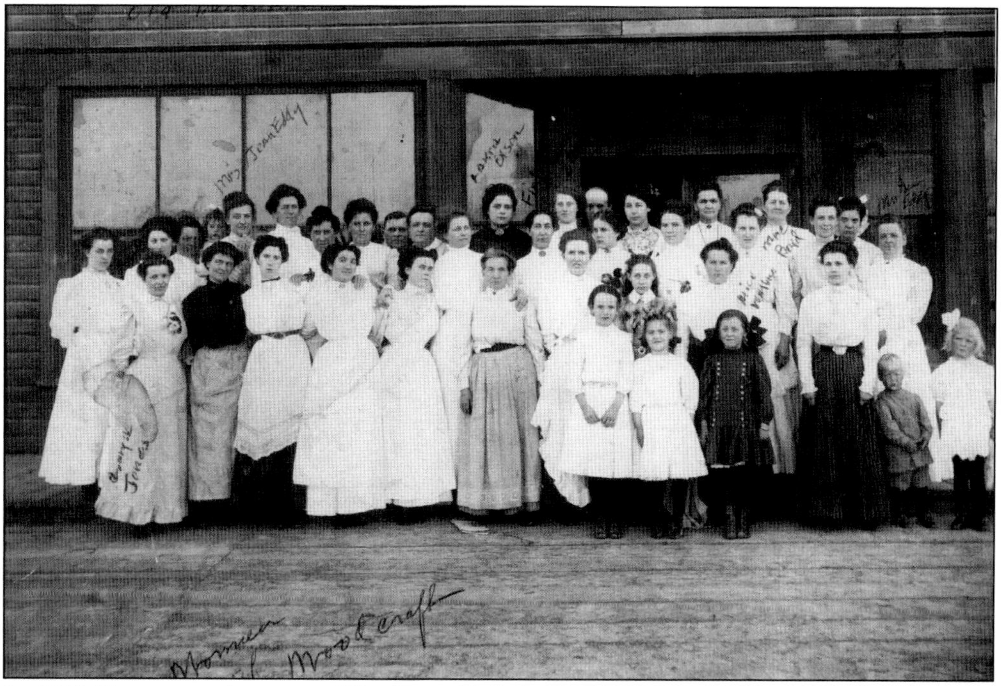

In 1908, Ruston was home to a Woodman Hall, located near North Fifty-second and Bennett Streets. The building later served as the first movie house in town. This large gathering of Ruston women includes a few children and two men tucked away in the back of the photograph. (TR.)

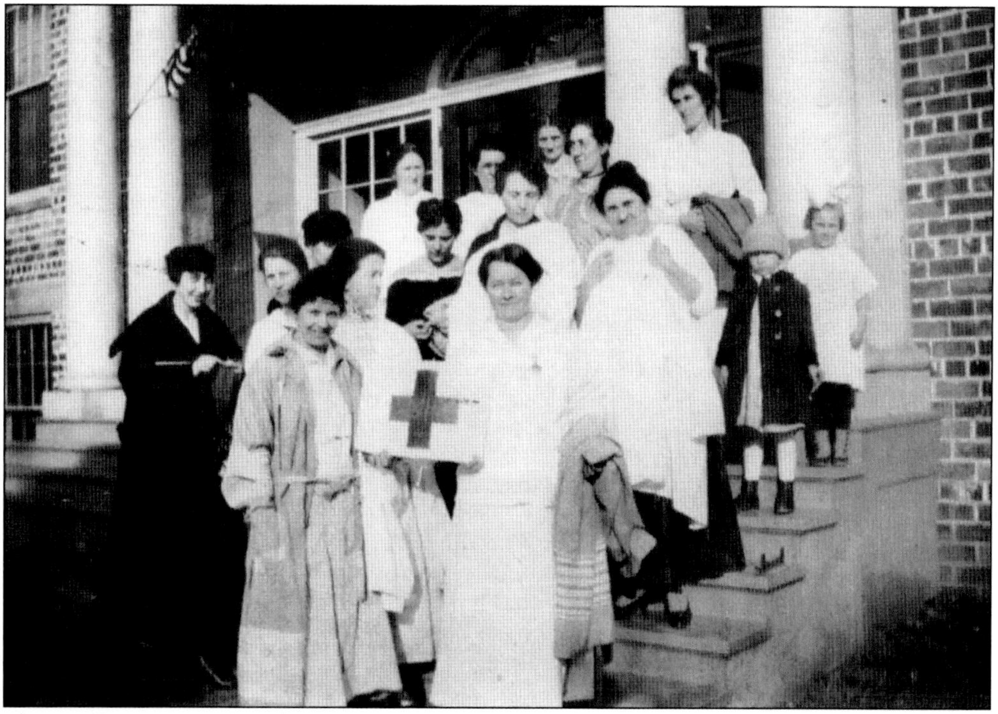

The small town contributed to the World War I effort with its own chapter of the Red Cross. The women of Ruston's chapter pose for this picture in 1918 at the smelter employee clubhouse. (TR.)

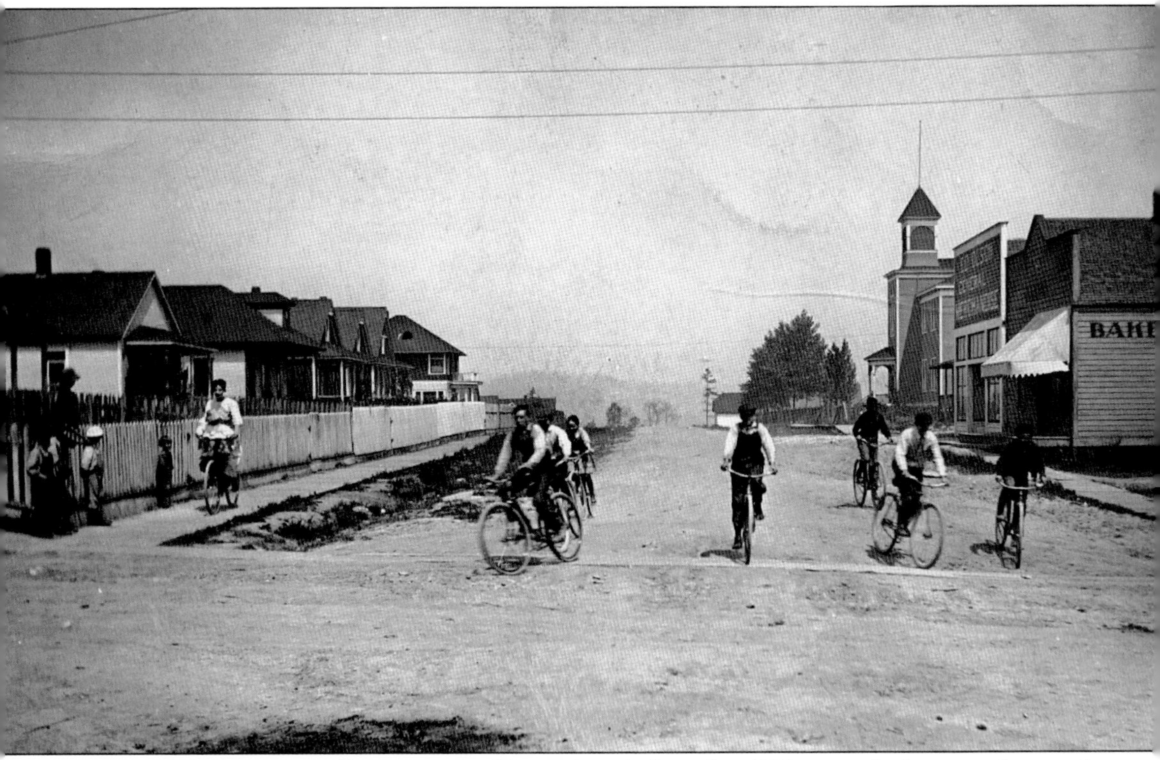

One of the most compelling pictures of Ruston's early days, this 1910 image, looking north toward Point Defiance, captures children at play along North Shirley Street. The commercial tone of the area is visible on the right side of the street, with Ed Olson's General Merchandise Store, Defiance Bakery, and the school in the distance. The children are, in no particular order, Earl Murphy, Art Erickson, Art Burkland, Dick Matthews, George Turner, Howard Murphy, and Lille and Bonita Turner. Although not seen here, one of the early homes in Ruston was built in 1890 and belonged to J.P. Garrison. Without much education, he moved from Texas to Old Tacoma. Garrison was sickly and not expected to live long, but he seemed to flourish in his new environment. He made his early living with a team of horses that he would hire out to clear logs from Point Defiance Park. By 1890, he had sold his horses and went to work for the smelter. Garrison was one of the first councilmen and also mayor. (Courtesy of Don and Beth Torbet.)

Three

SCHOOLHOUSE

Visitors who stand still enough under the porch at the old school building can almost hear the faint whisper of children's laughter as it echoes across the years. From PTA to school plays, to council meetings and movie nights, the building has served as the center of community activity for generations.

The first town council meeting was held on November 12, 1906, in the school on the bluff that overlooked the smelter. Mayor Austen presided with five new council members. G.H. Wallace was appointed clerk, and L. Martin was chosen as marshal. These same officials won their seats in that first election on December 7, 1906.

After the 1917 fire destroyed the first school, a new brick building was constructed in the same location. This new school was much larger and less susceptible to fire. Almost the entire block was dedicated to the new structure and play areas for the town's children.

Ruston has always fiercely held to its independence, even though Tacoma had grown to surround it by mid-century. One threat to the smaller town's identity arose in 1966, when the state cut off special aid to Ruston School because it was no longer considered "remote and necessary." The school was eventually incorporated into the Tacoma School District, and its doors were shut in 1986. After a battle with the district, the town regained ownership of the building and land, and the old school has been remodeled into office space.

Most recently, the former gym has been converted into a community center, named after former councilwoman Mary Joyce. Joyce led the fight to get ownership of the school returned to Ruston. After many decades away, town council meetings are once again held inside the building.

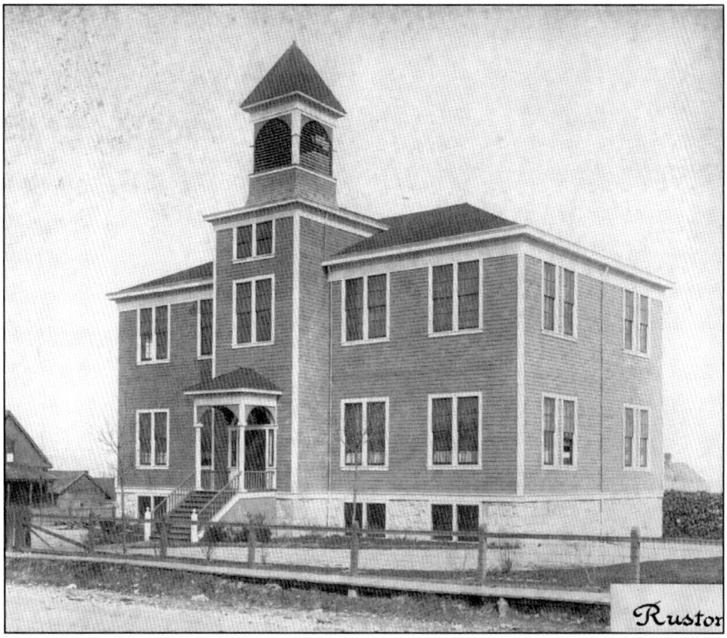

The shiny new school on North Shirley Street, shown in 1906, reflected the best of the bustling new town. Officials of the just incorporated town used this space for their meetings, setting direction for Ruston. Classrooms, which overlooked the expanding smelter complex, were filled with youngsters. (WSHS.)

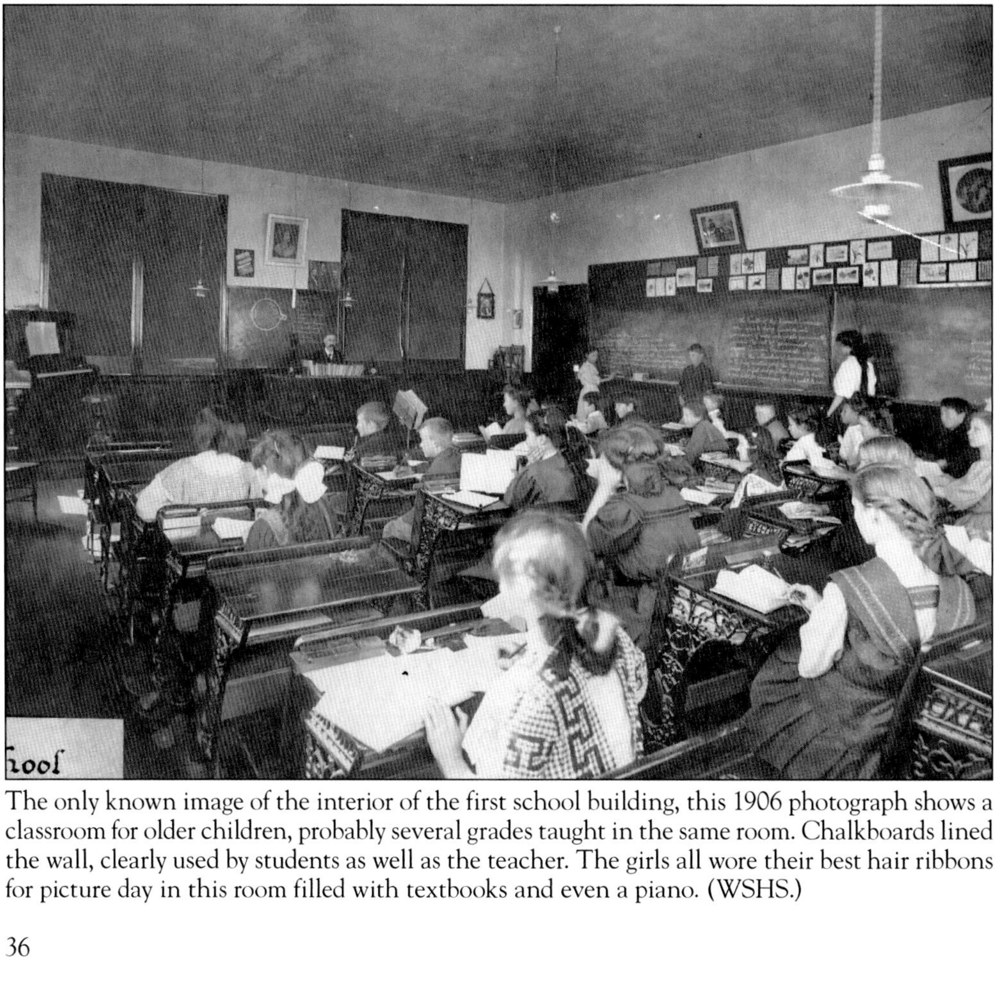

The only known image of the interior of the first school building, this 1906 photograph shows a classroom for older children, probably several grades taught in the same room. Chalkboards lined the wall, clearly used by students as well as the teacher. The girls all wore their best hair ribbons for picture day in this room filled with textbooks and even a piano. (WSHS.)

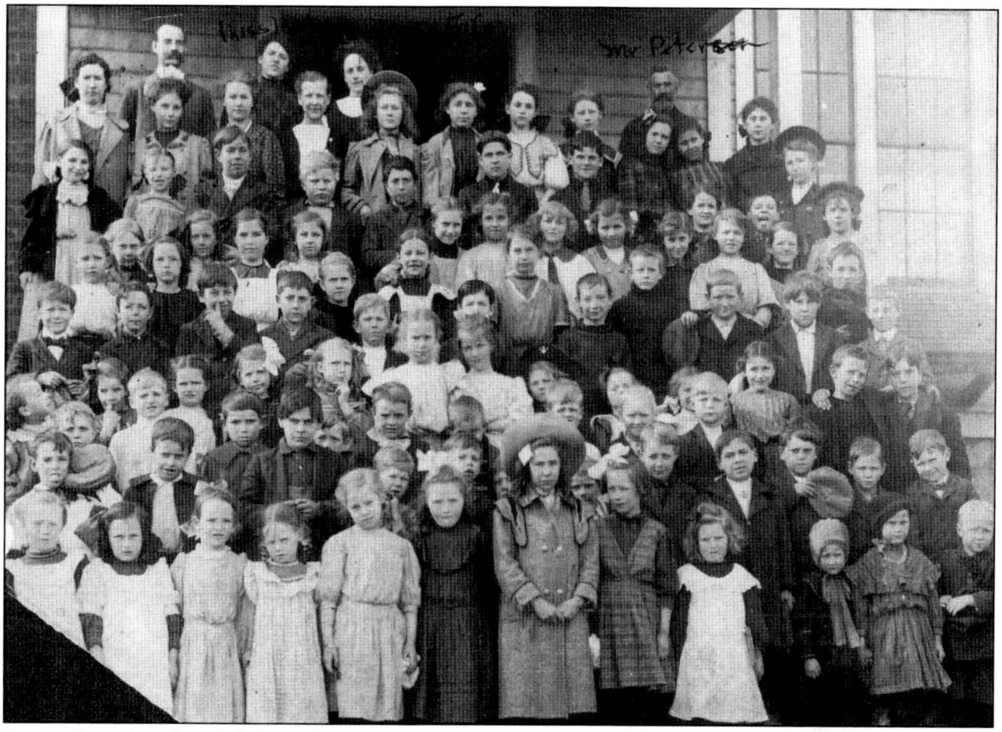

Ruston's early school did not have a shortage of children of all ages to fill its classrooms. This 1908 photograph of the entire school includes principal Mr. Groves, janitor Mr. Peterson, and teachers Misses Mater and Fife. The children bear the familiar last names of Olson and Johnson, as well as Gerud, Hurd, and Rumming. First names reflect the times: Zeke, Elmer, Pearl, Olga, Tillie, and Gretchen. (TR.)

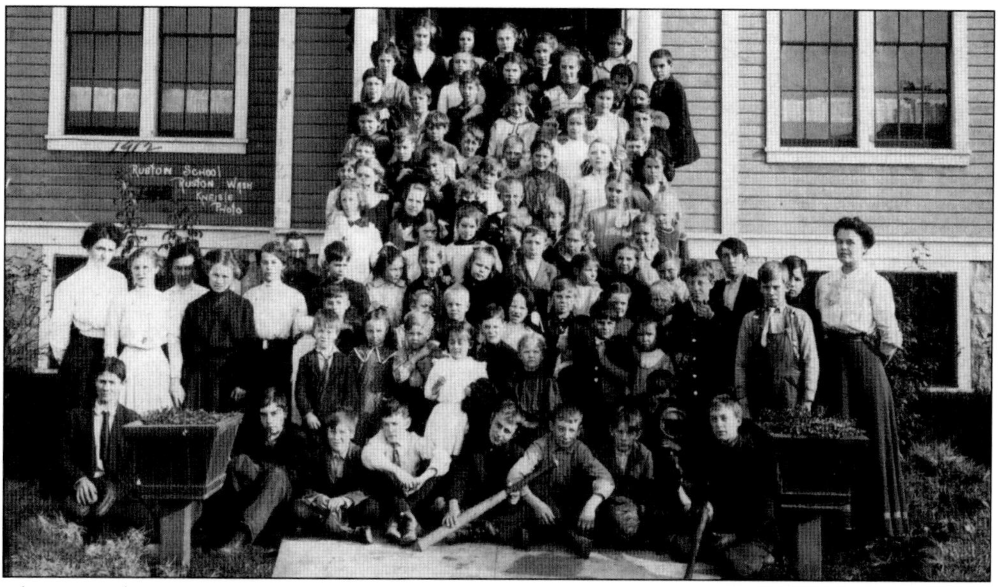

This 1912 photograph shows the full school, complete with flower boxes out front, with teachers Misses Martin, Moore, and Keeth. "Grandpa" Peterson is still the janitor. A few additional familiar names appear for these children, including Garrison, England, and Murphy. (TR.)

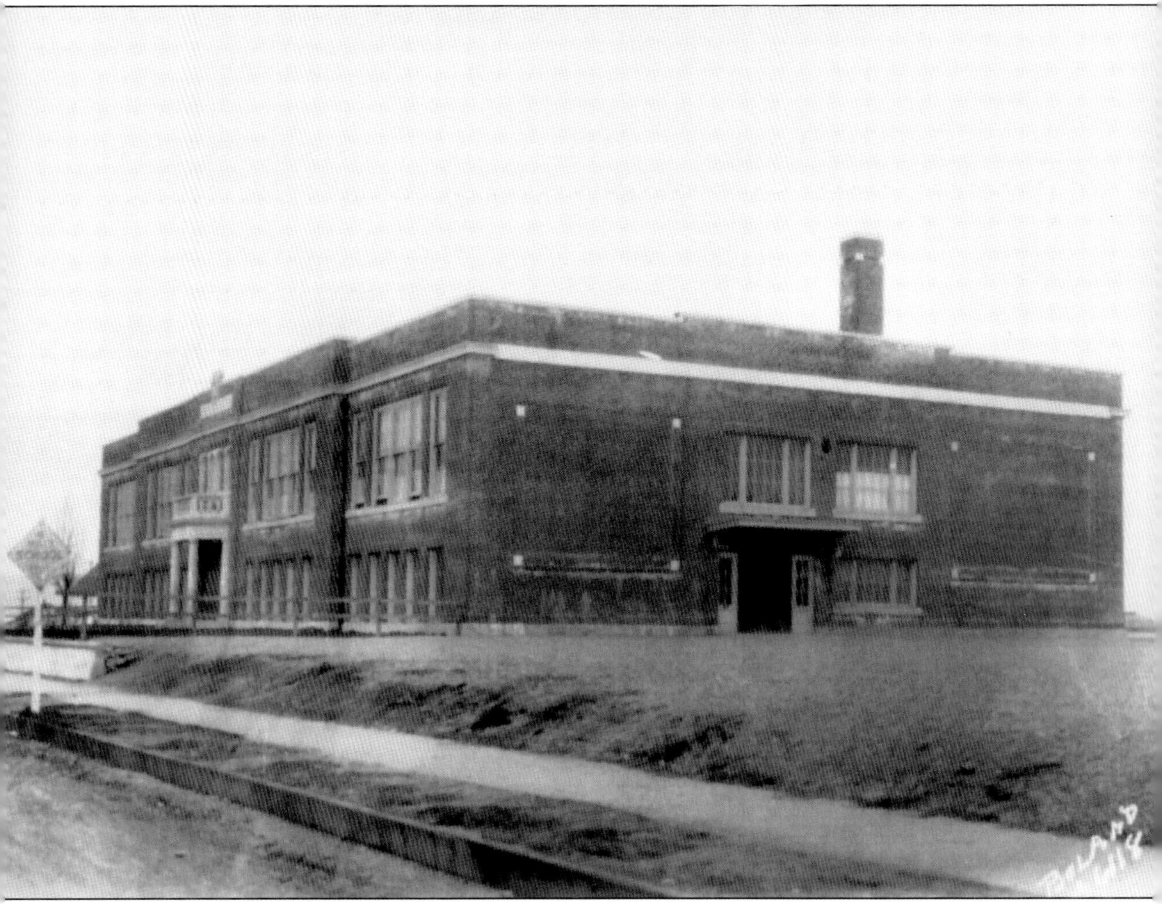

This 1924 picture shows the new Ruston School with expansive play areas on either side. Despite a dirt road out front, the new concrete sidewalks and retaining wall enhance the strong building. Stairwells were eventually added at the north and south entrances, but the front of the structure looks much the same today. Architects Hill, Mock, and Griffin are credited with the building's design. Major remodeling was done in 1967 and 1972. Ruston was forced to hand over the deed to the building to the Tacoma School District in March 1967, but the school continued to operate classes for kindergarten through eighth grade until 1986. After much cajoling, longtime Ruston council member Mary Krillich Joyce convinced the Tacoma School District to return the building to Ruston that same year. (TPL.)

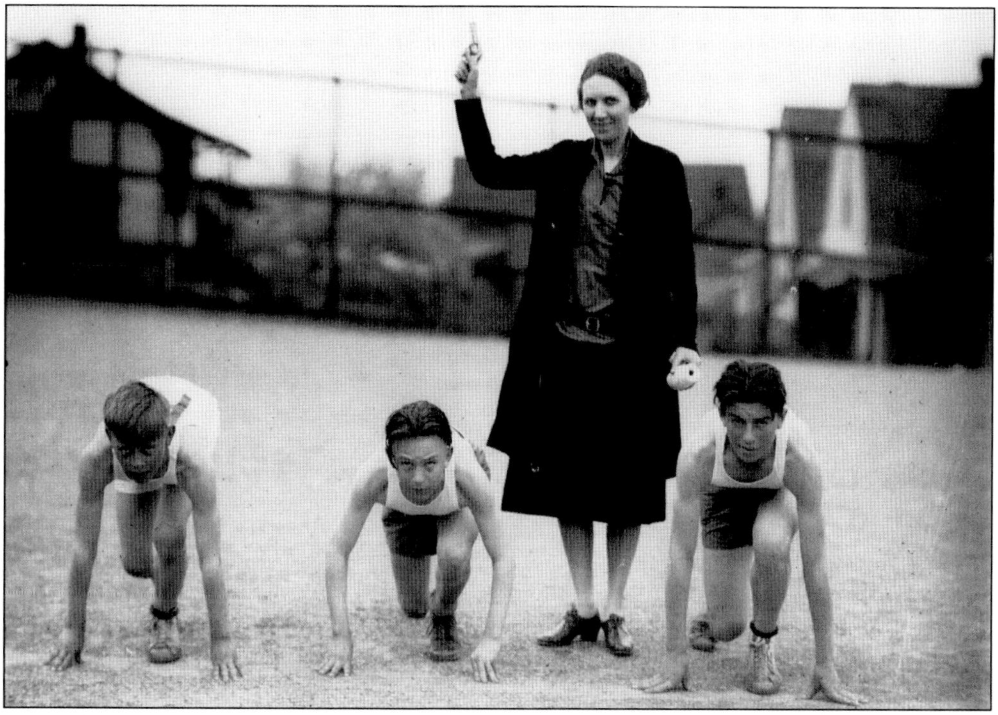

Ruston had a female school principal by 1928. Mrs. Lou Miller also served as track coach. From left to right are Richard Anderson (who was entering his first meet), Donald Nevers, and John Slavich (the latter were high-point winners of their classes the previous year). The boys pictured here, as well as Ruston girls, were training for a countywide grade school meet in Spanaway in April. (TPL.)

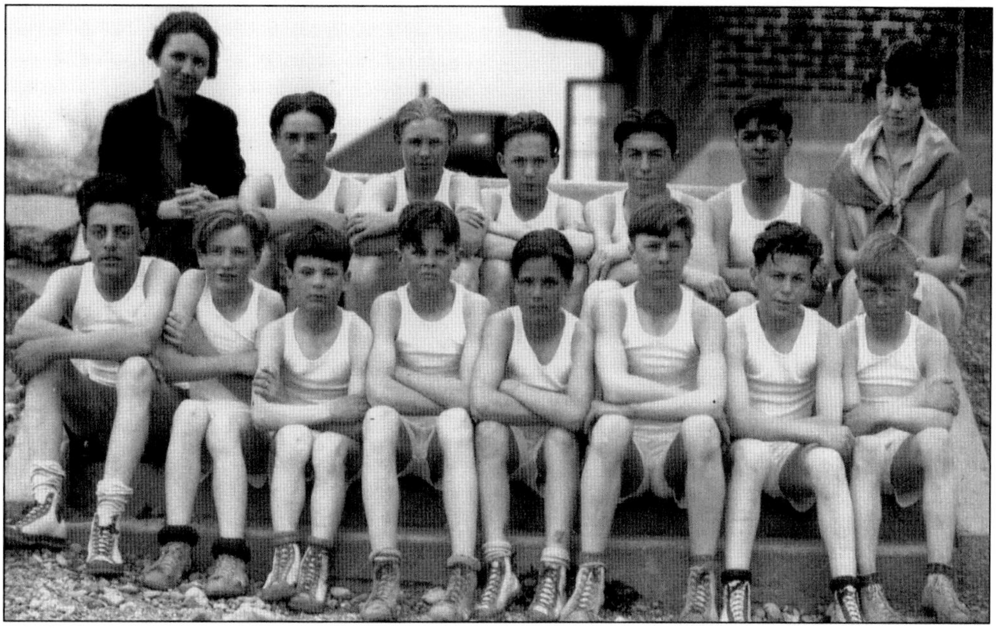

The boys' track team is captured on April 16, 1928. Miller's assistant is believed to be Gertrude Tenzler (second row, far right). The team is seated on the steps on the southeastern edge of school building. For competitions, boys were divided into three categories according to weight, height, and age. (TPL.)

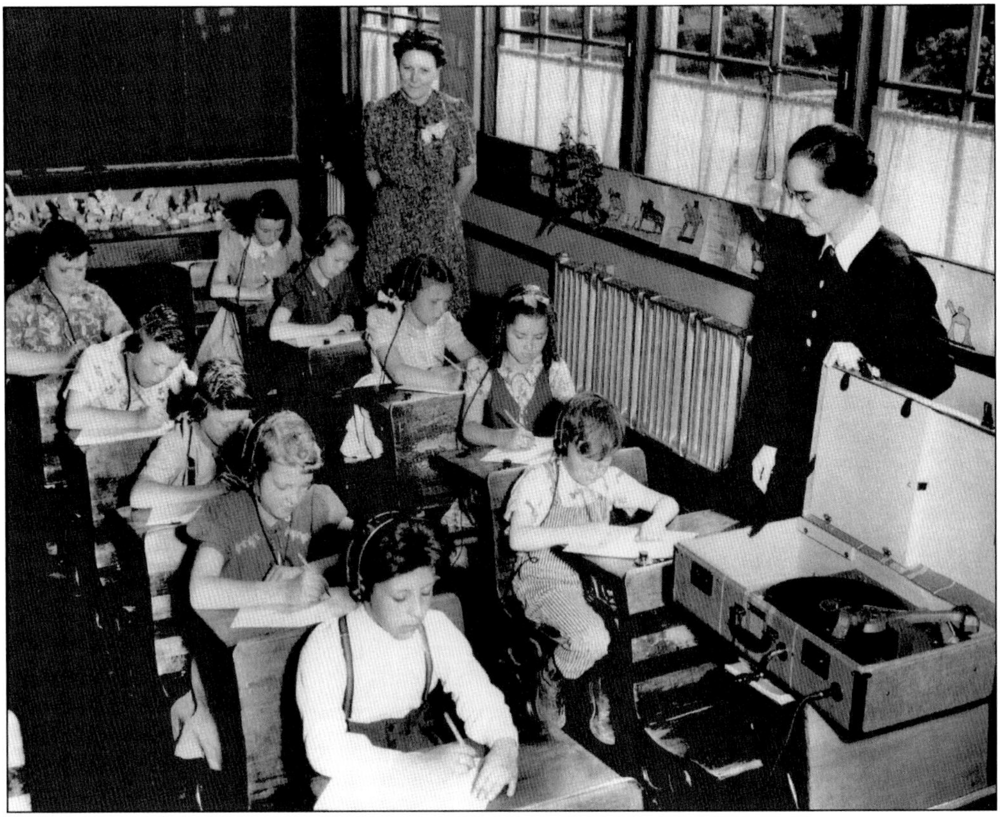

By 1941, technology was having a great impact on education. Ruston schoolchildren were testing new audio equipment from the local health department in this photograph. The nurse at the audiometer is Lillian Biehner. The children are, from front to back, (left row) Frankie Girolami, Marjorie Dimmen, Ned Face, and two unidentified students; (right row) Jimmy Tallman, Donna Canada, Margret Norton, Vida Fraley, and unidentified. The woman in back is unidentified. (TPL.)

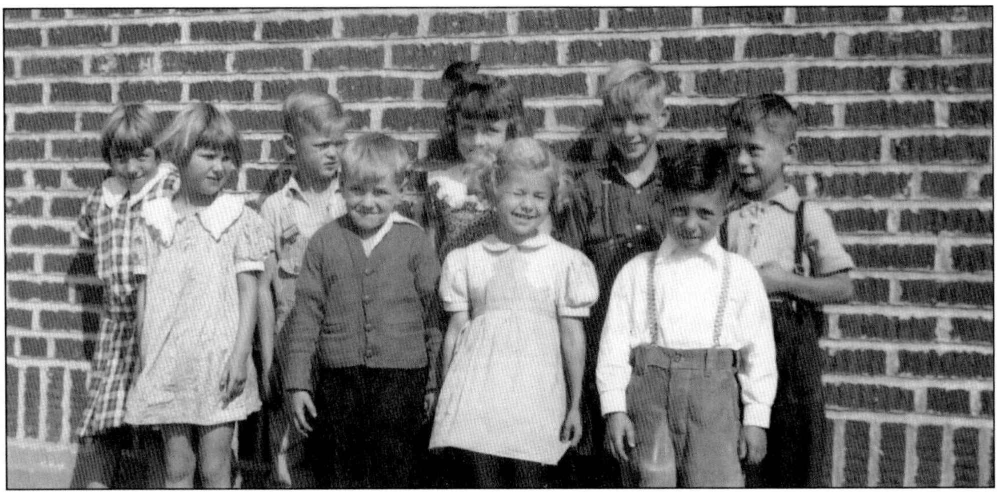

This group of children poses outside, in front of the brick wall of the school building in 1937. The young boy at the far right front appears to be Frank Girolami, who would go on to become a lawyer and served as a judge in Ruston for many decades. (Courtesy of the Tallman family.)

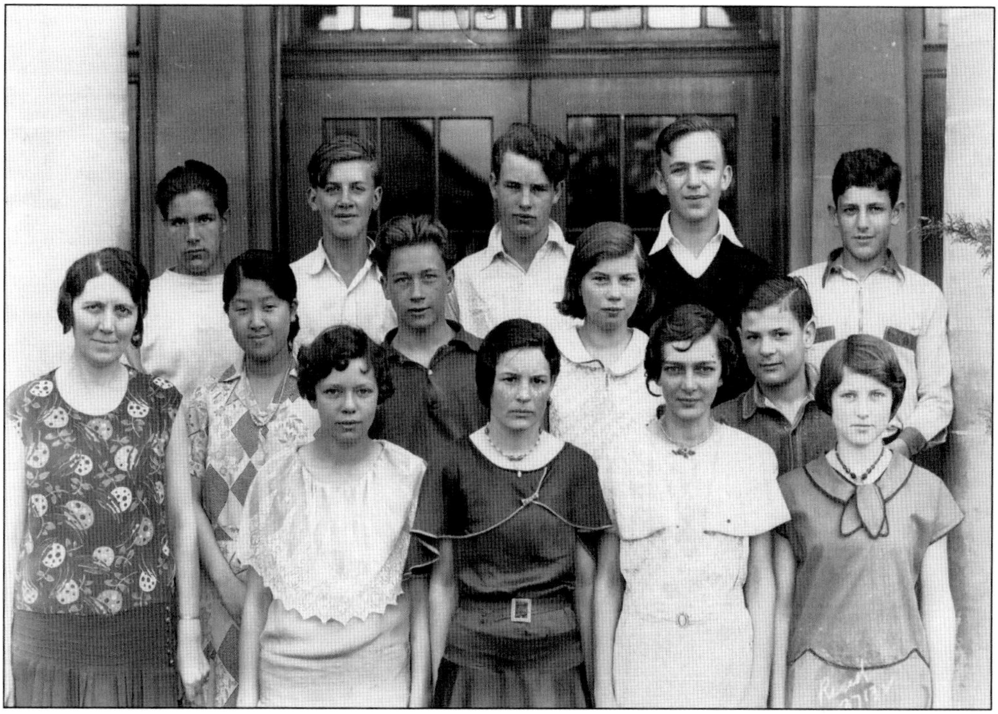

Gertrude Tenzler (first row, left) appears again in this undated photograph, apparently teaching one of the older classes. Ruston School only served children until the eighth grade. Everyone went to high school at Stadium or Lincoln, until Wilson High School opened in 1958. (Courtesy of the Tallman family.)

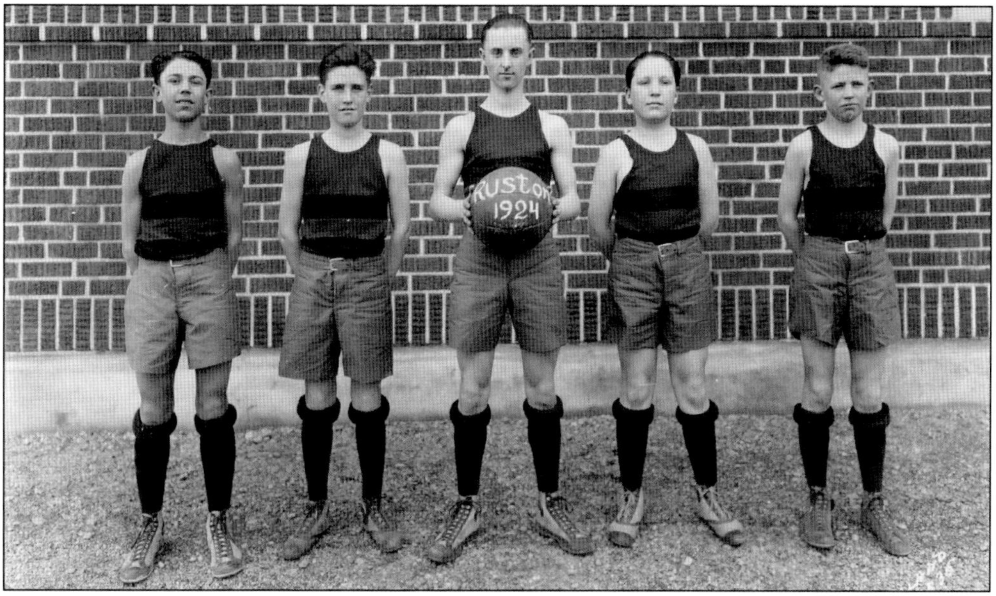

Sports teams from Ruston were known to be rough and tough. As an industrial town with fathers who worked manual labor, the young men grew up with raw strength as a prized virtue. Players from other schools were often intimidated when it was time to compete with Ruston. This 1924 photograph shows one such basketball team. (Courtesy of the Tallman family.)

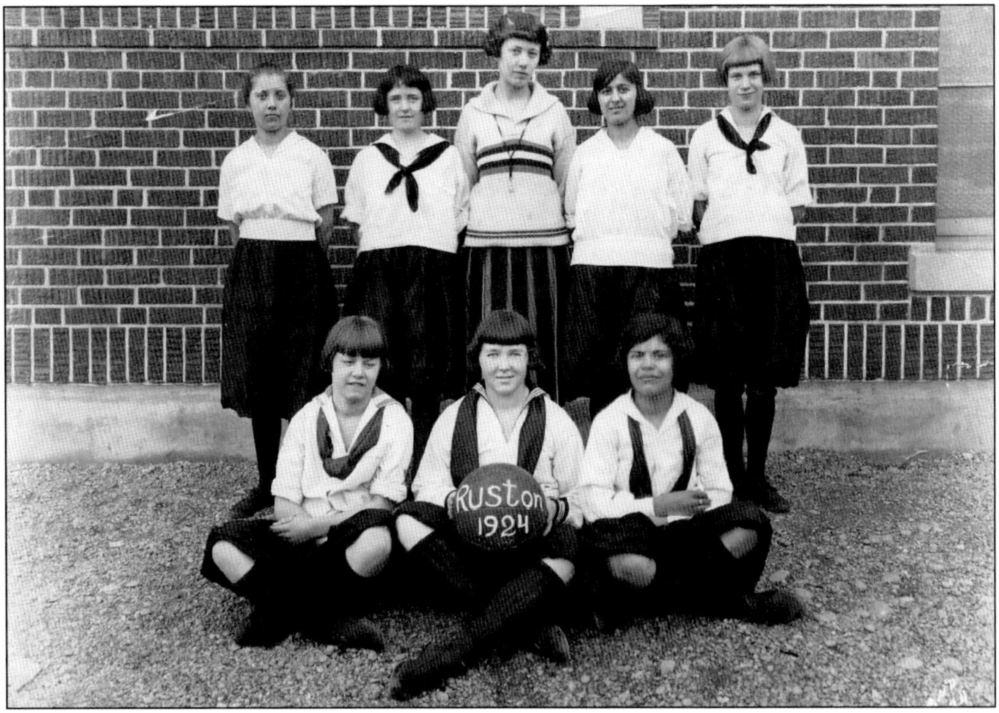

It is unclear if the reputation for toughness extended to the girls. It seems hard to imagine this 1924 team, pictured in dresses and scarves, as rough. The coach standing in the center of the second row may be a younger Gertrude Tenzler. Like the men in the early photographs of smelter work crews, this sports team is diverse. (Courtesy of the Tallman family.)

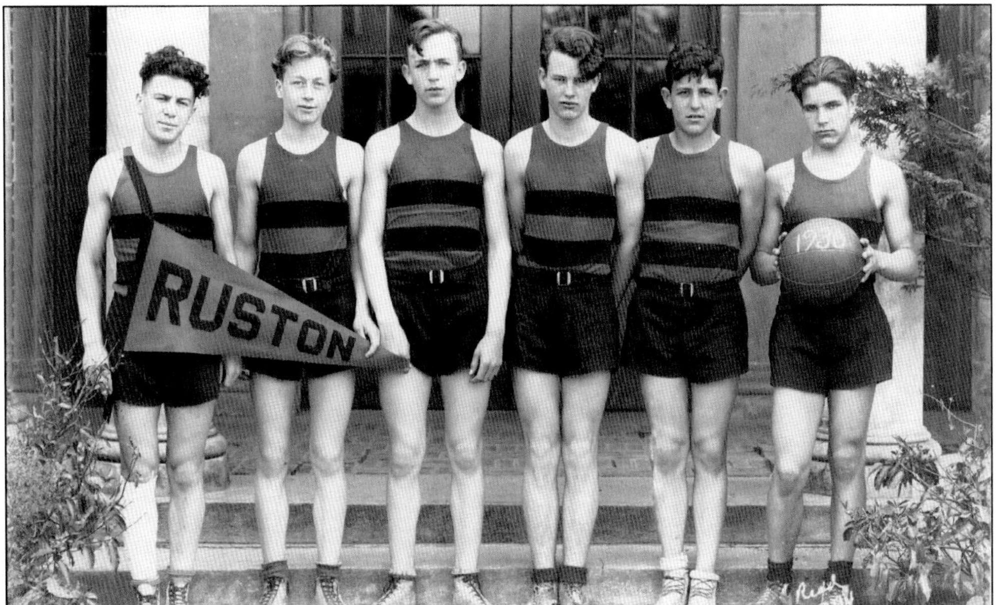

Sporting a Ruston banner, members of this 1930 boys' basketball team stand tall in their uniforms. They appear to be posing on the steps of the school in front of the same doors that still grace the entrance of the building today. (Courtesy of the Tallman family.)

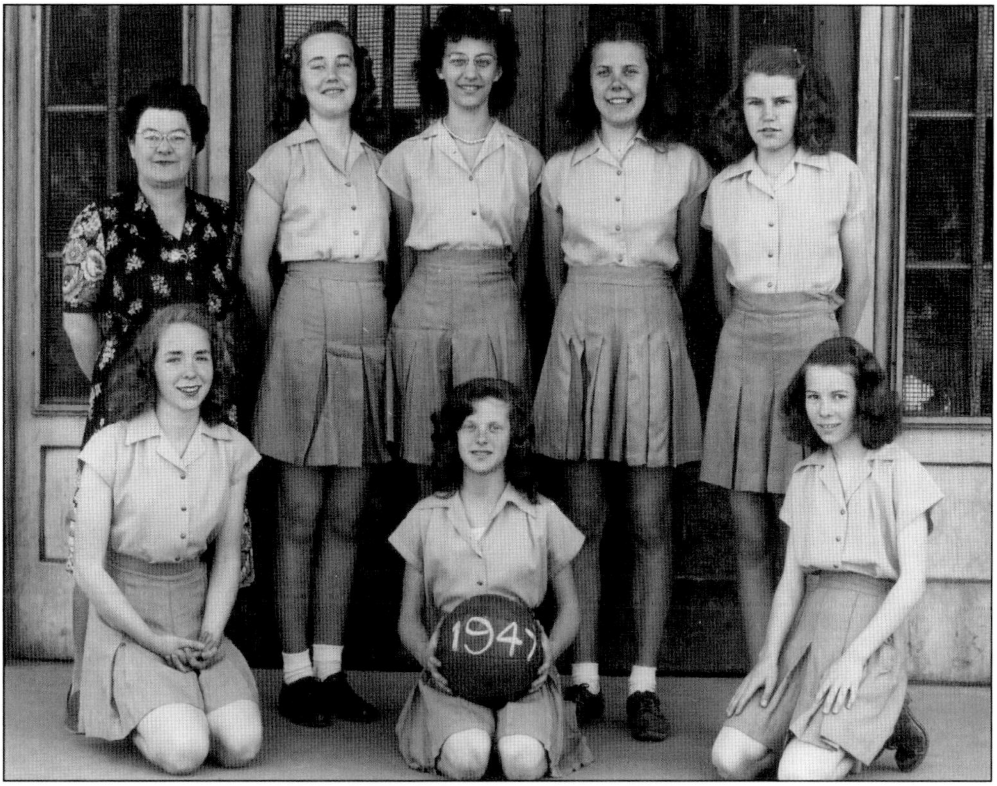

By 1947, styles had changed, but Ruston School continued to produce active sports teams for both boys and girls. This girls' team wears skirts and has players much taller than the coach. (Rod Larson.)

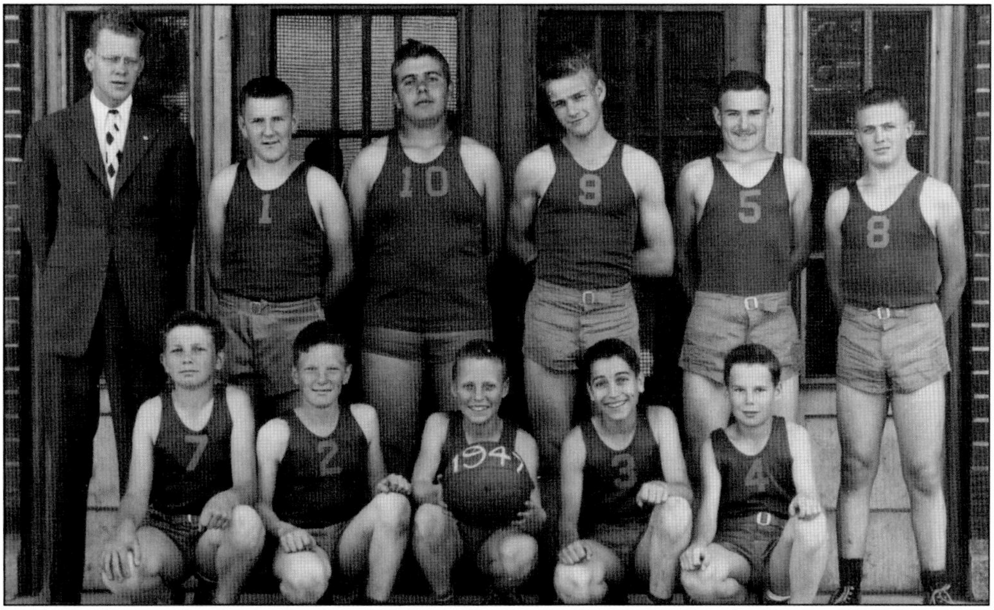

The 1947 boys' team includes some older-looking young men, one even sprouting the start of a moustache. But the coach is a head taller than even the oldest boy. Rod Larson (far left) was not only the coach but also served as principal of the school for decades. (Rod Larson.)

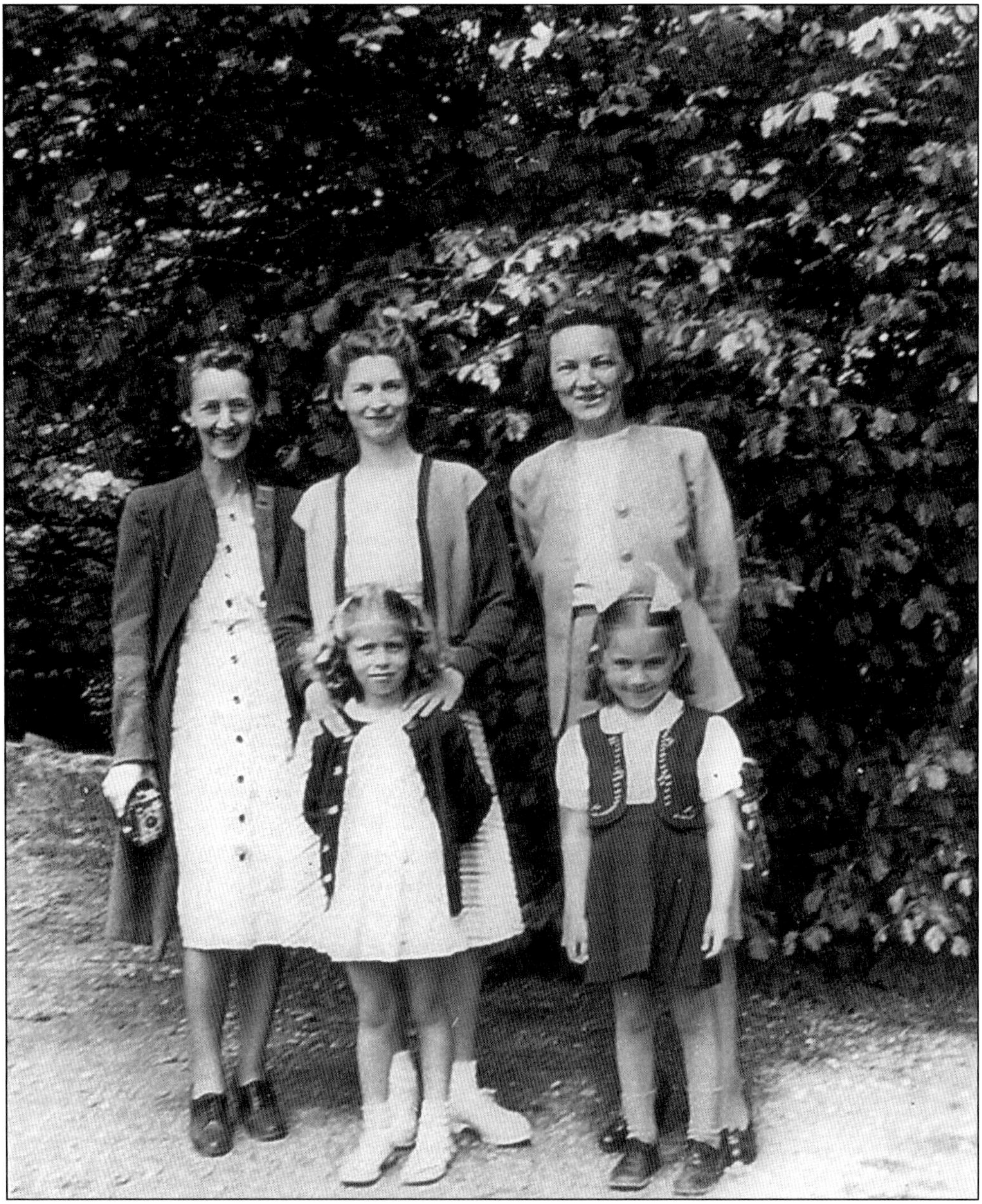

This photograph of a 1948 Ruston School picnic at Point Defiance Park features a young Rose Matesa (far left), who lived in Ruston until her death in 1995, at age 91. When Tacoma received the military reservation that was to become Point Defiance Park, the area was described in an early journal as "covered with a forest of giant Douglas Firs—some over 200 feet in height and as much as 9 feet in diameter, and with huge red cedars and hemlocks, white alder, swamp cedar, Madonna, soft maple, yew, birch and chiltim formed a jungle with a low growth of huckleberry, fern, sala and Oregon grape." Long before European settlers reached this shore, other people gathered around ancient campfires on Ruston beaches. The area was familiar to the original native population, who harvested clams from local beaches. At the entrance to Gig Harbor, there existed a large village, which appears to have been inhabited by the Puyallup tribe, on what became known as Hylebos Creek in Tacoma. (Carol Gore.)

The 1948 picnic was clearly fun for Jerry Kingbury (left) and Ronnie Adams (right), seated on either side of an unknown pal. School groups from across the South Sound continue to flock to the park at the end of each year, often visiting the zoo or playing at Owen Beach. (Carol Gore.)

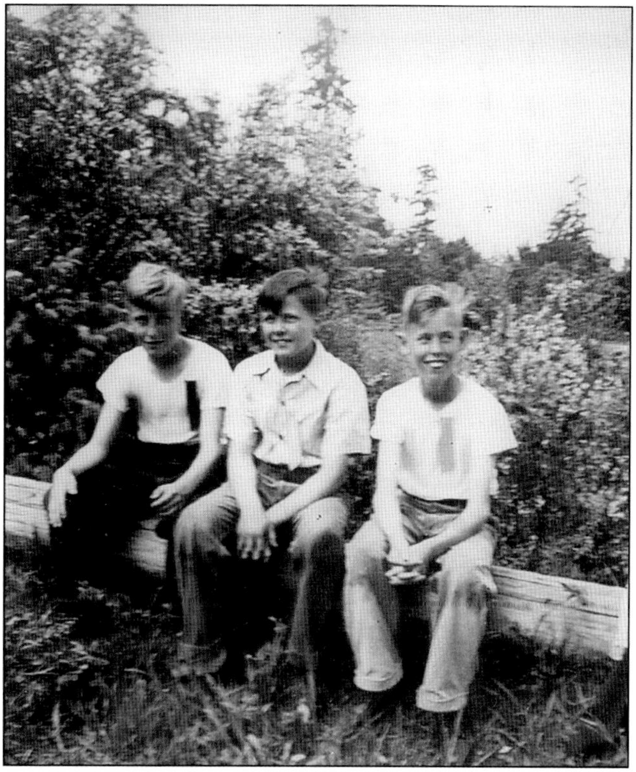

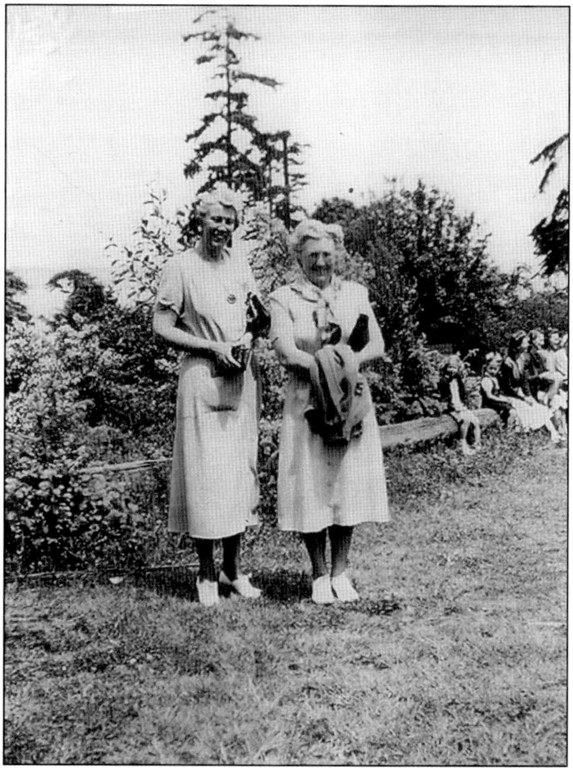

Teachers Misses Parsons (left) and Garges are seen in numerous Ruston School classroom pictures over the years. It appears both spent a great deal of their teaching careers working with the town's youth; they are shown here at Point Defiance Park in 1948. (Carol Gore.)

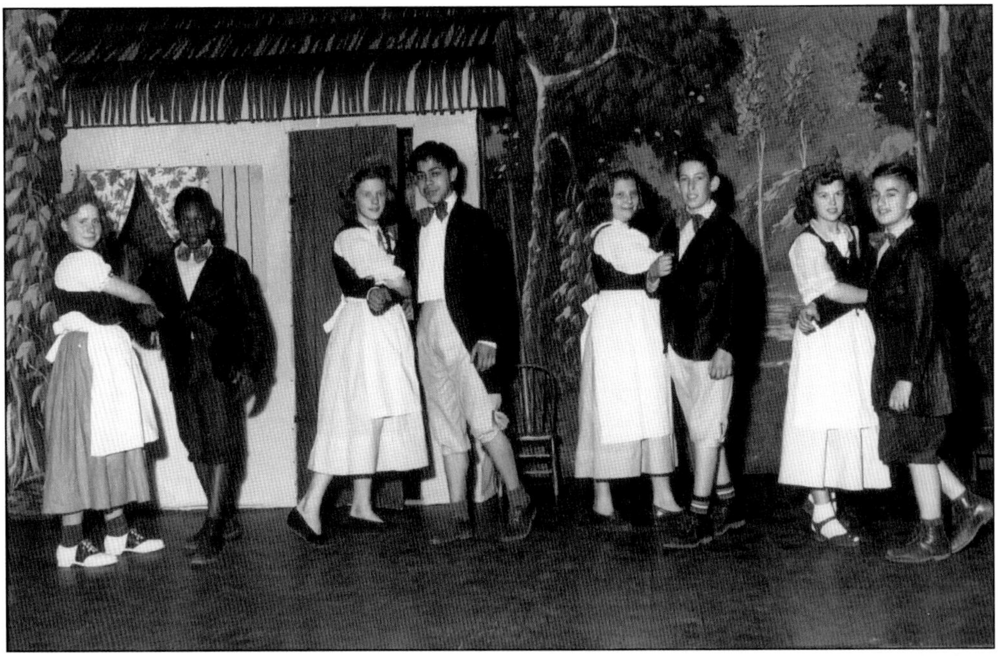

Before the era of television entertainment, Ruston children reportedly put on some the best dramatic school plays around. This undated photograph shows the stars of one such production, complete with elaborate costumes and stage sets. The school gym is equipped with a full stage. (Carol Gore.)

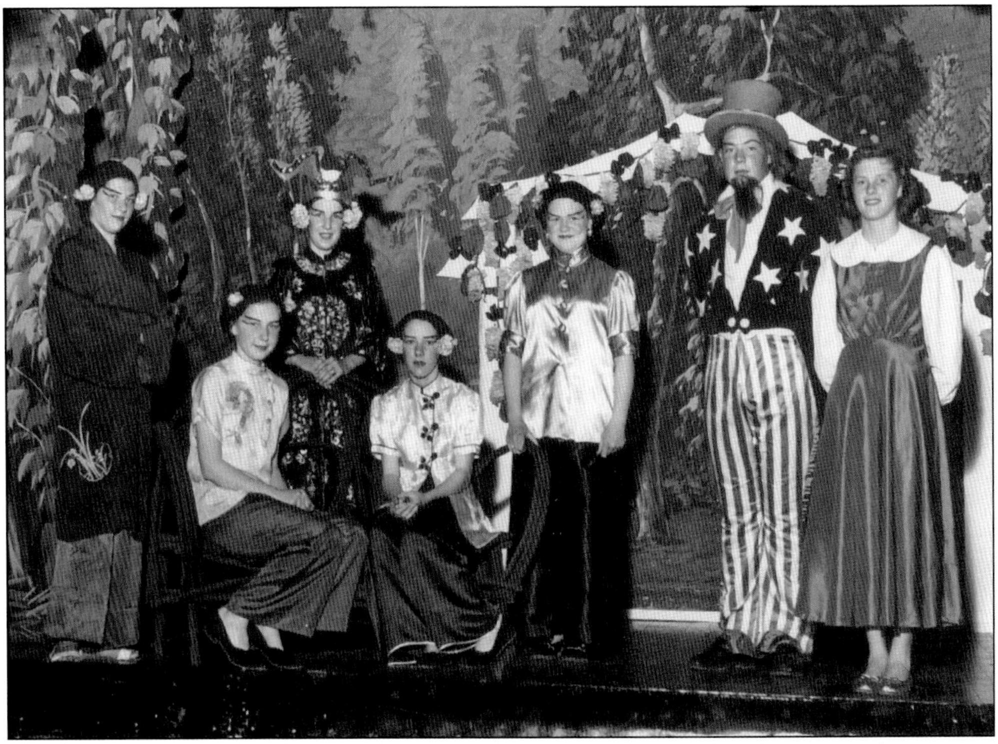

The 1949 play was set in the exotic Far East and had a patriotic theme. (Carol Gore.)

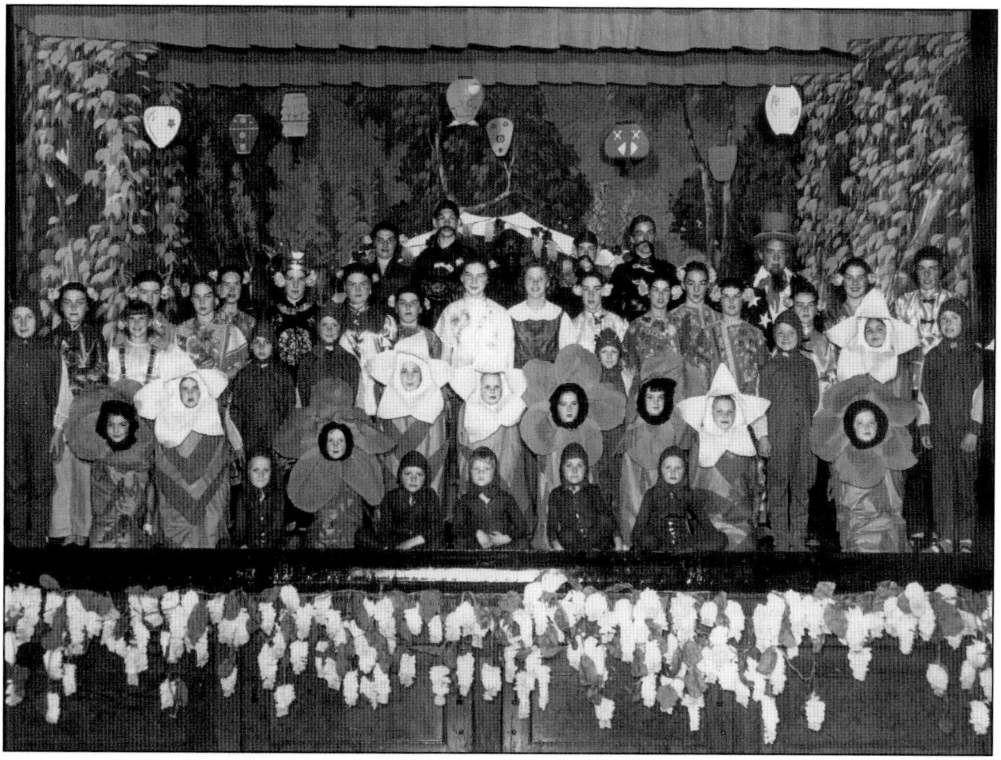

It was clear the whole school, with all ages of children, got involved in the plays. Parents and the extended community all enjoyed the entertainment. (Carol Gore.)

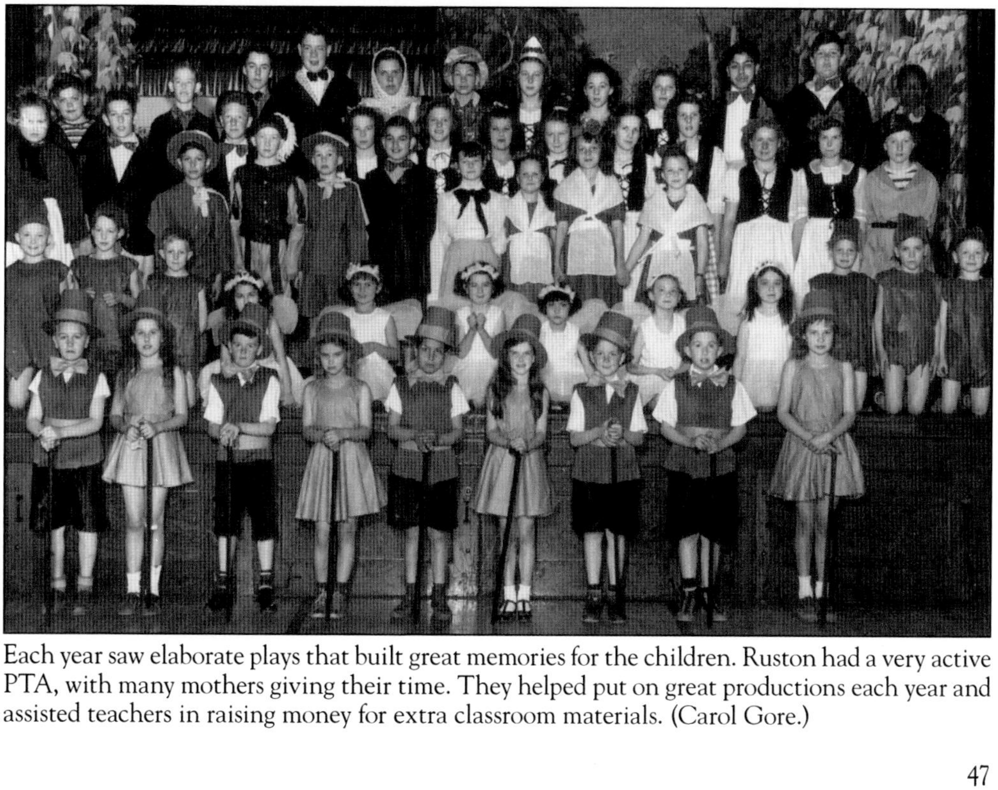

Each year saw elaborate plays that built great memories for the children. Ruston had a very active PTA, with many mothers giving their time. They helped put on great productions each year and assisted teachers in raising money for extra classroom materials. (Carol Gore.)

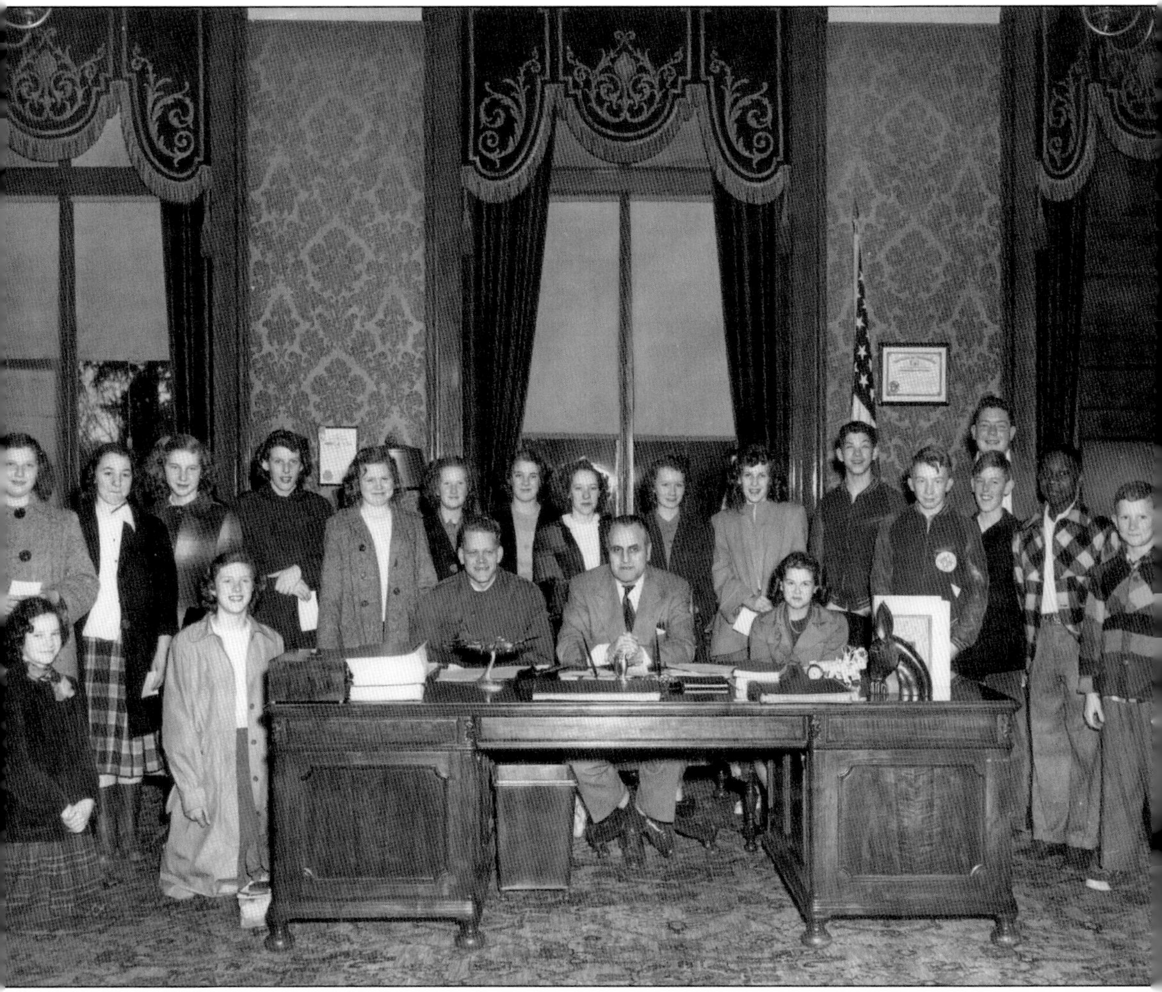

In 1949, the older Ruston classes went to visit Gov. Monrad Wallgren of Washington State. The youth all appear excited to be in the company of the state's highest leader. Principal Rod Larson is seated to the left of the governor. (Carol Gore.)

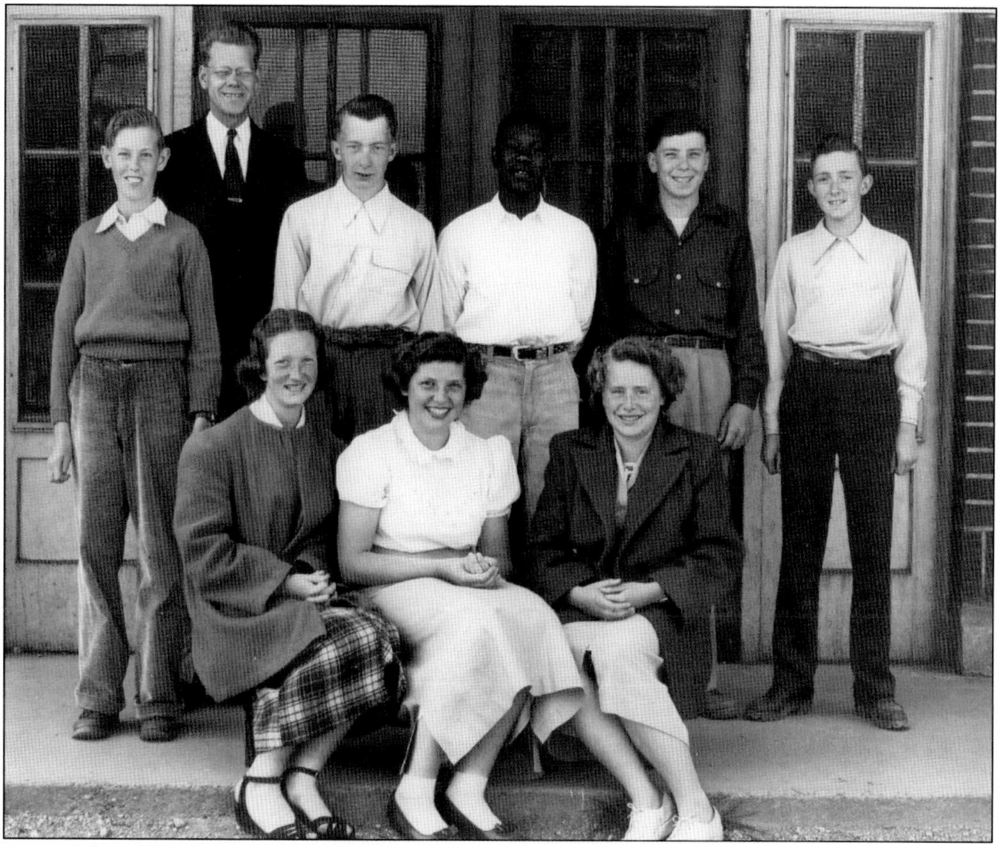

One of the older classes, probably seventh and eighth grade combined, is pictured in 1950 with principal Rod Larson. The classes were much smaller than in today's schools. In addition to his duties as principal and coach, Larson also taught. (Carol Gore.)

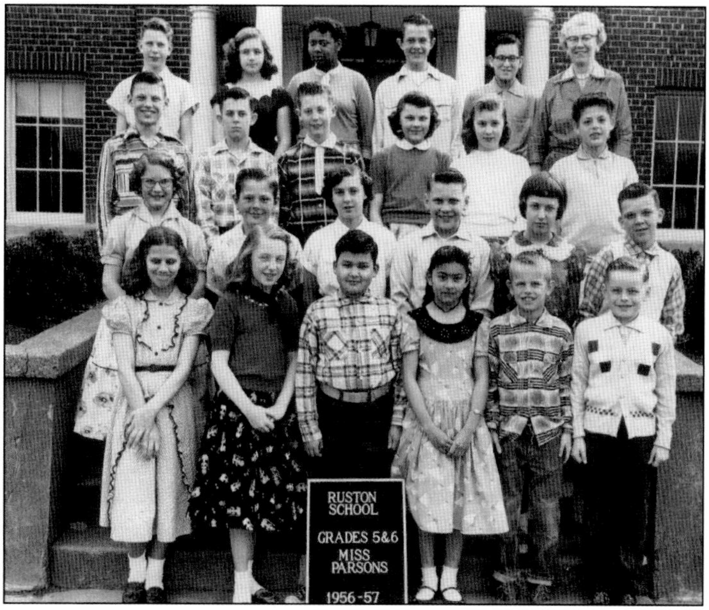

One of the families with deep roots in town is the Bundrock clan. Clarence Bundrock moved to Ruston after World War II brought him to Point Defiance to work the military crash boats. He married Roberta O'Leary, raised a family, and remained in Ruston until his death in 2009. Daughter Shirley is pictured in this 1957 photograph (far left, second row). Miss Parsons (far right, fourth row) is still teaching at the time. (Roberta Bundrock.)

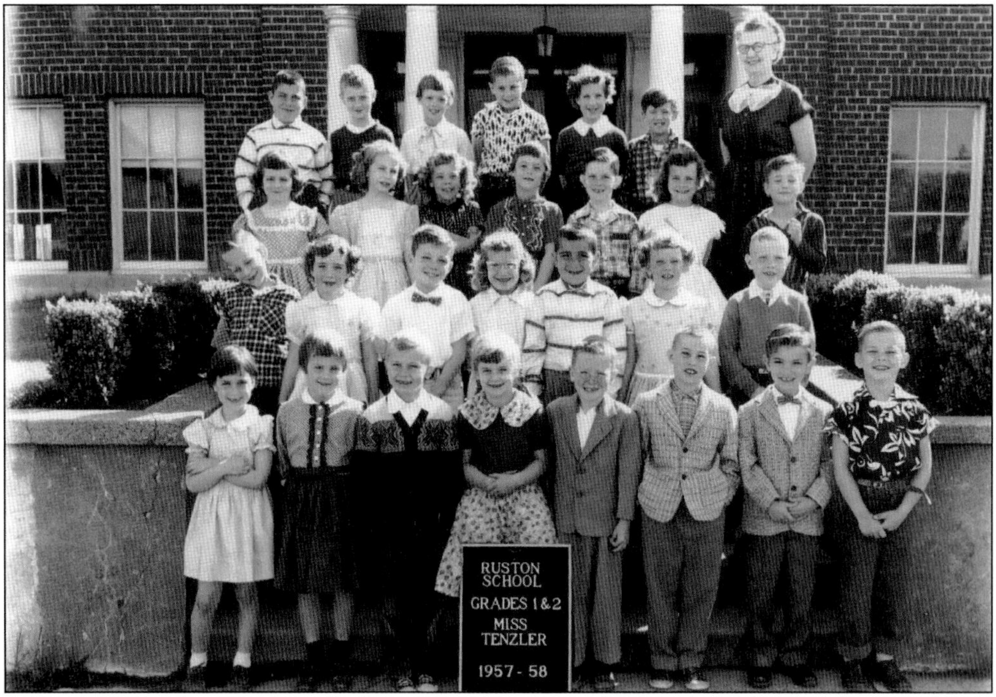

A teacher named Miss Tenzler is pictured in 1958 with a class of first and second graders. There is no way to confirm if this is the same Gertrude Tenzler shown in 1928 as the young assistant for the Ruston boys' track team. If this is the same woman, she devoted over 30 years to children in Ruston. (Roberta Bundrock.)

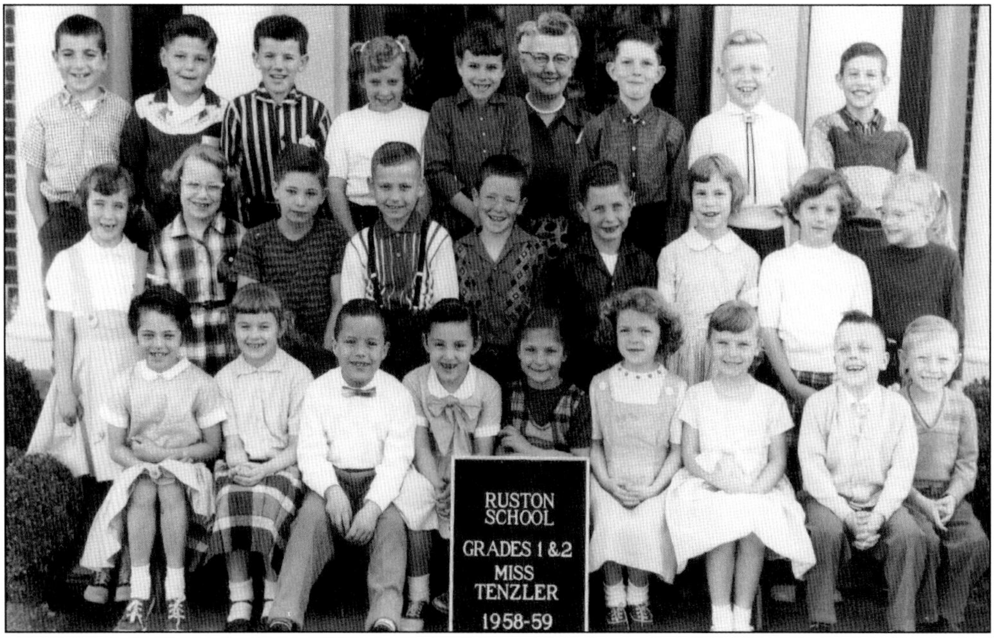

A year later, Tenzler is shown with this group of happy children. The joy on these faces brings memories of the innocence of childhood, when laughter came easily, and the world was new. (Roberta Bundrock.)

The name Ruston is unusual enough that the spelling was apparently difficult in this 1959 eighth-grade picture. The front of the school building looks identical 50 years later, down to the tree out front—with the exception of the fine-looking car parked street side. These cars are now only seen in area antique collections. (Roberta Bundrock.)

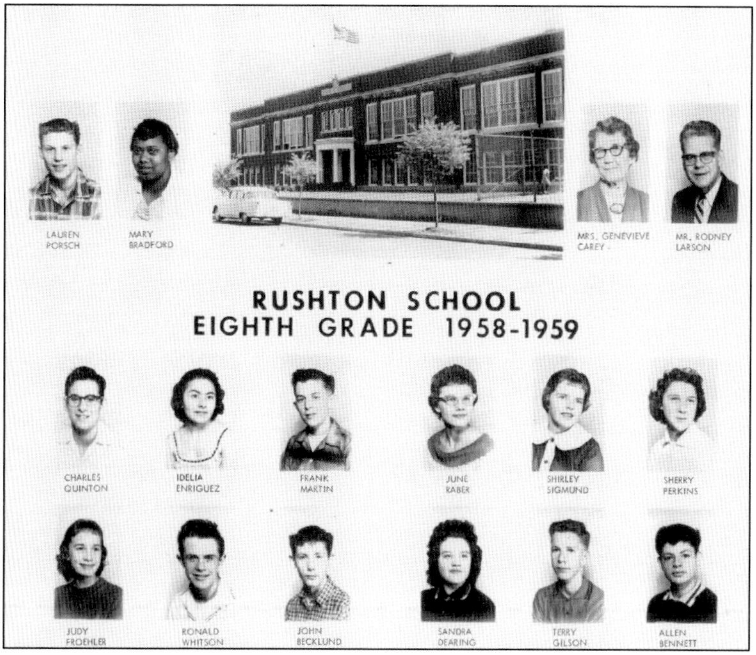

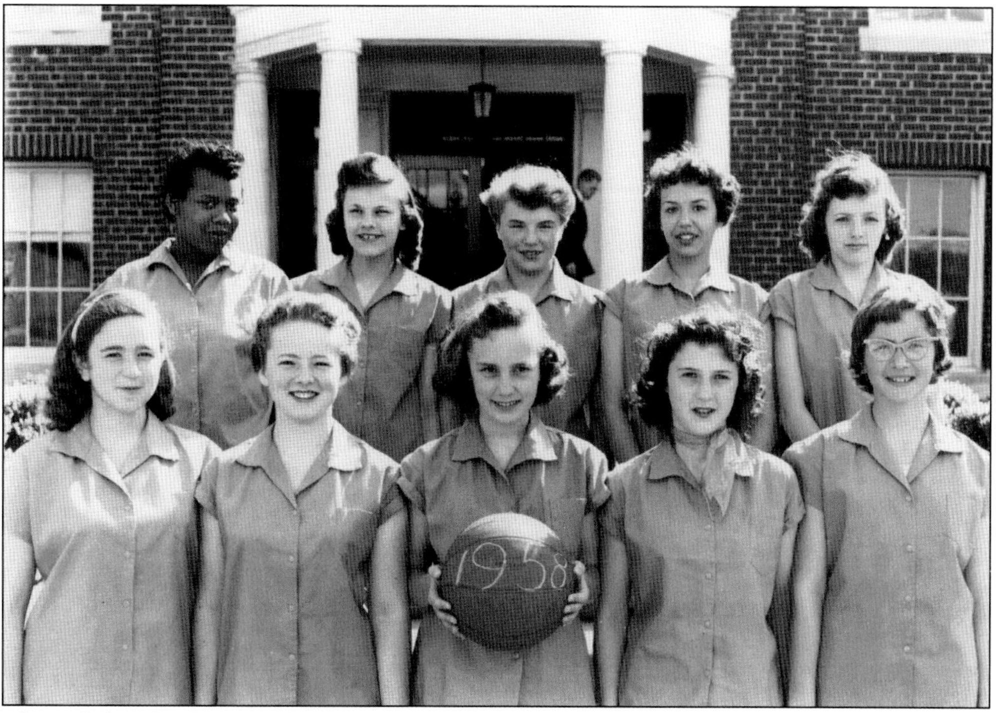

The stylish girls of Ruston basketball are shown in this 1958 photograph. Principal Rod Larson can be seen on the front porch of the school, behind the girls. Pictured from left to right are (first row) Vicky Giberson, Anneka Gerlings, Judy Froehlers, Sherry Perkins, and Shirley Bundrock; (second row) Mary Alice Bradford, June Raber, Bonnie Holgrins, Jo Ann Eberts, Carolinn Raber. (Roberta Bundrock.)

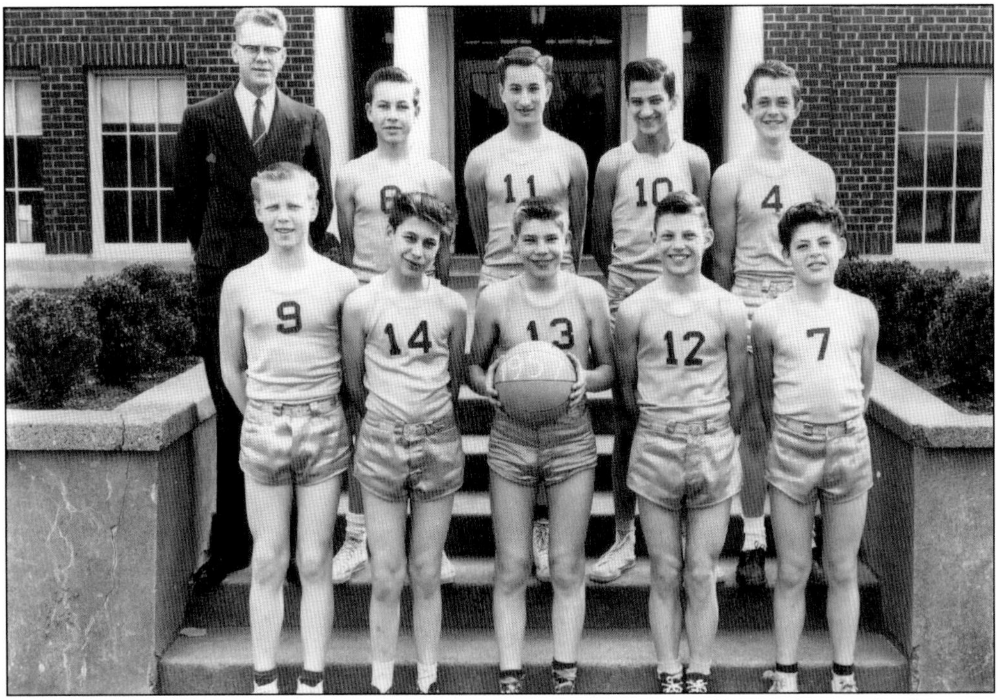

The 1957 boys' basketball team shows hairstyles of the era, especially number 14. Rod Larson remained active in the school in many facets, coaching teams in addition to acting as principal and teacher. He was beloved by alumni at the 2008 Ruston School Reunion; Larson was able to attend, even though he was well past his 90th birthday. (Rod Larson.)

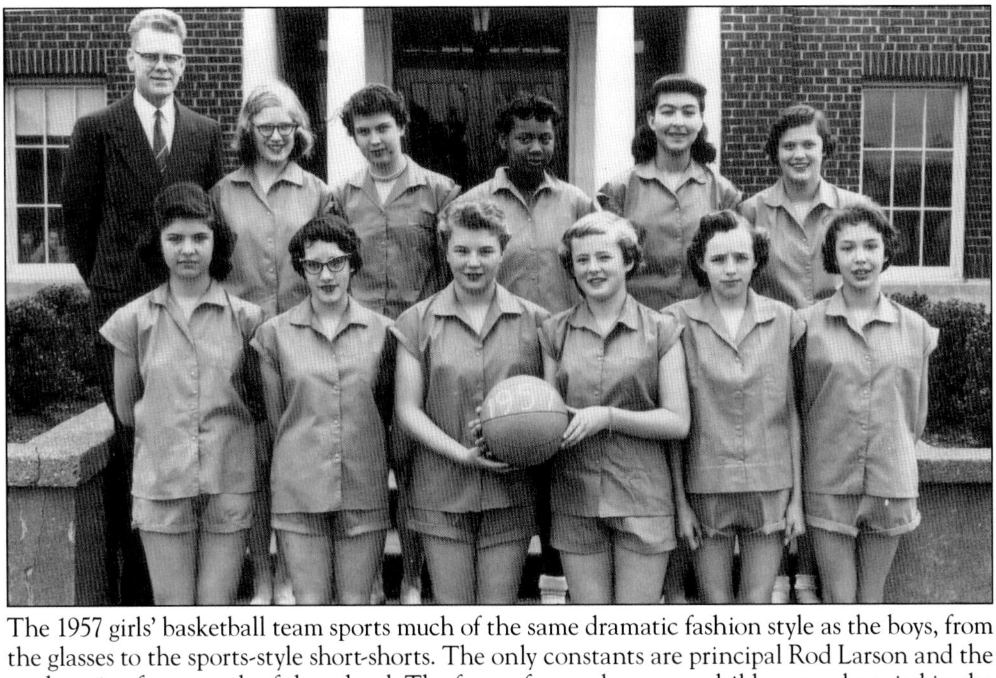

The 1957 girls' basketball team sports much of the same dramatic fashion style as the boys, from the glasses to the sports-style short-shorts. The only constants are principal Rod Larson and the unchanging front porch of the school. The faces of several younger children can be spied in the window to the left of Larson. (Rod Larson.)

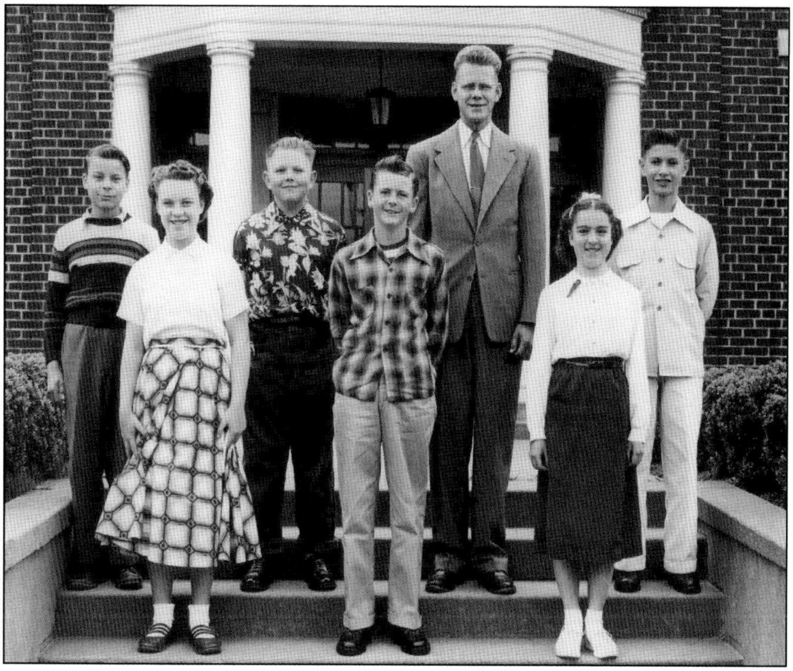

This undated picture confirms again the smaller class sizes often seen in the town's only school. (Rod Larson.)

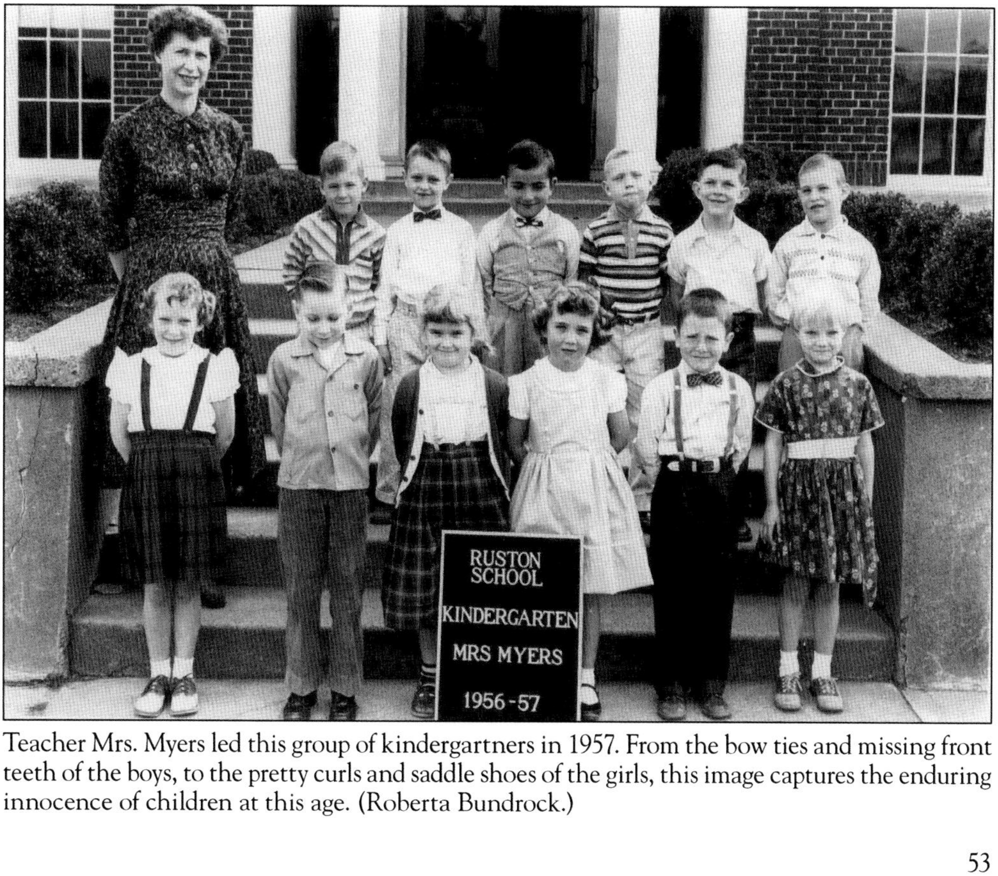

Teacher Mrs. Myers led this group of kindergartners in 1957. From the bow ties and missing front teeth of the boys, to the pretty curls and saddle shoes of the girls, this image captures the enduring innocence of children at this age. (Roberta Bundrock.)

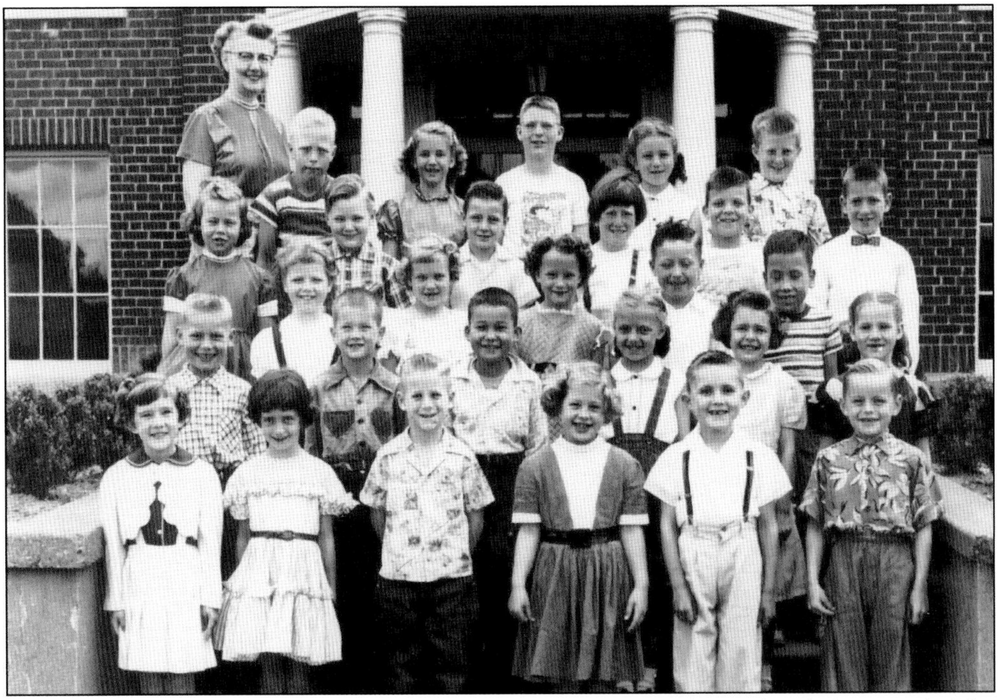

Miss Tenzler leads another troupe of first and second graders in this undated photograph. The different personalities are apparent on the faces of the children, from the older boys in back to those in front. (Roberta Bundrock.)

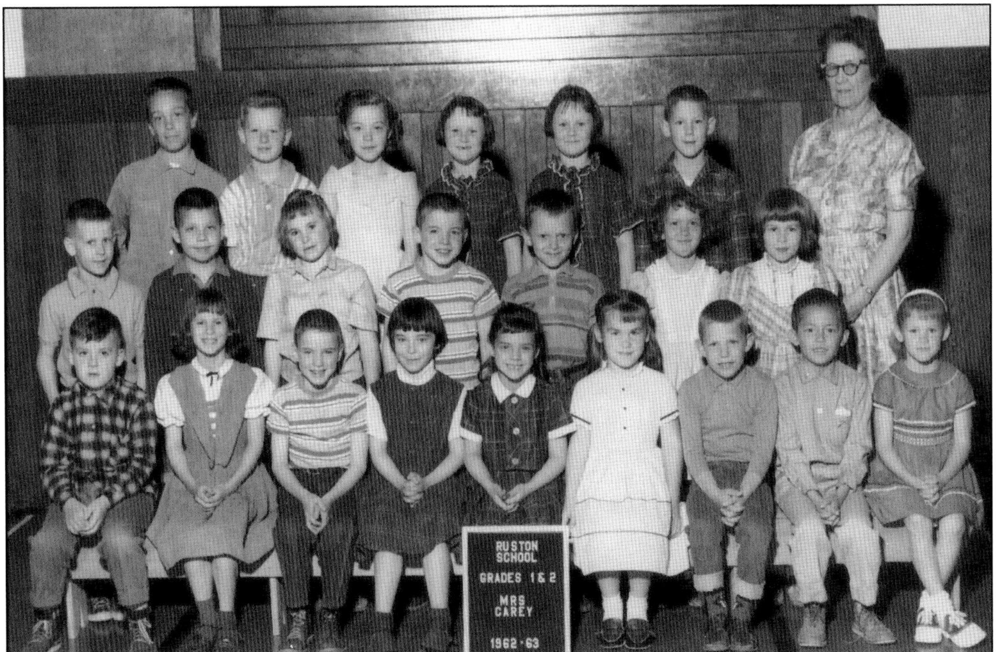

By 1962, Mrs. Carey was teaching the first and second grades. The location for pictures had moved indoors, into the gym, and the school had a pair of identical twin sisters (third row, center). (Carol Gore.)

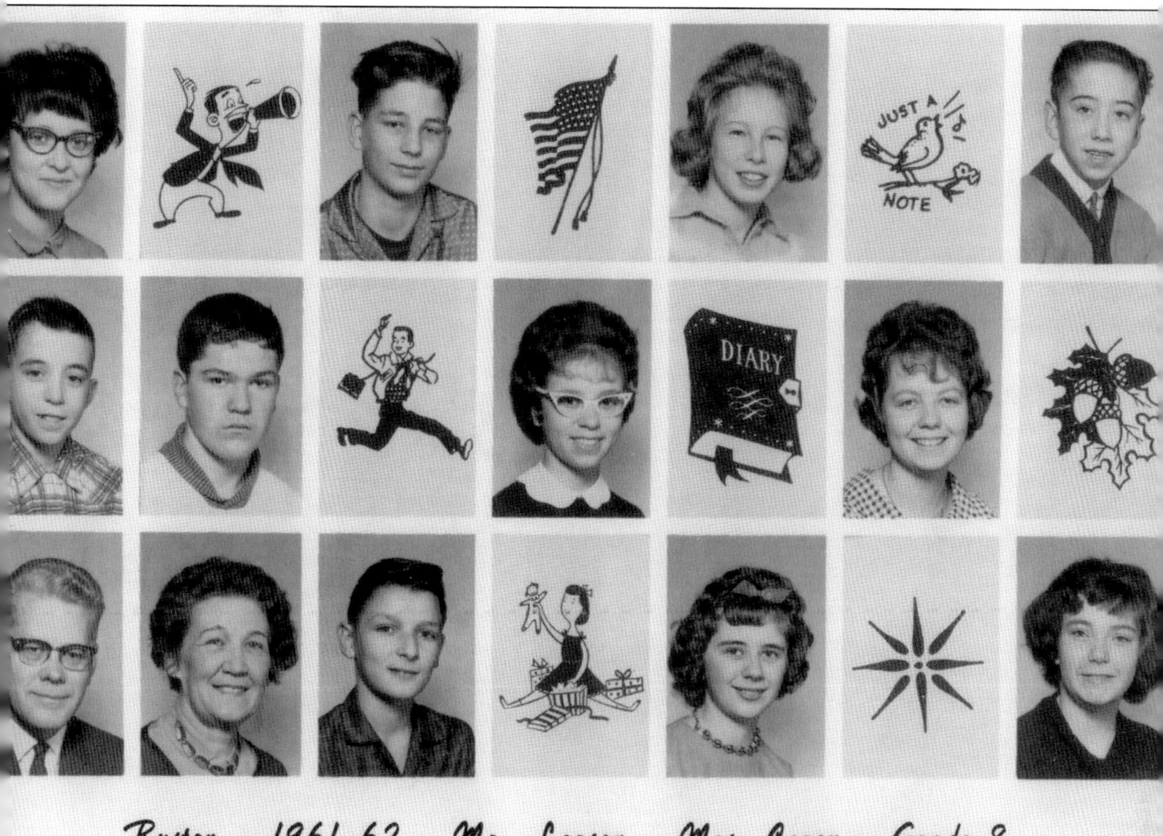

Ruston – 1961-62 – Mr. Larson – Mrs. Carey – Grade 8

The fathers of these Ruston School students would have been working by the time they had reached the ages of the eighth graders pictured. Industrial jobs in smelting and refining were tough, dirty, sweaty work, but they paid well. Many of these men spoke of working hard so they could send their children to college in hopes of a better career. Early Ruston children remember Charlie, son of George Krillich. Born in 1908, by the time he was 70, his routine included regular stops at The Brick to cash a check and buy candy. He then wandered the streets of Ruston, passing out treats to local children. His brother Ned was on the Metropolitan Park Board for a time. Local resident Mary Joyce, daughter of one of the Krillich brothers, spent much of her childhood delivering groceries for the family business. (Carol Gore.)

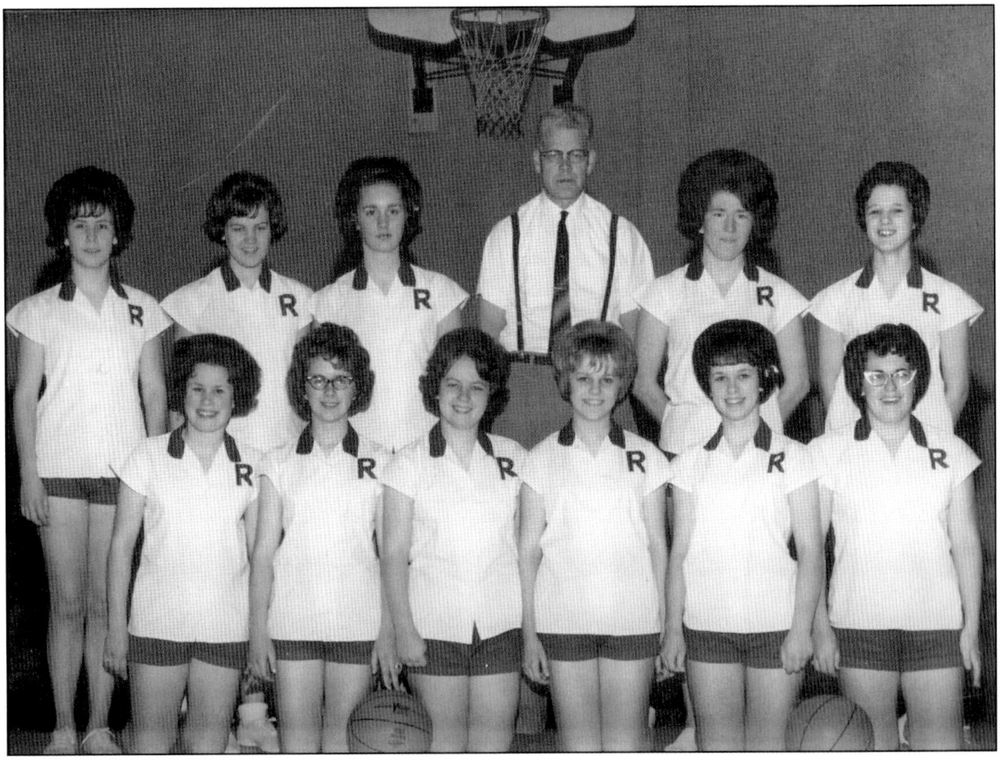

Rod Larson continued to coach basketball for decades. This 1963 team, pictured in uniforms that proudly display an *R* for Ruston, won the county championship. (Carol Gore.)

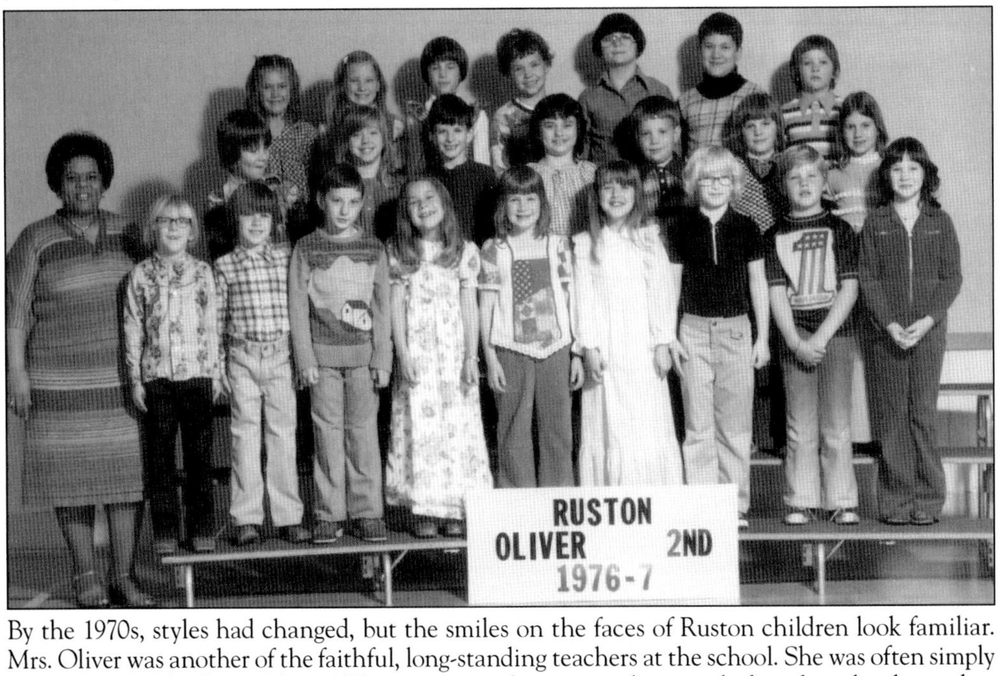

By the 1970s, styles had changed, but the smiles on the faces of Ruston children look familiar. Mrs. Oliver was another of the faithful, long-standing teachers at the school. She was often simply referred to as "the best." This 1977 image was taken just eight years before the school was shut down. (Carol Gore.)

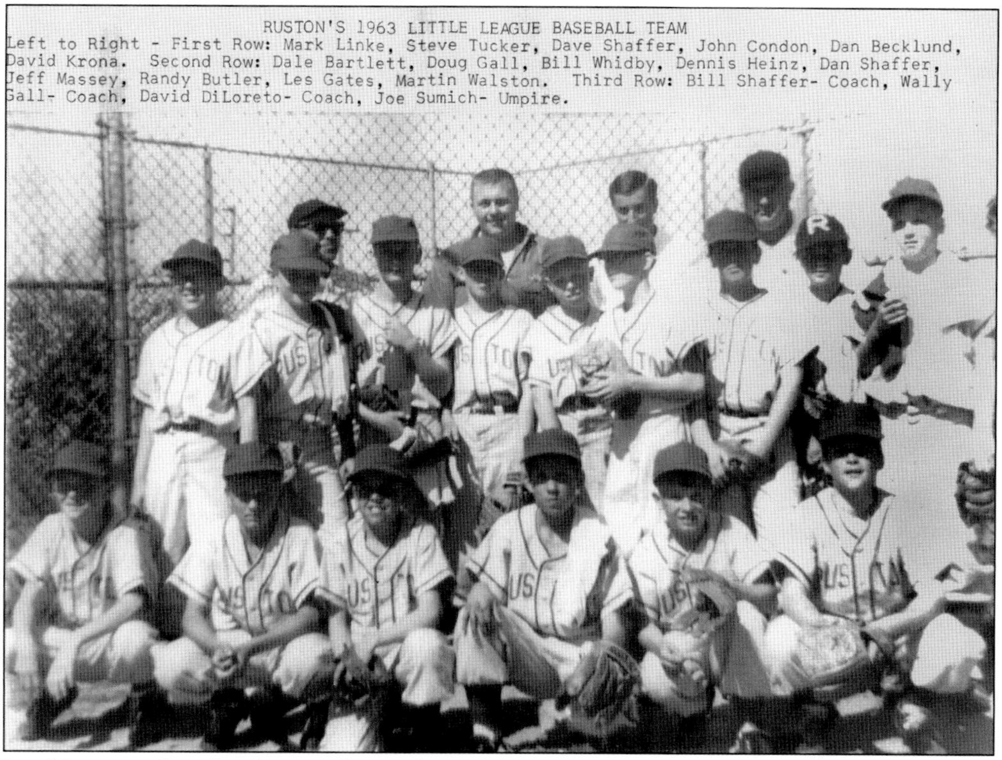

In addition to the school teams, Ruston hosted extracurricular sports squads like this 1963 Little League team (above). Once again, the names of the children were familiar, with aunts, uncles, and siblings all settling in town to raise their families and work at the smelter. The Shaffers owned the gas station on the corner of North Fifty-first and Pearl Street for decades. The Linkes raised many children in town. There was more than one DiLoreto home in Ruston at the time. Steve Tucker (first row, second from the right) is now one of the town maintenance men. The smelter was an integral part of the community and often sponsored local teams, such as this 1973 girls' softball team (below). Even with an injury (far left), the members still showed up for this team photograph. (Above, TR; below, KP.)

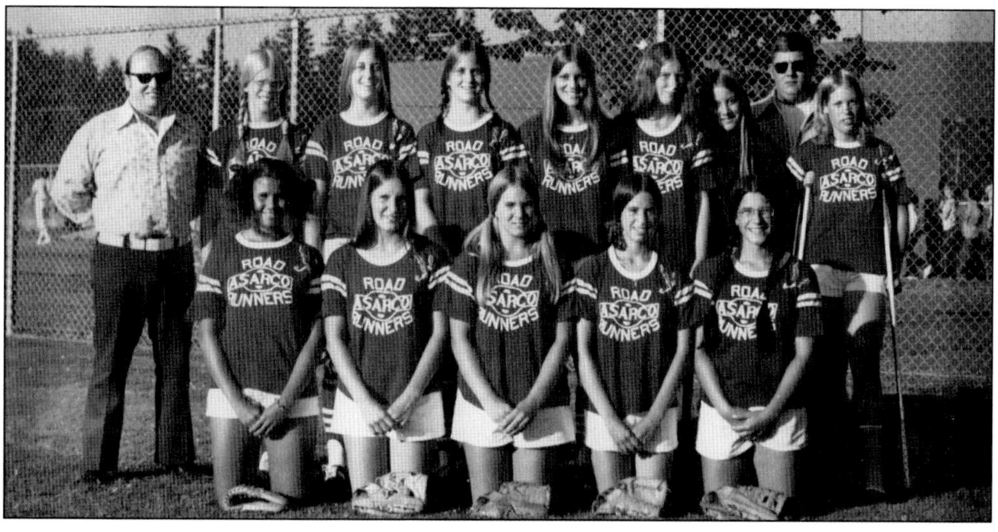

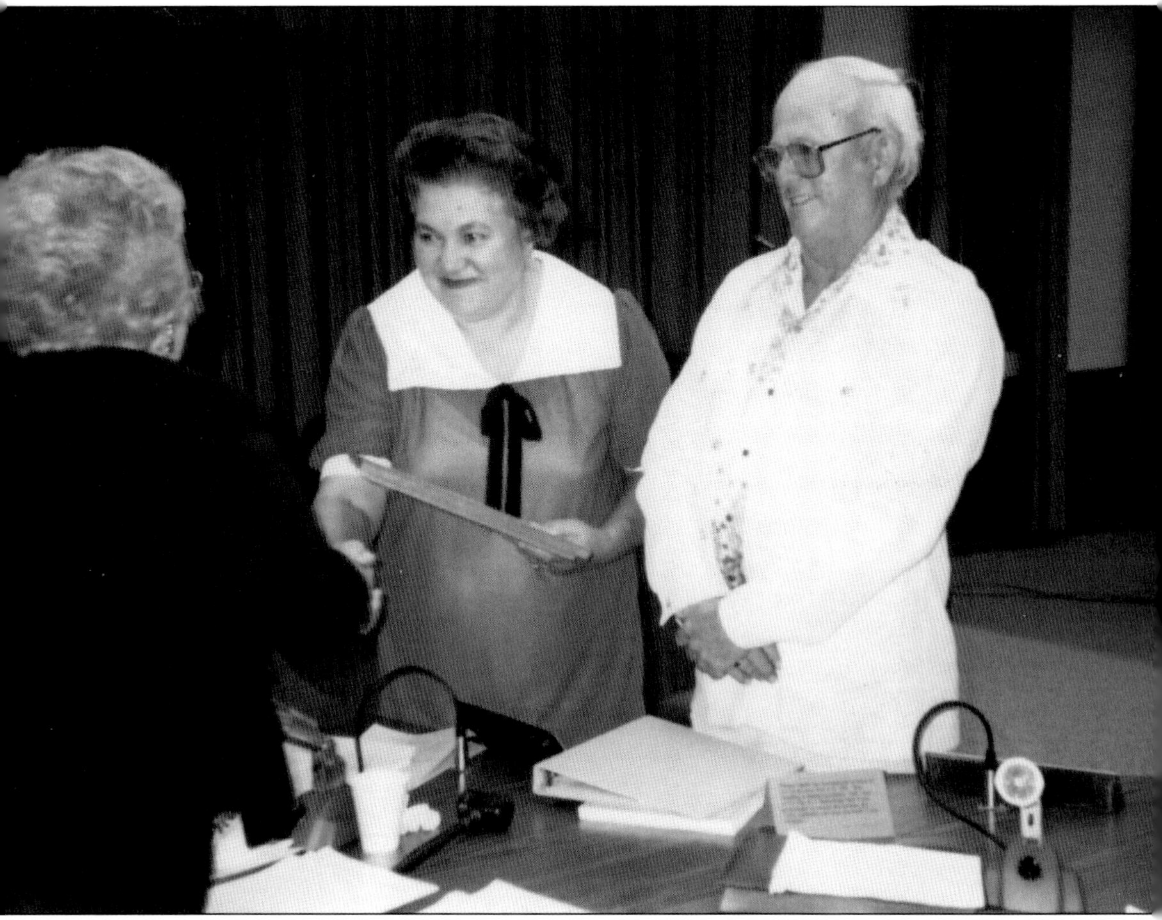

Longtime councilwoman Mary Joyce fought hard to convince the Tacoma School District to return the school building and adjacent land to Ruston after it closed the school. She is seen in 1986, along with mayor Pete Brudevold, accepting the deed for the school from school board president Cathy Pearsall-Stipek. Joyce grew up in Ruston. She is the daughter of one of the Krillich brothers who operated a grocery store and boardinghouse on North Forty-ninth Street for many years in the early 1900s. Joyce married Tacoma police officer Bert Joyce, raised five sons, and dedicated over 40 years to Ruston as a council member. Ruston has seen its share of tragedies over the years. Mayor Brudevold was murdered while in office in 1988. The tragedy shocked the small town. Brudevold's killer was soon captured and sentenced. (TR.)

Four

SMELTER STACK

The most memorable structure in Ruston over the past century has been the smelter smokestack. Built in 1917, it stood 571 feet tall on the bluff overlooking the smelter. It was constructed in just nine months, using teams of horses to cut a deep circular base into the clay soil. At the time, it was the tallest stack in the world. But the record did not stand long. An earthquake caused damage that later required the removal of the top 10 feet.

The stack received its share of attention over the years. A new coat of paint was news, and the smokestack was even used as the site of a wedding in 1929. It was a popular symbol for protesters, with environmental groups putting their messages on it. Even after the fires cooled under the stack, banners were hung by the daring few. A local family hung a remembrance of their deceased mother in 1991. The night before the stack was demolished, even with sticks of dynamite in its brick, a foolhardy radio fan hung a sheet promoting a "blast the stack" party.

The collapse of the giant tower captured, in one moment, both the past and future of the tiny town. The stack was imploded on January 17, 1993, eight years after the smelter closed its doors. Spectators numbering to 100,000 gathered in Ruston to watch the event from land and water. In just eight seconds, the stack fell to the sound of boat horns and yells—and the bittersweet tears of many.

For some, the demise of the smelter stack signaled only good things. But for longtime Rustonites, it was a symbol of a larger community's rejection of its industrial base, which had built not only Ruston, but also Tacoma. It was a foreshadowing of the lean years ahead, of struggling to survive without businesses to tax or employees to house. While many in Tacoma were applauding as the dust cleared, some locals were quietly mourning the end of an era and wondering about the future of the little town. Yet despite the odds, Ruston survives.

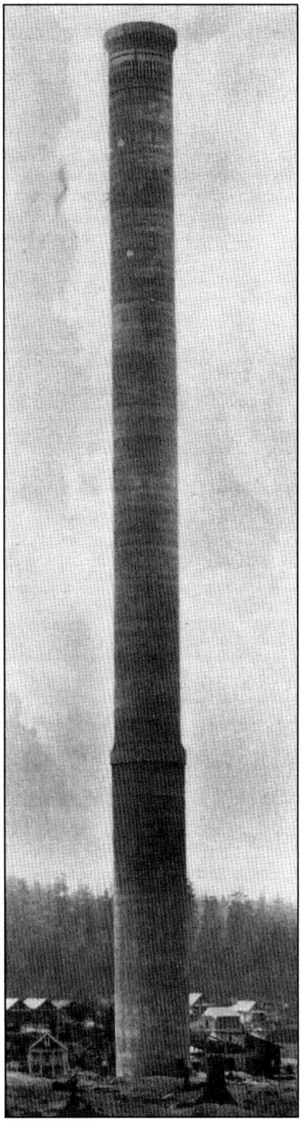

Early smelter operations used a variety of stacks throughout the plant site. In 1906, ever-expanding operations built what was then the tallest concrete chimney in the world, at 317.5 feet. After the purchase by the Guggenheim industrial empire a few years later, this towering stack was replaced by an even taller version in 1917. (TPL.)

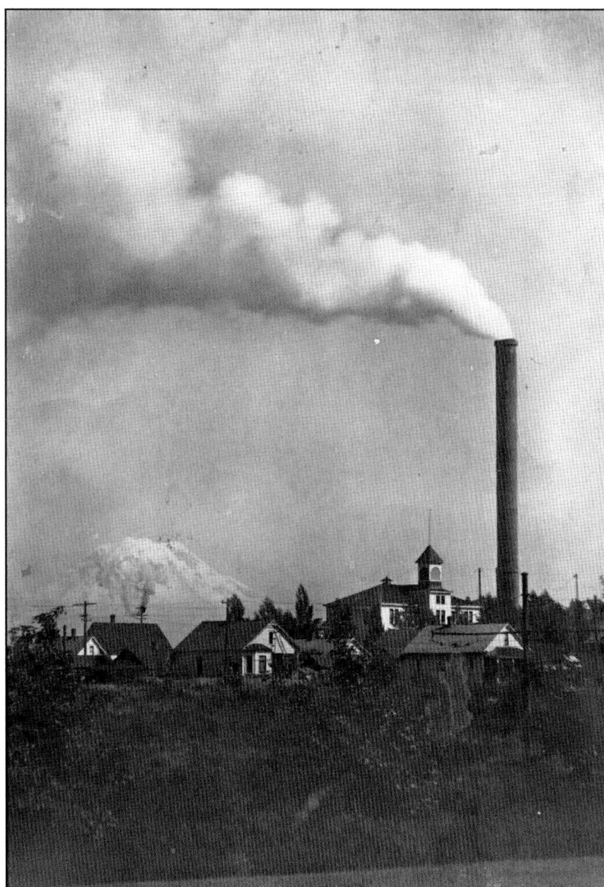

The stack towers over the town skyline in this 1908 photograph. As early as 1890, a local newspaper noted, "the subject of the disposal of the smoke from the smelter has not yet assumed any importance in Tacoma, though the big smelter just north of the city has been in operation for some time, the matter is likely to force itself upon the popular mind sometime in the future." (TR.)

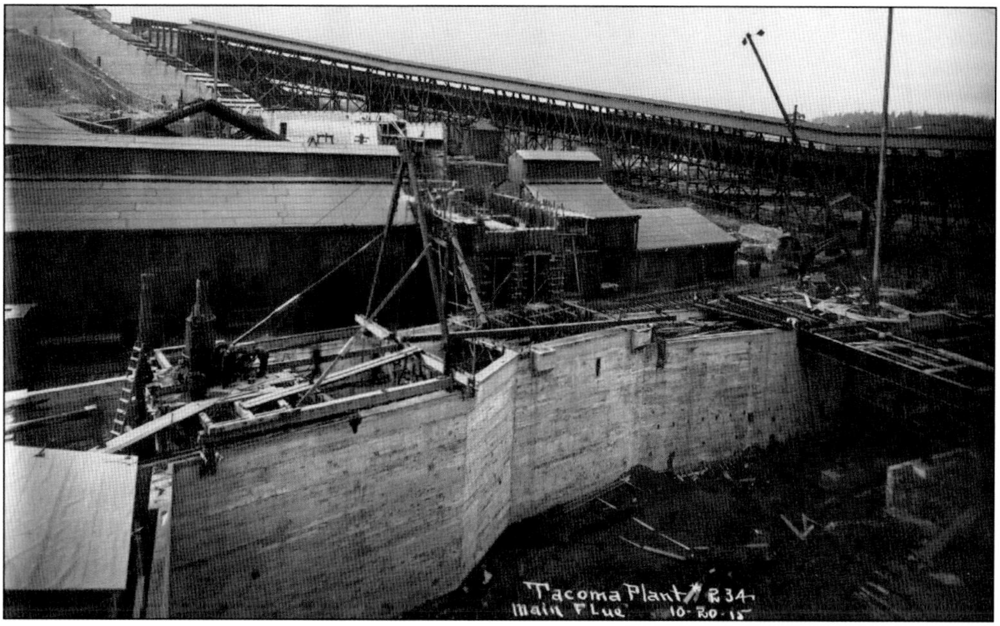

Images of housing or businesses in Ruston are hard to find in the public record, but pictures of the smelter are everywhere. The major upgrade of the smelter as it was integrated into the American Smelting and Refining Company (ASARCO) was well documented in photographs. This 1915 picture shows the new flute being constructed to carry smoke and gases up to the stack for dispersion. (KP.)

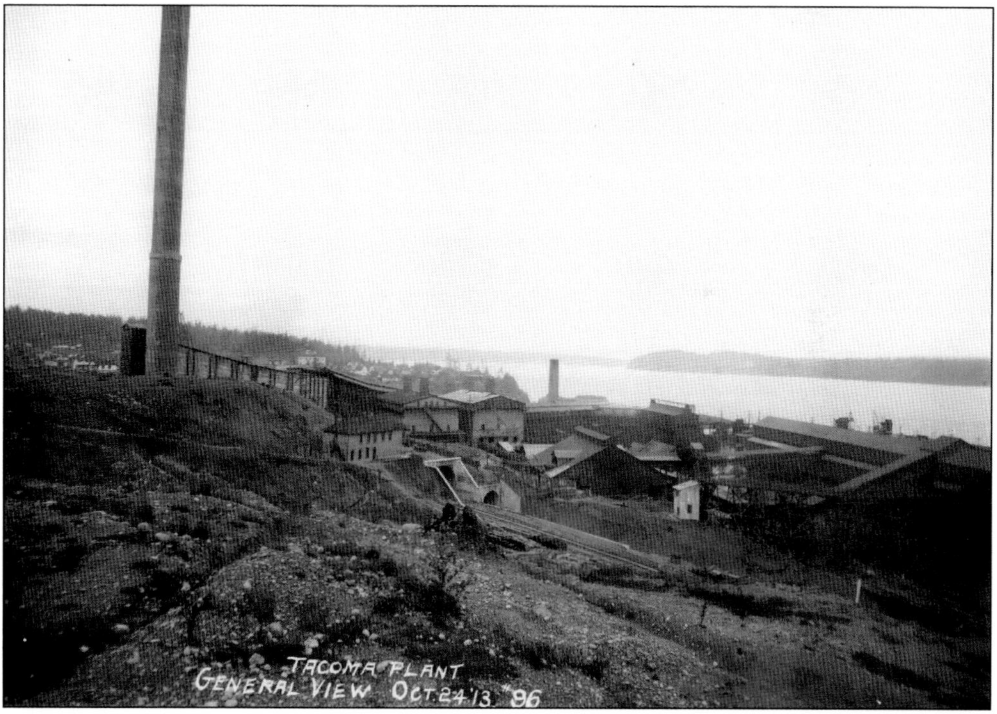

This west-looking view offers a glimpse of Ruston just beyond the stack. At the time of this photograph in 1913, it appears all the housing is centered around the smelter and stops at about Pearl Street. The first school building on North Shirley Street dominates the town skyline. (KP.)

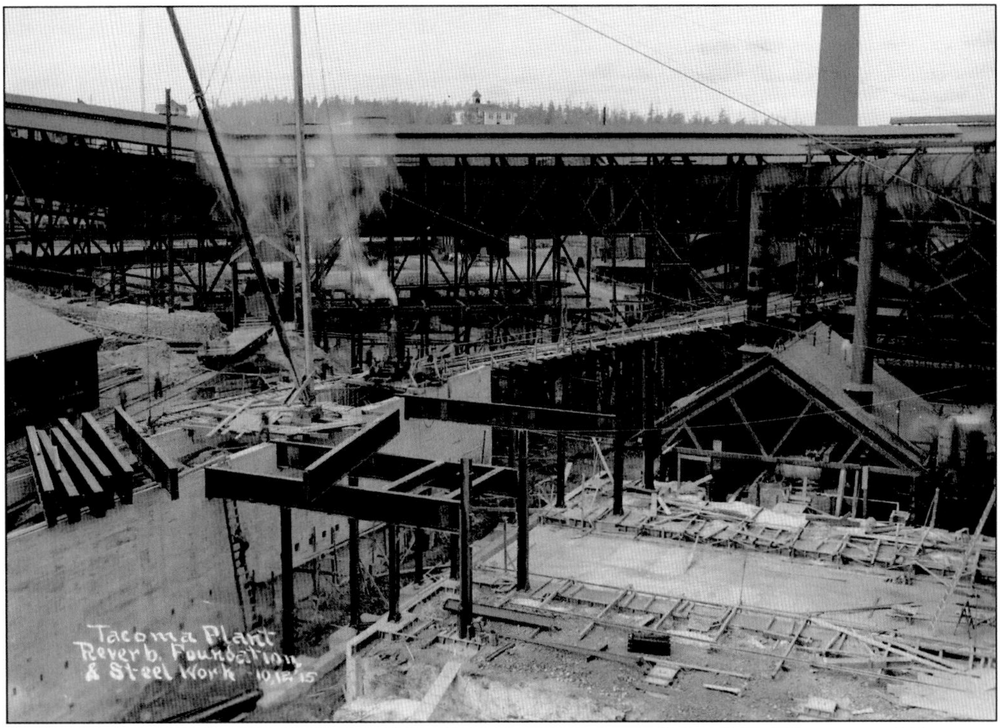

Giant structures dominated the smelter grounds, even in 1915. Looking east toward Bennett Street, the main flue is seen. The top of the original school building stands just above the flue on the horizon. (KP.)

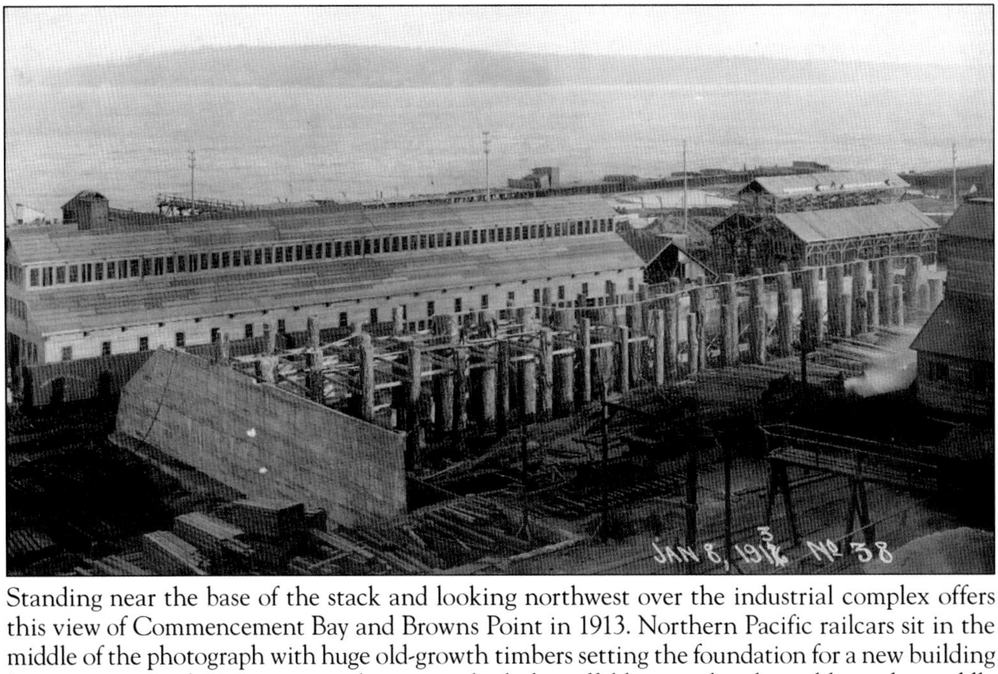

Standing near the base of the stack and looking northwest over the industrial complex offers this view of Commencement Bay and Browns Point in 1913. Northern Pacific railcars sit in the middle of the photograph with huge old-growth timbers setting the foundation for a new building being constructed. Two men standing on makeshift scaffolding are barely visible in the middle of the timbers. (KP.)

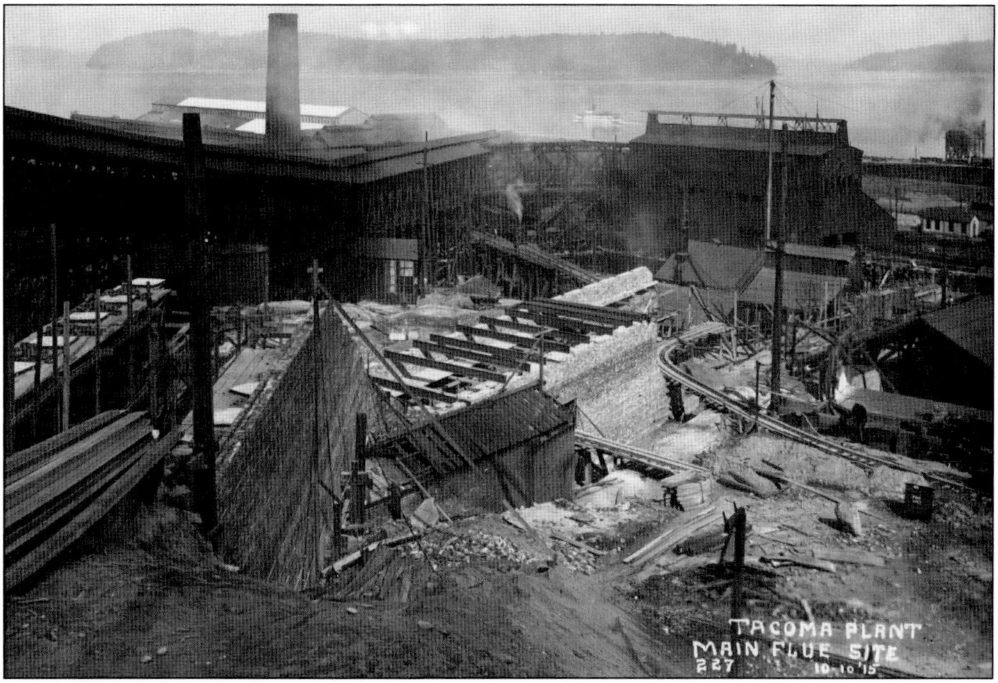

A smaller stack in the lower smelter area is still standing in this 1915 photograph, looking north towards Vashon Island. A boat can be seen making its way toward the Narrows. A steam engine sits on the raised tracks in the center of the picture. (KP.)

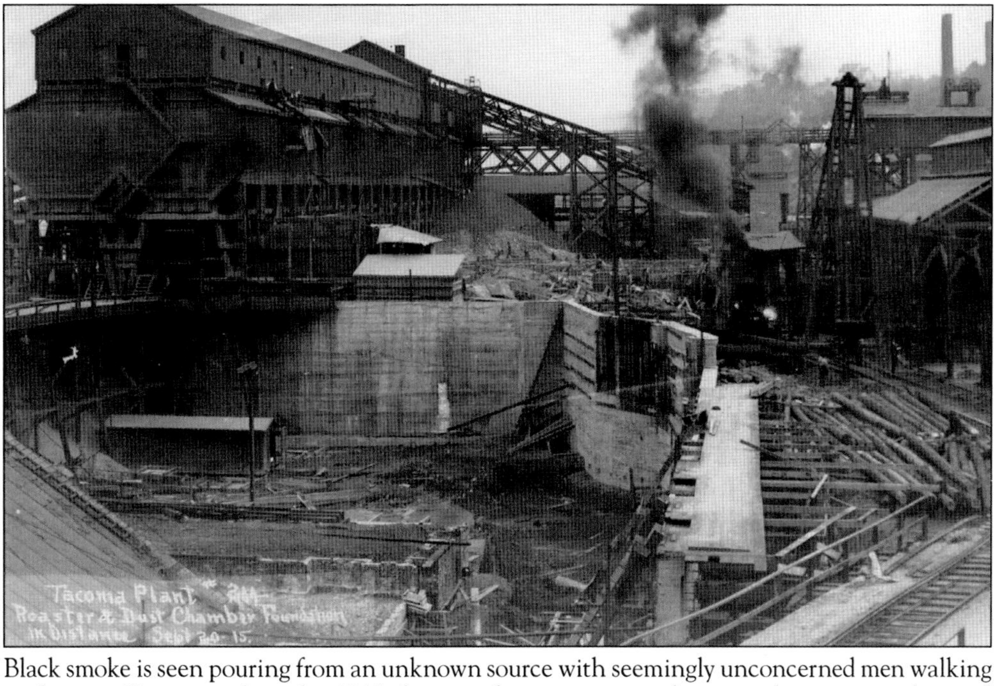

Black smoke is seen pouring from an unknown source with seemingly unconcerned men walking in the area. Even as early as this 1915 photograph, attempts were being made to capture dust and other pollutants before they were released up the stacks, with the construction of one of the first baghouse buildings at the Tacoma Plant. (KP.)

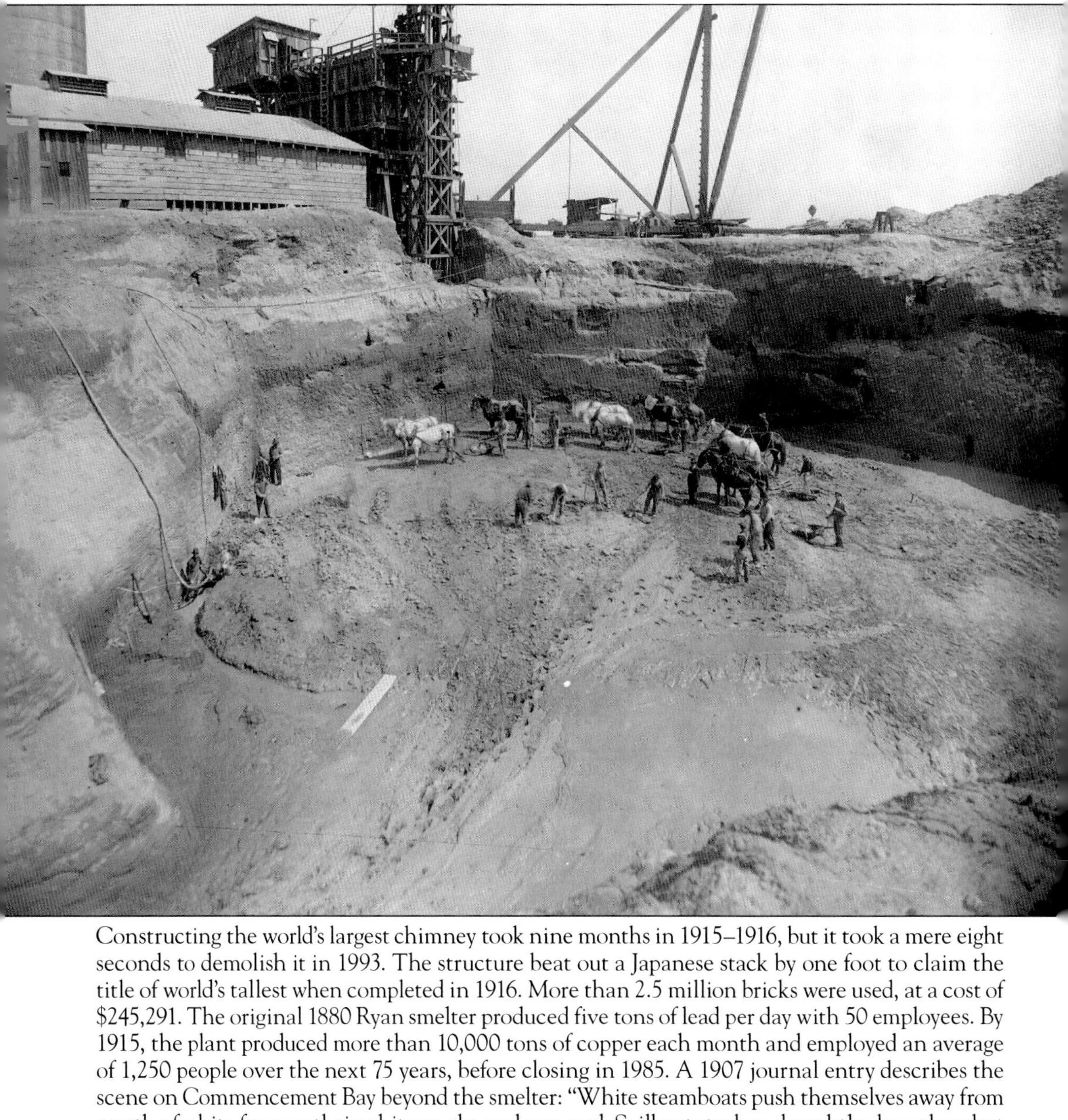

Constructing the world's largest chimney took nine months in 1915–1916, but it took a mere eight seconds to demolish it in 1993. The structure beat out a Japanese stack by one foot to claim the title of world's tallest when completed in 1916. More than 2.5 million bricks were used, at a cost of $245,291. The original 1880 Ryan smelter produced five tons of lead per day with 50 employees. By 1915, the plant produced more than 10,000 tons of copper each month and employed an average of 1,250 people over the next 75 years, before closing in 1985. A 1907 journal entry describes the scene on Commencement Bay beyond the smelter: "White steamboats push themselves away from a path of white foam as their white smoke curls upward. Sailboats tack and naphtha launches dart by. Rowboats with fishing parties and graceful Racine canoes float and drift over deep waters. Or perhaps the vanishing Puyallup or Nisqually Indian, in narrow, peculiarly pointed canoe, dug from a cedar tree, paddle along, with his household goods, on a visit or seek a change of fishing grounds." (WSHS.)

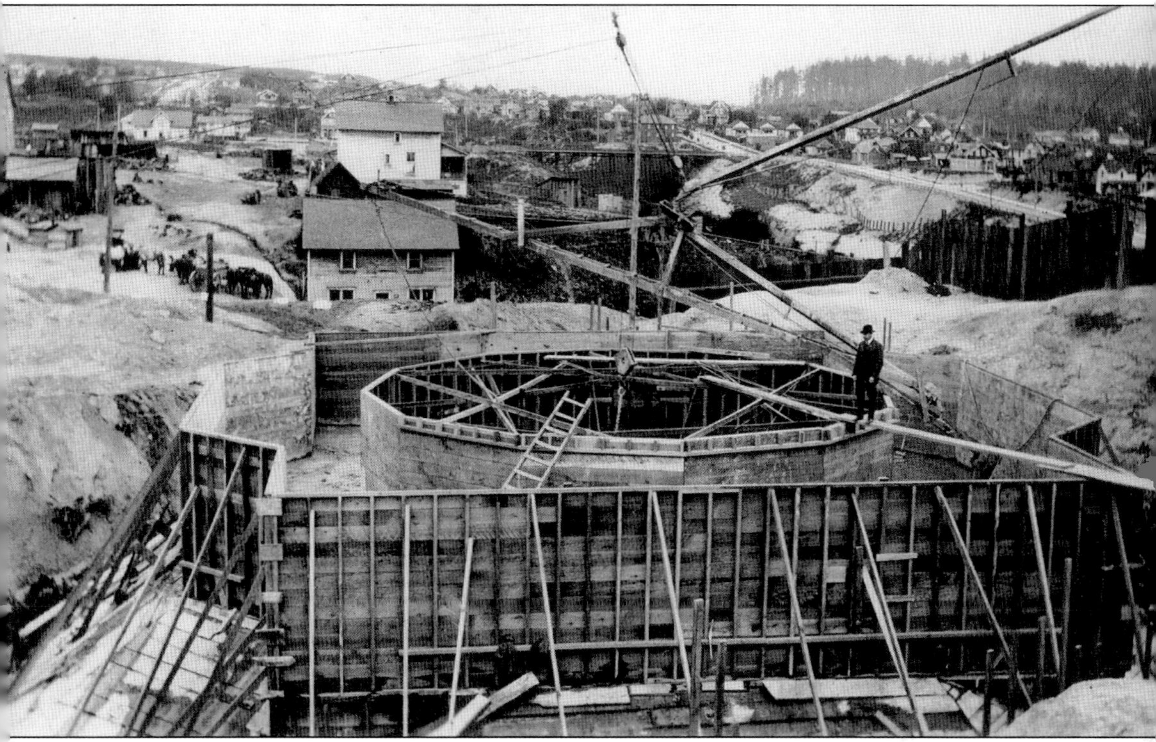

Horses were the primary means used to carve out the hole for the base of the tall stack. In this 1915 photograph, a businessman inspects the construction. The beginnings of North Fifty-first Street can be seen to the left, behind the stack. Just up the hill, North Fifty-first Street intersects with North Pearl Street, a bustling center of commerce even at the time of this picture. A few years before, a Mr. Chambers, of Ruston, donated "plank enough" to the committee to build a crossing over the intersection, and the marshal was "authorized to take the matter in hand and see that the crossing was put down in a substantial manner." An old wooden bridge in the center of the picture connects the north and south ends of town before the Nelson-Bennett Train Tunnel was constructed. (WSHS.)

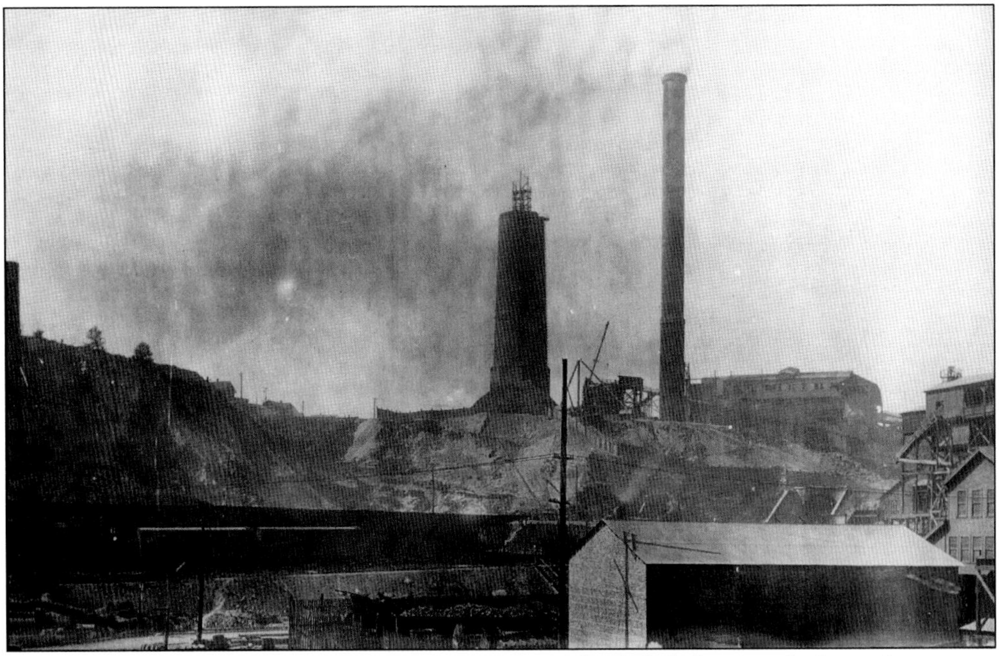

This faded photograph shows the large smokestack mid-point in its construction. The smaller stack is still standing. The train tunnel can be seen to the left with its earthen cover. Maintaining the hillside enabled the flues to be constructed on solid ground, rather than building tall, raised structures for the massive tubes. (KP.)

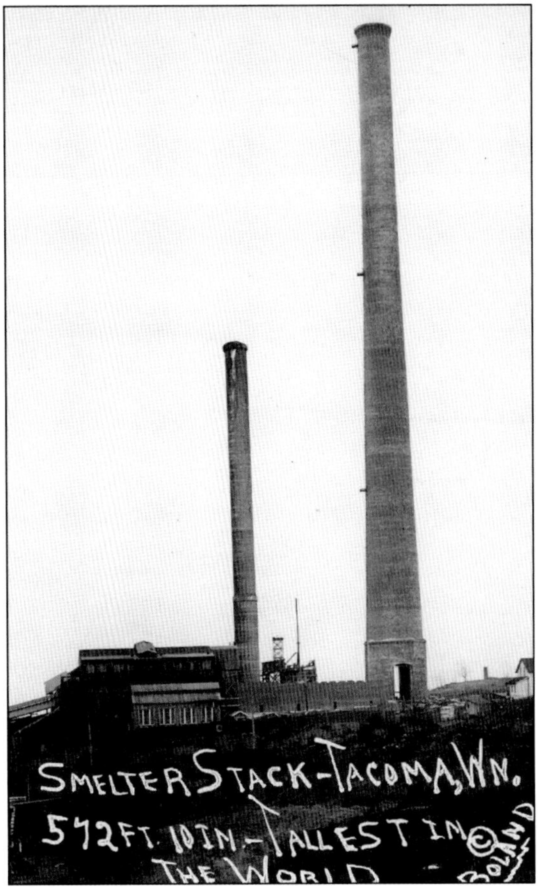

The stark difference in height is striking in this photograph, taken just before the obsolete, smaller stack was demolished. The new stack is measured down to the inch and served as bragging rights not only for Ruston, but for the entire Greater South Sound community. Until it was felled, the huge stack would appear as a major landmark on maps and was used for navigation by both water vessels and airplanes. (WSHS.)

The shiny, new stack could be seen from all around the area, as evidenced in this 1917 photograph taken shortly after construction was complete. The notation on the bottom of this postcard states it was the second tallest stack at the time. It appears some other industrial giant had already captured that elusive title of "world's tallest stack." (TPL.)

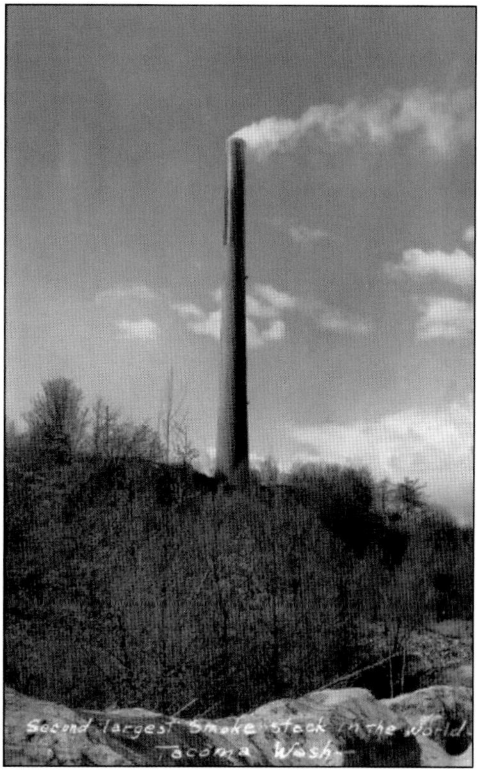

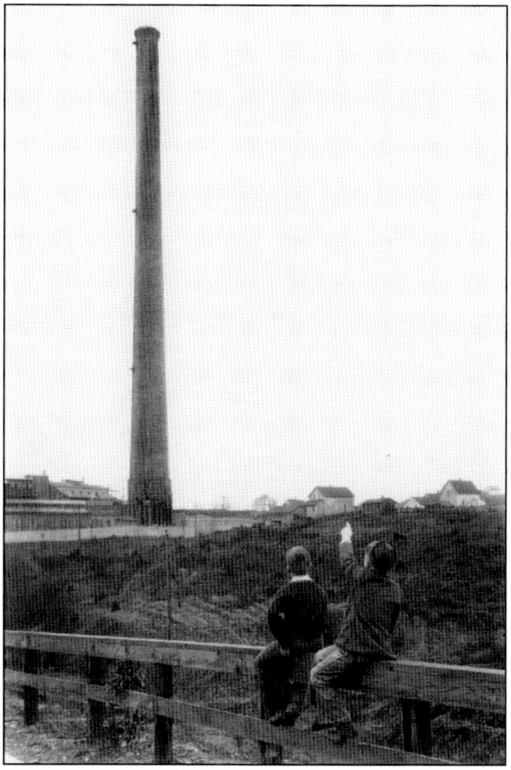

These two unidentified young boys appear to be impressed with the tall smelter stack in 1931 (looking east from Fifty-first Street). The view across the cooling pond has changed dramatically in the last 80 years. Land that once housed three-story buildings and the giant chimney now sits mostly vacant, awaiting construction of single-family homes on top of the buried stack base. (TPL.)

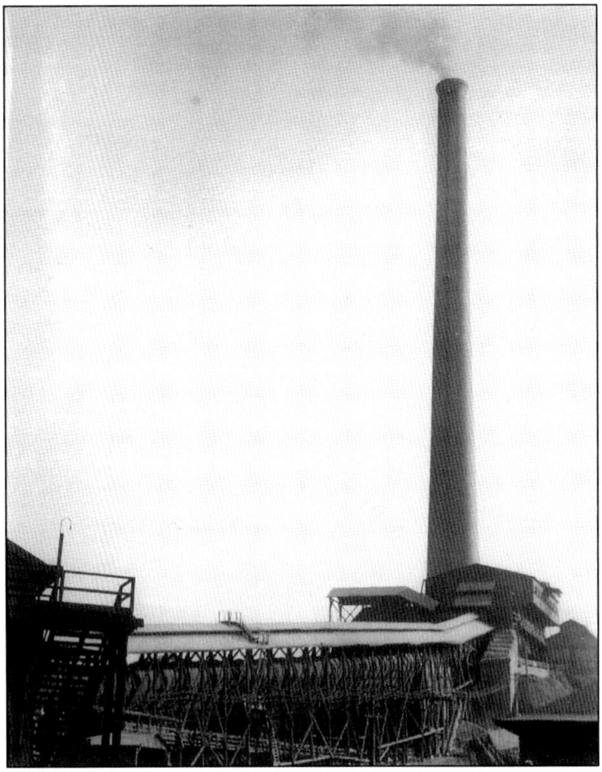

By 1929, the giant flue construction was complete and the smelter was back to full capacity as one of the world's leading copper producers. This picture was taken at the bottom of Baltimore Street looking south. (KP.)

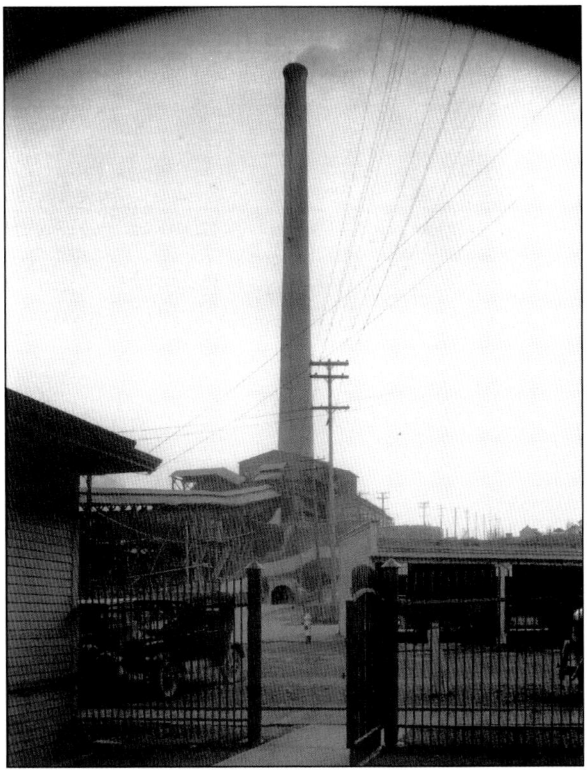

The view had not changed much by 1935. The tunnel that ferried cars under the hillside was seeing increased use by actual vehicles instead of horses, although most of the laborers walked to work. According to one resident, at shift change "the sidewalks were just black with men." (TPL.)

Operations at the base of the stack remained much the same as well. Houses still stood within shouting distance of the industrial complex. A maintenance ladder with resting platforms can be seen up the side of the giant stack. The cured lip at the top of the stack would be damaged in an earthquake and the top 10 feet removed. (TPL.)

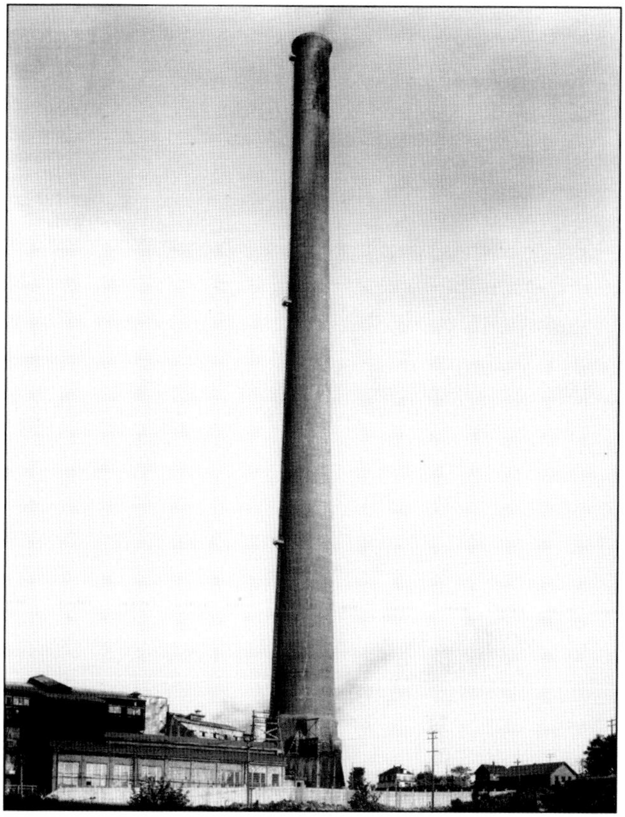

For those strong and brave enough to climb the stack ladder, the view that awaited them was like no other, except perhaps from an airplane. This maintenance photograph from the top of the smokestack shows the scene looking south over Commencement Bay in the early 1970s. (KP.)

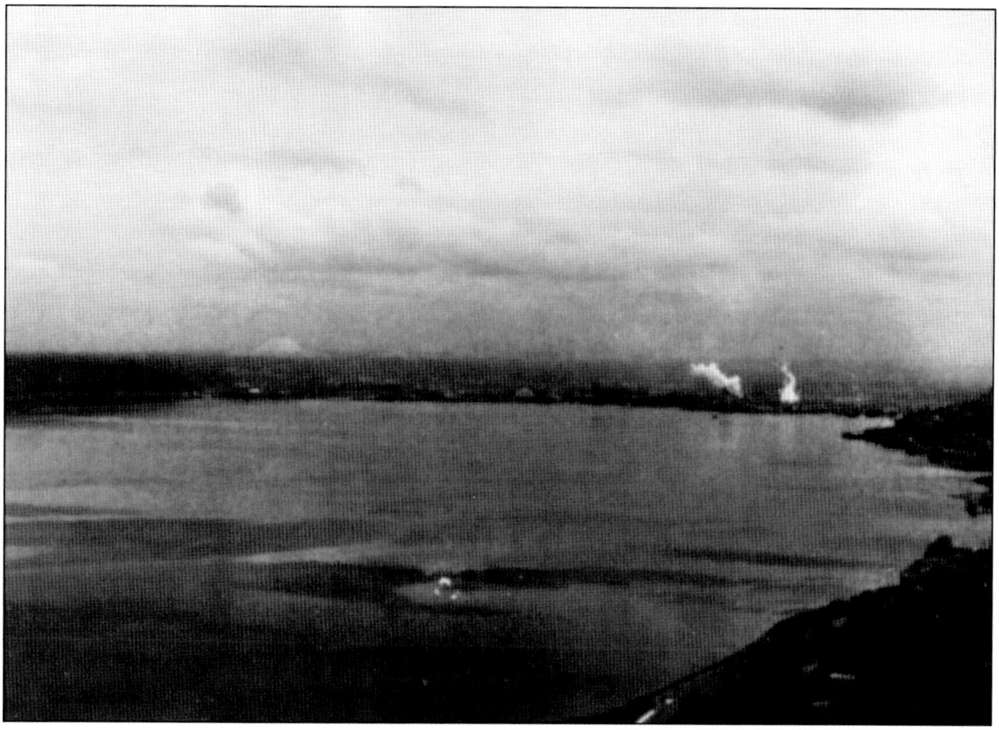

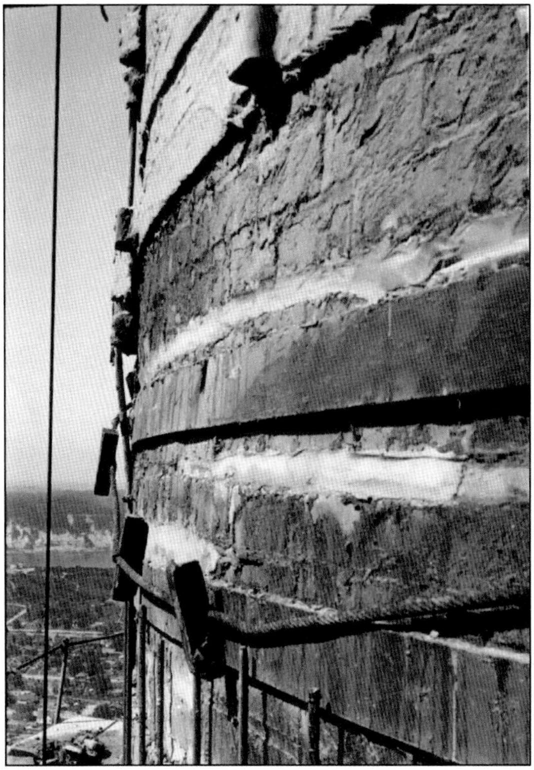

The purpose of a climb up the ladder was to perform inspections of the giant tower. This 1950 image shows the condition of the reinforcing wire bands that were placed around the brick. In a view toward the west, the bluffs along the opposite side of the Narrows near Gig Harbor can be seen in the distance. (KP.)

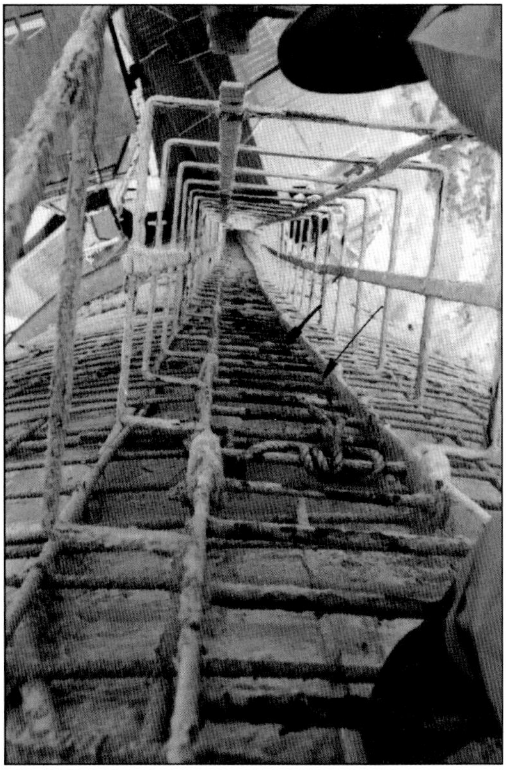

Not only was it important to watch the condition of the stack, but the ladder needed constant maintenance as well. The arrows point to some rungs that needed attention. It clearly took a hearty soul to stomach this climb. (KP.)

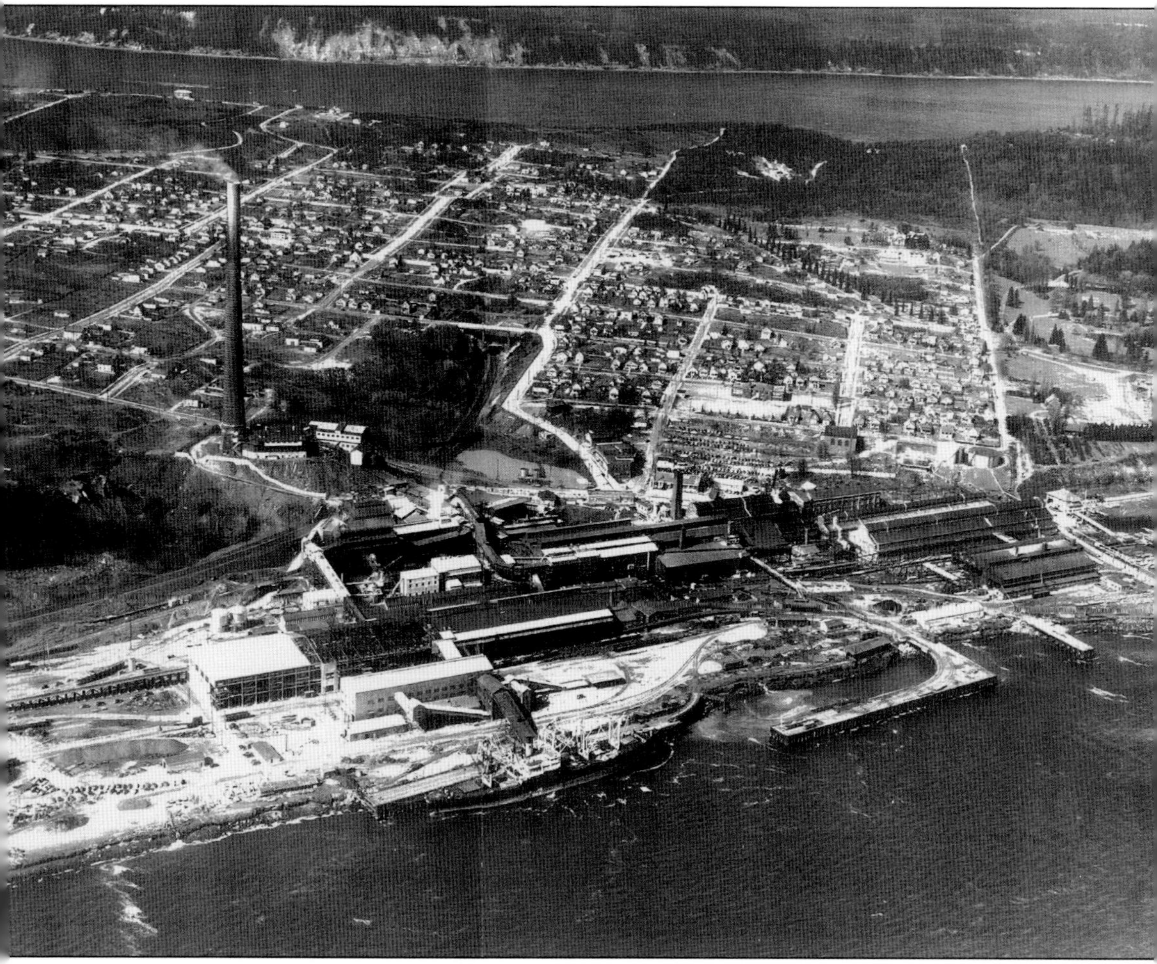

This undated photograph shows not only the smelter complex but the town as well. This location on the Ruston shoreline offered unique features, like a deepwater port and access to a major rail line. Housing was starting to fill in by now along the neatly laid blocks. The hotels and commercial buildings are still standing at the bottom of North Fifty-first Street. The town's municipal dump can be seen on the hillside, just west of the stack, on land that would eventually be turned into a park using a trust fund bequeathed by William R. Rust. The American Dream of each family having its own car was being realized by more and more smelter employees, as evidenced by the large parking area just below Bennett Street and at the south end of the plant. (KP.)

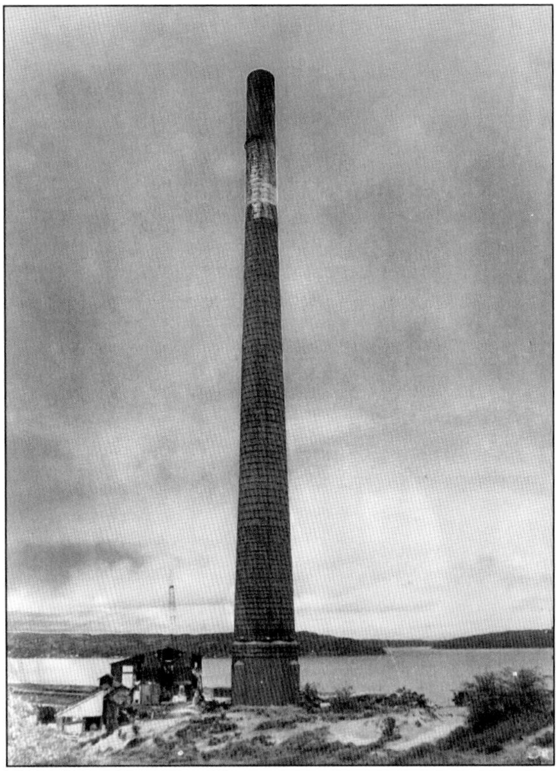

Looking north over Vashon Island in 1987, the stack stands tall at the then shuttered smelter. The adjacent buildings are in disrepair, or demolition had begun. This hillside has now been cleaned up and is ready for new single-family homes. (Sherri Forch.)

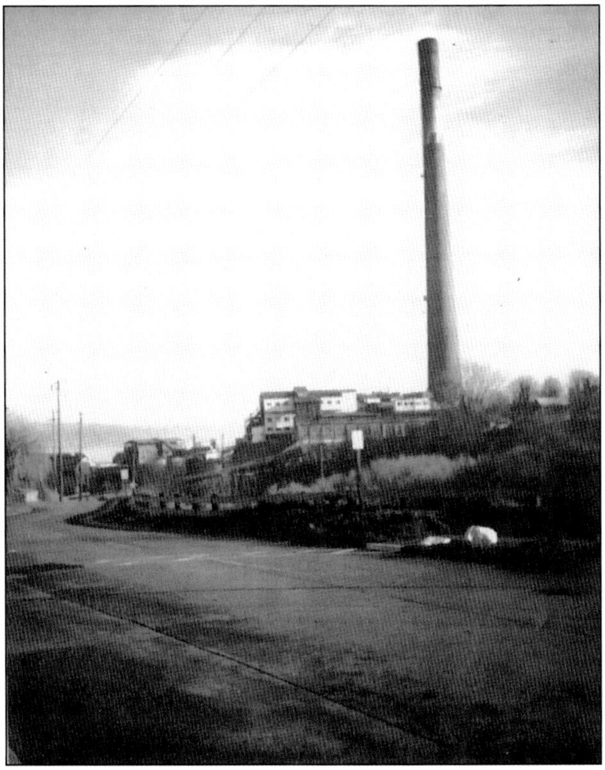

The view looking southeast over Commencement Bay at the intersection of North Fifty-first and Winnifred Streets was once filled with tall buildings and the towering smokestack. A small glimpse of the bay can be seen in the background. (Don and Beth Torbet.)

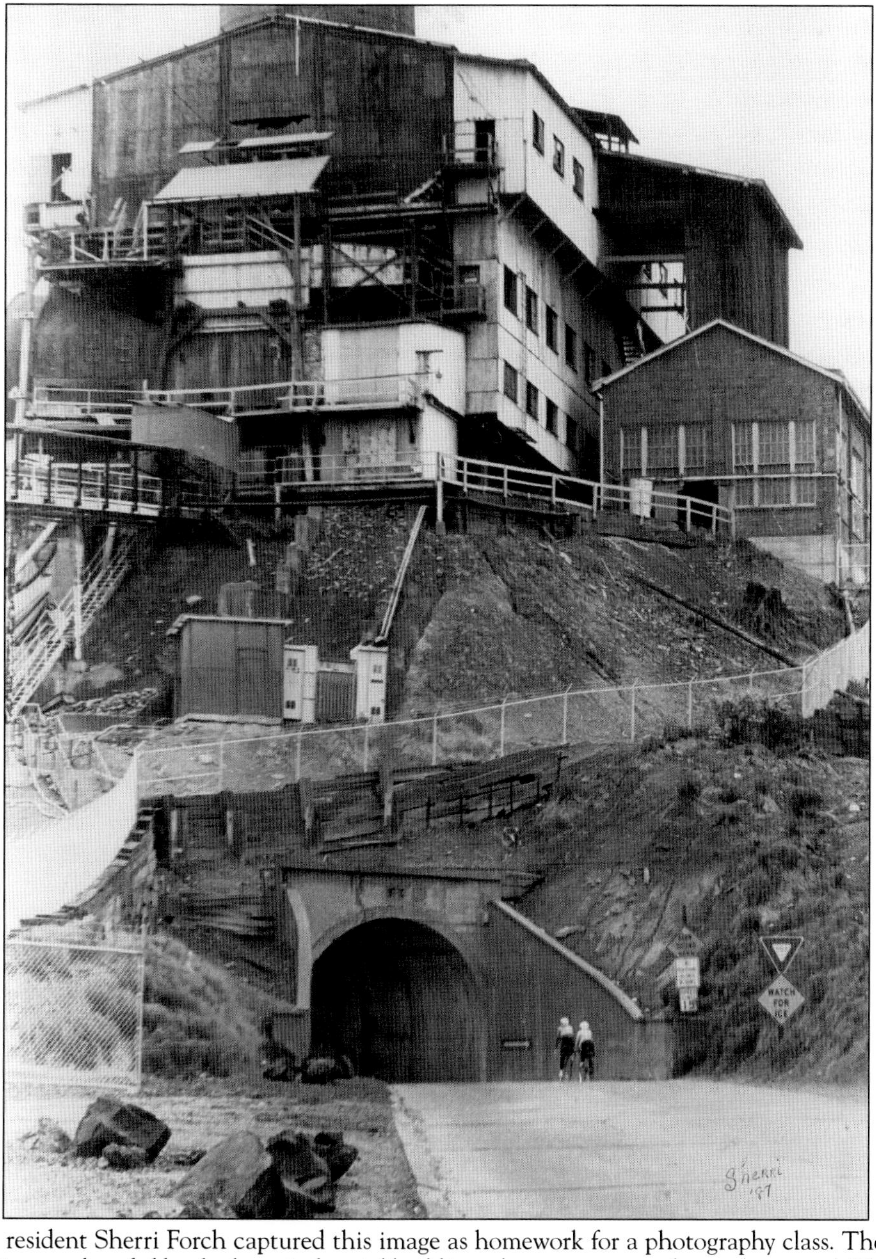

Local resident Sherri Forch captured this image as homework for a photography class. The two bicyclists are dwarfed by the huge industrial buildings that once towered over the tunnel. The old wooden fence had probably stood for decades. The car tunnel is still used today, but it is slated for closure in 2011 as a new, wider road is built around the base of the hillside. The difficult corner at this end of the tunnel caught many a large truck over the years, sometimes twisting trailers as they became trapped against the narrow walls. The extraction process usually brought out the locals to watch the show. Originally, Ruston Way on the other side of the tunnel was a wooden-plank road that extended north from Old Tacoma to give access to the many logging mills that lined the shoreline; it was built over the year-round water flows at Garfield, Mason, and Puget gulches. When the permanent road and rail line were built in the early 1900s, construction dammed the water flow of the various gulches. (Sherri Forch.)

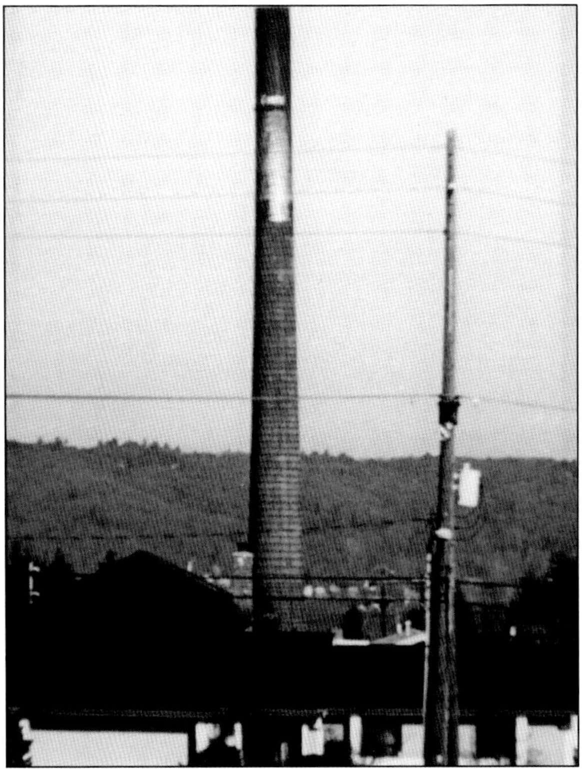

The morning of January 17, 1993, dawned clear and cold. An estimated 100,000 people gathered in Ruston or on boats offshore to watch the historic implosion of the smelter stack. These photographs were taken at Vassault Park, about a mile south of the stack. (E.T. Gatlin.)

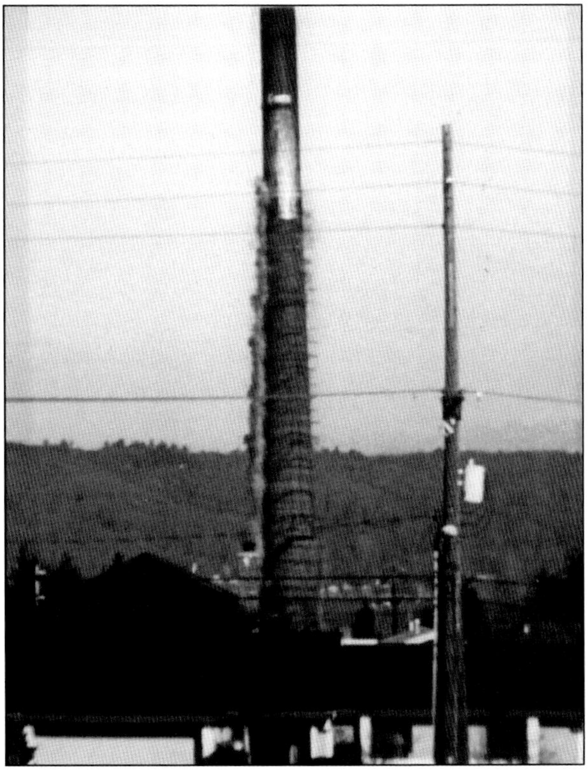

This series of images was taken by professional photographer E.T. Gatlin. He was not planning to fight the crowds to record the stack demolition, but as he was heading out to the store, he decided on a whim to stop and capture the historic event. He used a 105-millimeter lens freehand to photograph the stack's final moments. (E.T. Gatlin.)

The first set of explosives snapped the reinforcing bands around the brick, and dynamite buried inside the stack walls was detonated in a carefully scripted dance to bring the giant tower down upon itself. (E.T. Gatlin.)

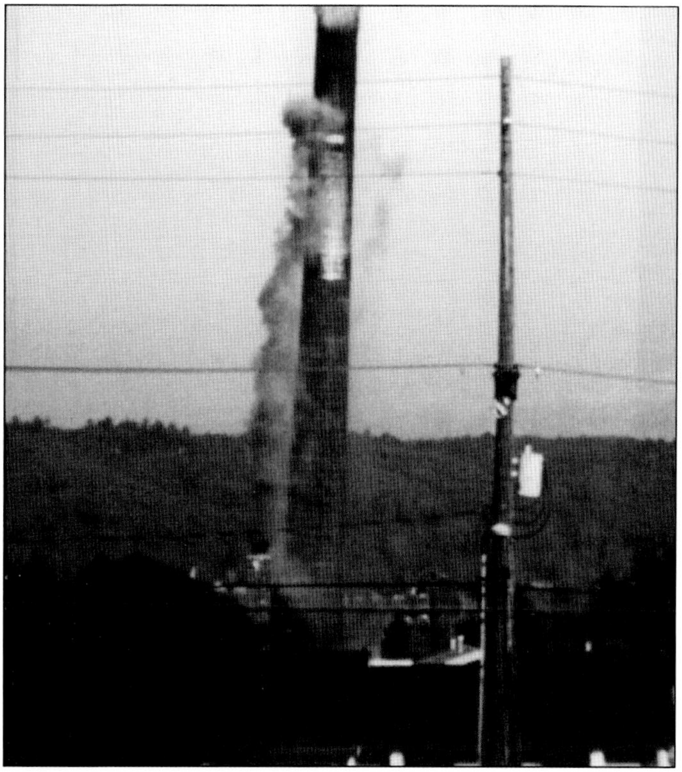

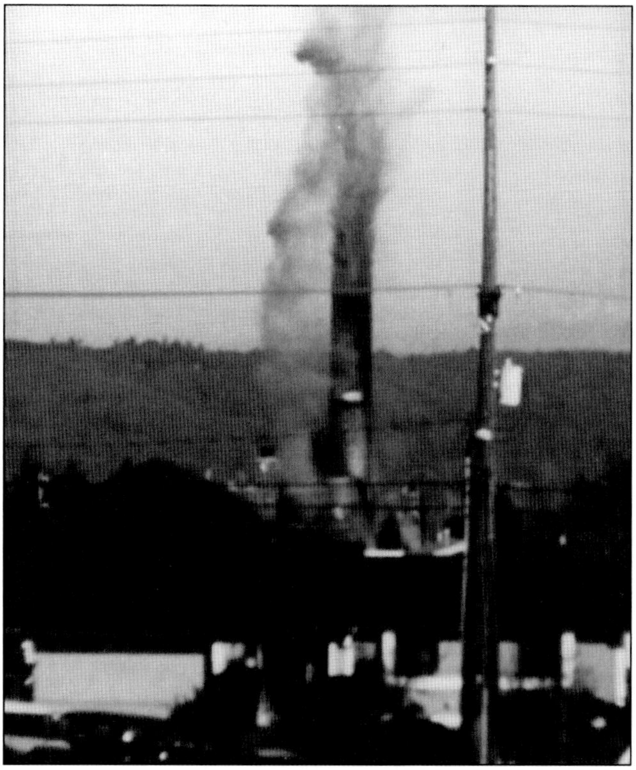

In the stack foundation alone, 120 tons of steel reinforcing rails and 5,908 cubic yards of concrete were used. In addition to the 2.5 million paving bricks in the chimney, 2,800 tons of sand and fire clay were among the building materials. (E.T. Gatlin.)

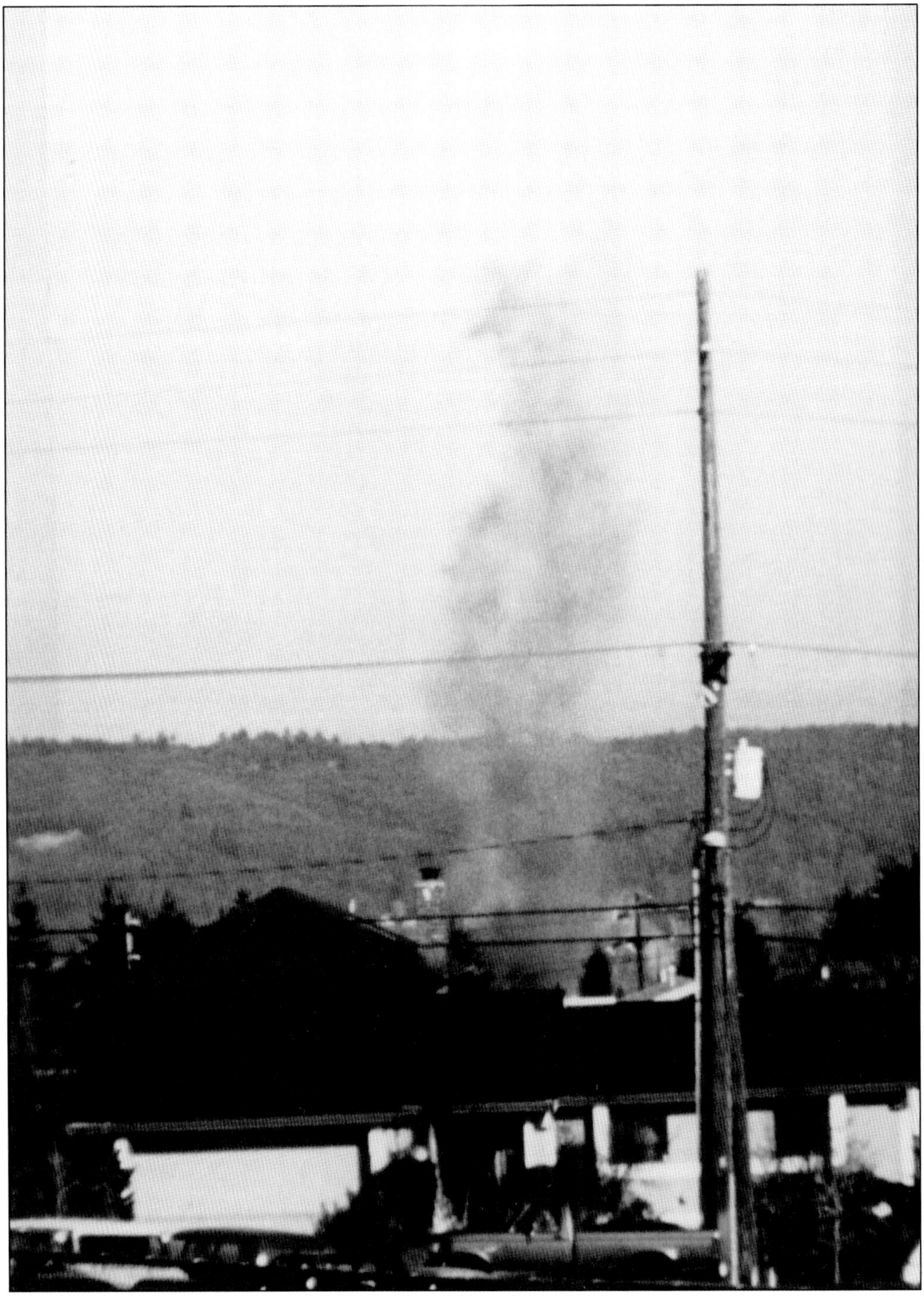

In the end, the stack fell gracefully as planned in eight short seconds, signaling an end of an era not only for the ASARCO Tacoma Smelter, but for Ruston as well. As the dust cleared, a new landscape emerged with unknown hurdles and an uncertain future. A tough transition lay ahead, but somehow Ruston has survived and is ready to move into a new era of prosperity. (E.T. Gatlin.)

Five

SMELTING

Most locals never set foot inside the huge smelter buildings, saw the fires burning, or felt the heat of the molten ore. The ancient craft of refining metal was well developed, just beyond their sight, inside Ruston's ASARCO smelter.

Copper ore was first mined from the earth and processed into finely crushed concentrates where much of the non-metal material was removed. Upon arrival at the ASARCO Tacoma Smelter, each load was tested and sorted. Metallurgists mixed each batch and sent it to the roasters for preheating to burn off excess sulfur, which was captured and sold.

This material, called calcine, was then sent to the reverberatory furnace for the final melt. Nicknamed "Reverb," the furnace, which was constantly vibrating, was 110 feet long, 28 feet wide, and 12 feet deep, with gas burners that kept the internal temperature at 2,700 degrees Fahrenheit. The heavier copper-iron sulfide, called matte, would settle on the bottom and be transported in 17-ton ladles via overhead cranes to the converters. After more processing to remove the iron and any remaining sulfur, the melt was about 98.7 percent pure copper. The unused material, called slag, hardened into a black rock that was poured along the shoreline, extending the smelter landmass into Commencement Bay.

For copper to efficiently conduct electricity as wire, 99.9 percent purity is needed. The Ruston facility also operated an electrostatic refinery. The molten copper from the smelter was poured into anodes, which are large sheets weighing 530 pounds. The giant sheets were hung in sulfuric-acid-filled tanks the size of football fields. Cathodes, thin sheets of pure copper, where hung between each anode. As an electrical current passed through the tank over 28 days, purified copper moved from the anode to the cathode. The final step was to remelt the pure copper into the form needed by customers, usually oblong bars of about 500 pounds each, ready for shipment around the world.

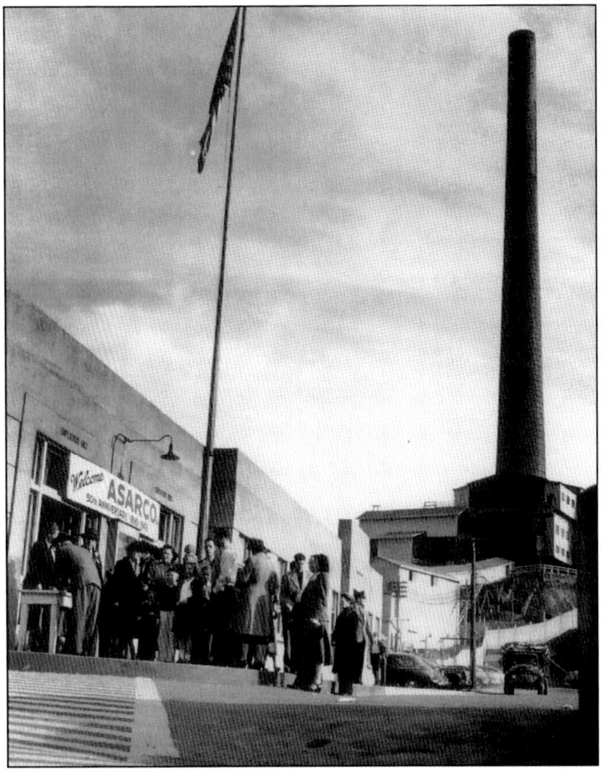

The year 1949 marked the 50th anniversary of the ASARCO Tacoma Plant. The company celebrated along with the larger community. Pictured is one of the many parties and open house events in front of the smelter gates at the bottom of North Fifty-first Street. (TPL.)

One of the first stops for the concentrated ore was the Fine Ore Bins building, where the material was stored in batches according to its chemical makeup. Huge cranes with buckets operated from overhead to move the concentrates. This large building was the last to be demolished in 2005. (KP.)

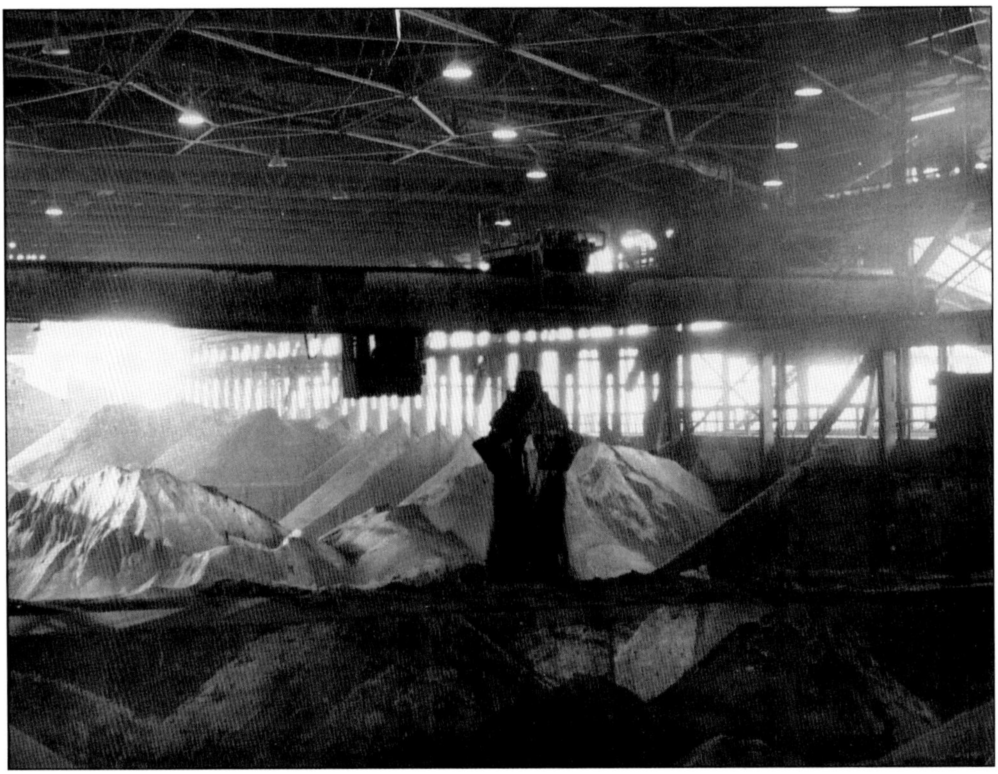

The molten copper, not yet pure enough for use, was skimmed from the bottom of the furnaces into huge ladles for transport to the next step in the refining process. (KP.)

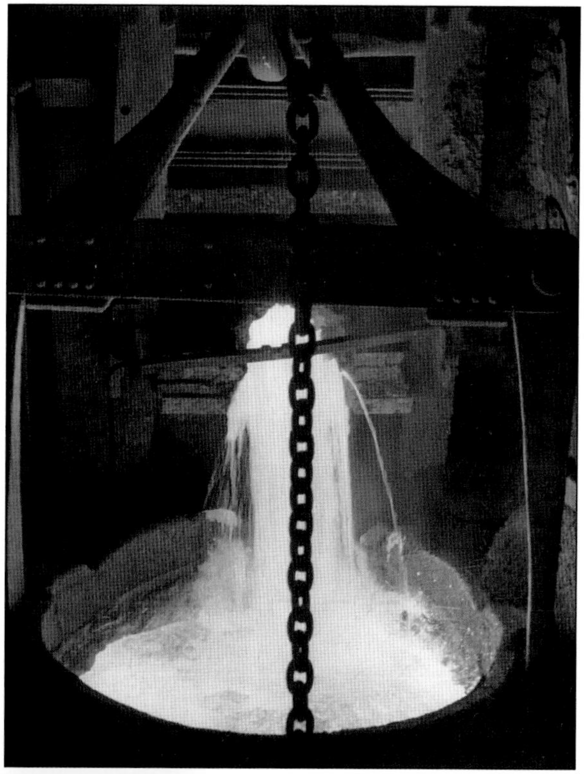

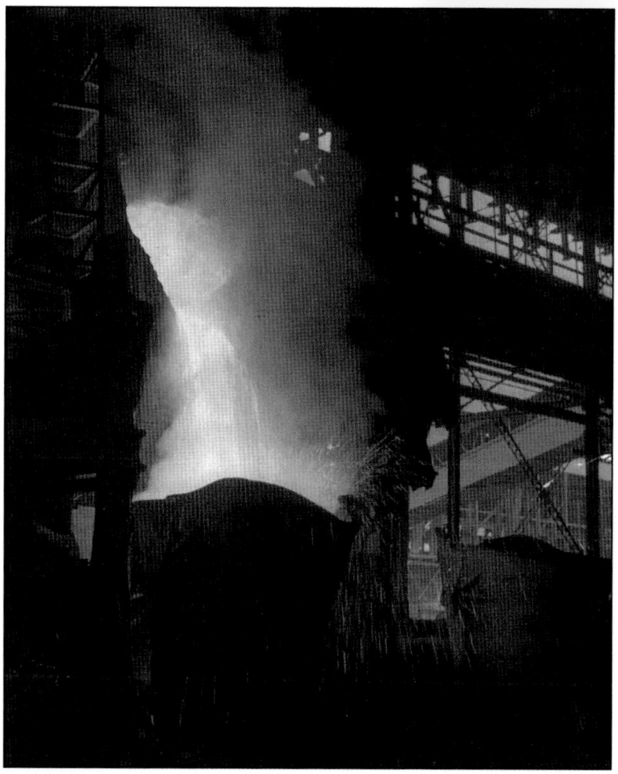

These ladles, pictured in the 1970s, looked much the same as those used in the 1890s when the smelter first opened. The heat from the furnaces and molten material was intense and created gases and dust that were captured and reused as much as possible. (KP.)

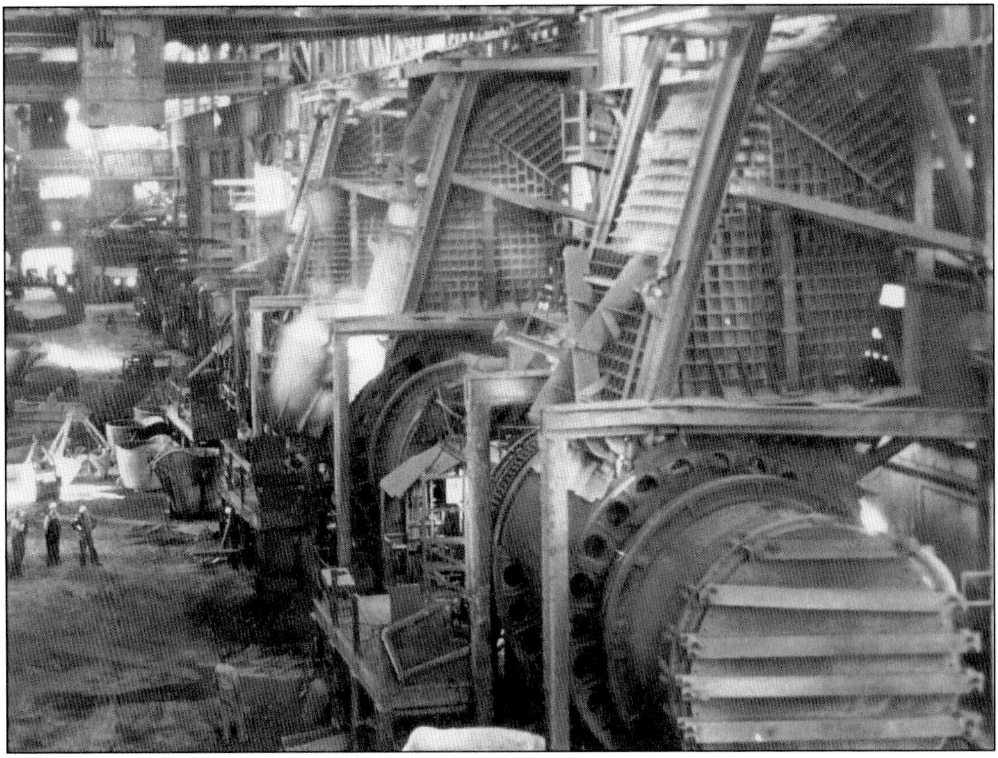

The row of four converters received the copper matte via overhead cranes. Each converter was 13 feet in diameter, 30 feet long, and lined with brick. Silica was added to the matte and air was blown through the molten bath to burn off sulfur and oxidize the iron. (KP.)

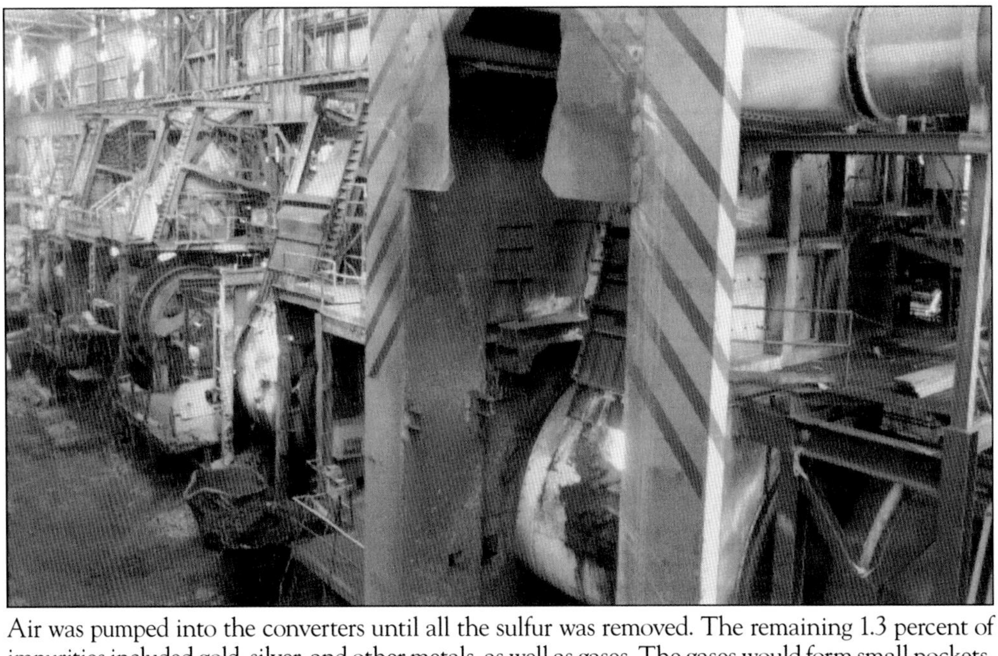

Air was pumped into the converters until all the sulfur was removed. The remaining 1.3 percent of impurities included gold, silver, and other metals, as well as gases. The gases would form small pockets, or blisters, as the metal solidified. The product was known as blister copper because of this. (KP.)

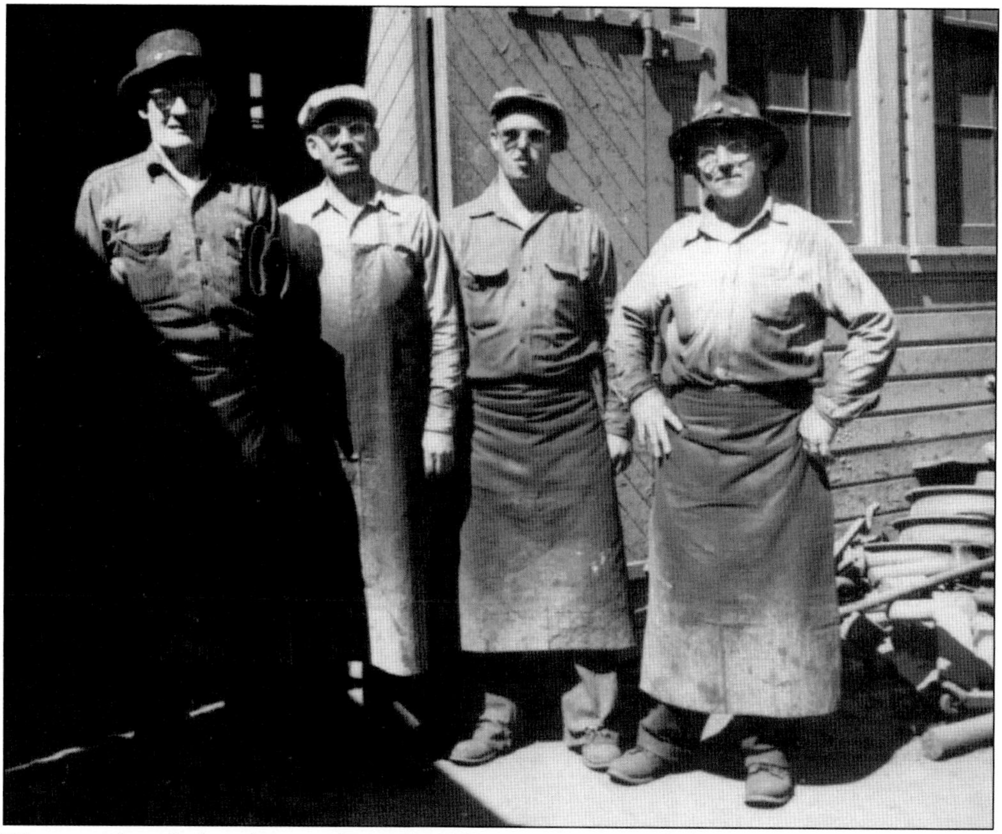

These unidentified workers in the early 1950s wear aprons to help protect them from molten material. Modern-day wear is much improved for both safety and comfort. (KP.)

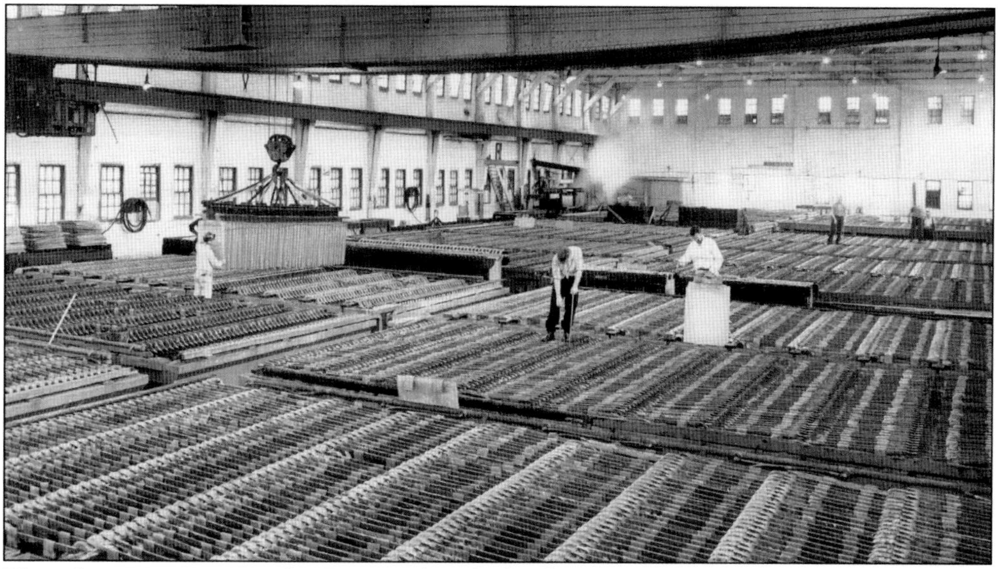

The refining operation at the Tacoma Plant had at least two large buildings to house the huge acid tanks. Each batch was constantly monitored. Large overhead cranes were used to move the massive plates. (KP.)

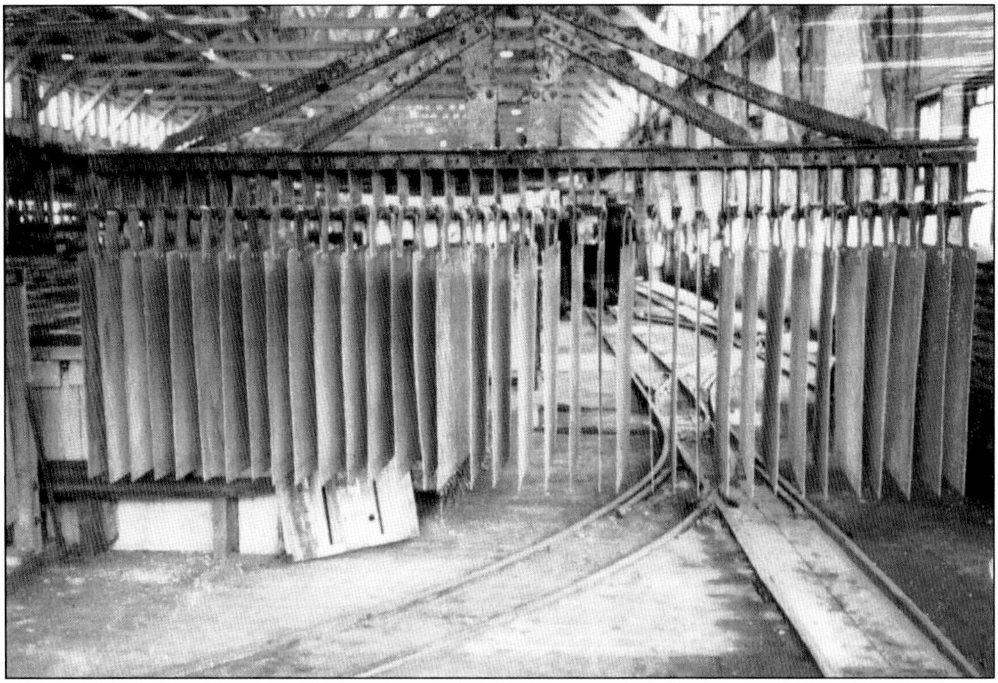

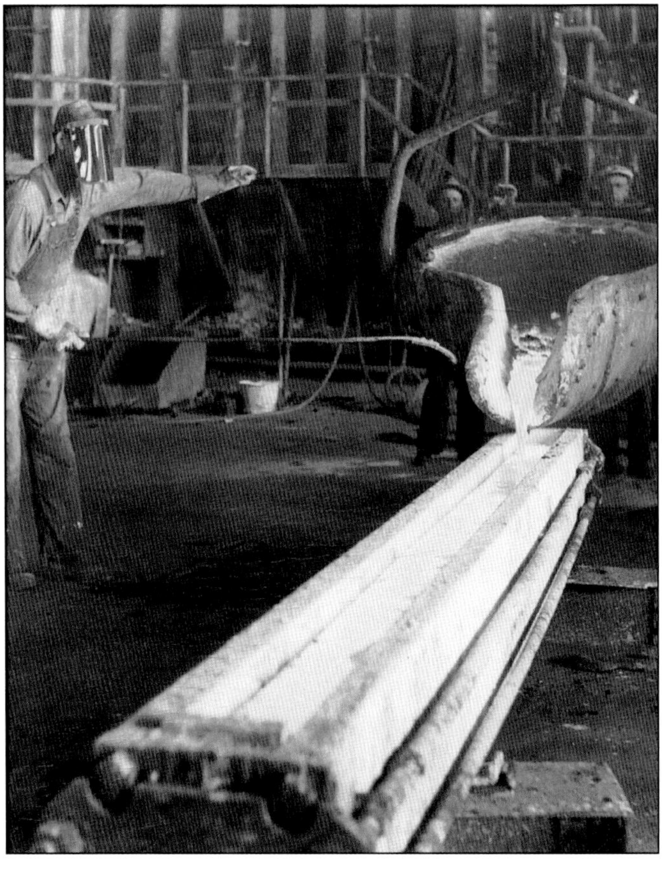

Cathode plates are pictured, probably in the 1950s. These were hung in the acid tanks next to the anode plates to attract the pure copper when the electrical current was applied. Each sheet weighed several hundred pounds when the process was complete. (TR.)

The final product could be made into a variety of shapes in the special castings department. This 1957 photograph shows the molten copper being poured into a long, thin rectangle. (KP.)

These wire bars, sometimes called ingots, were usually the final form for copper from the Tacoma Plant. The last step after the copper hardened was to strip off any rough edges before shipment. (TR.)

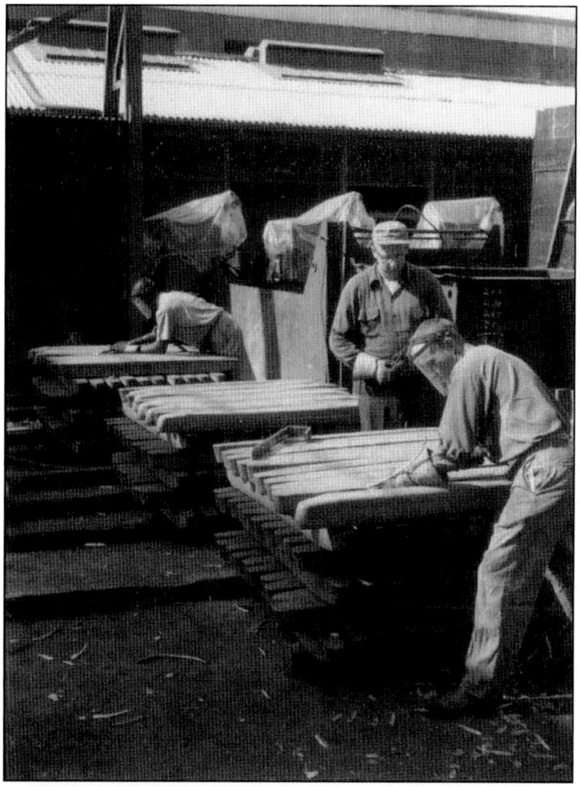

Besides the heart of the operations inside the large buildings and furnaces, much of the 67-acre plant site was used to sort and prepare the various by-products for shipment. (KP.)

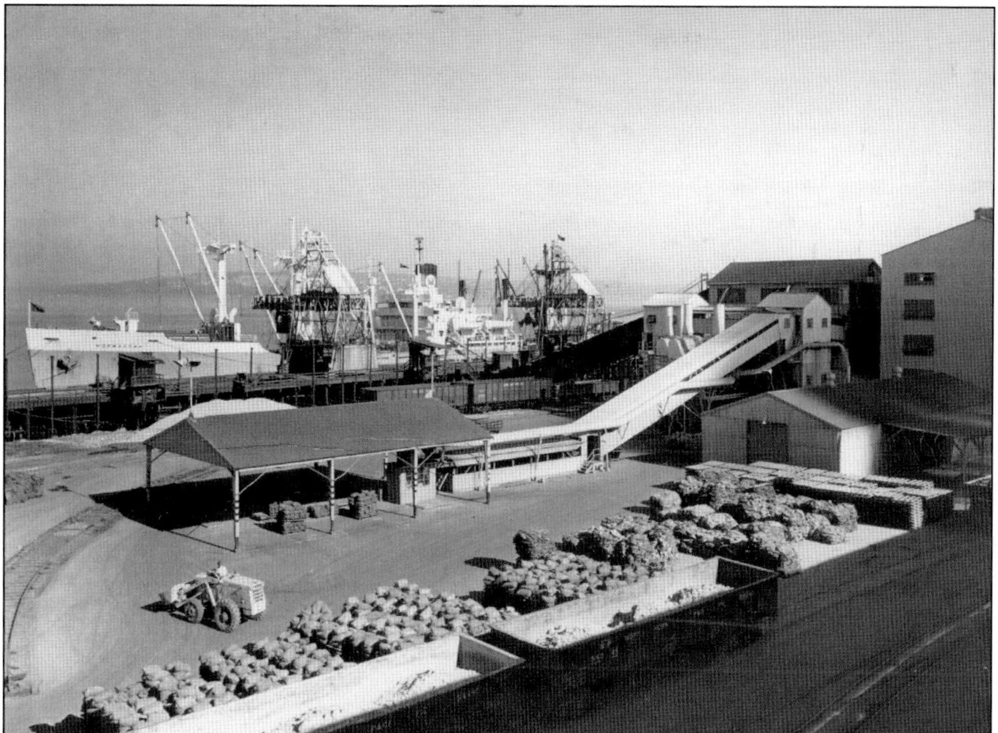

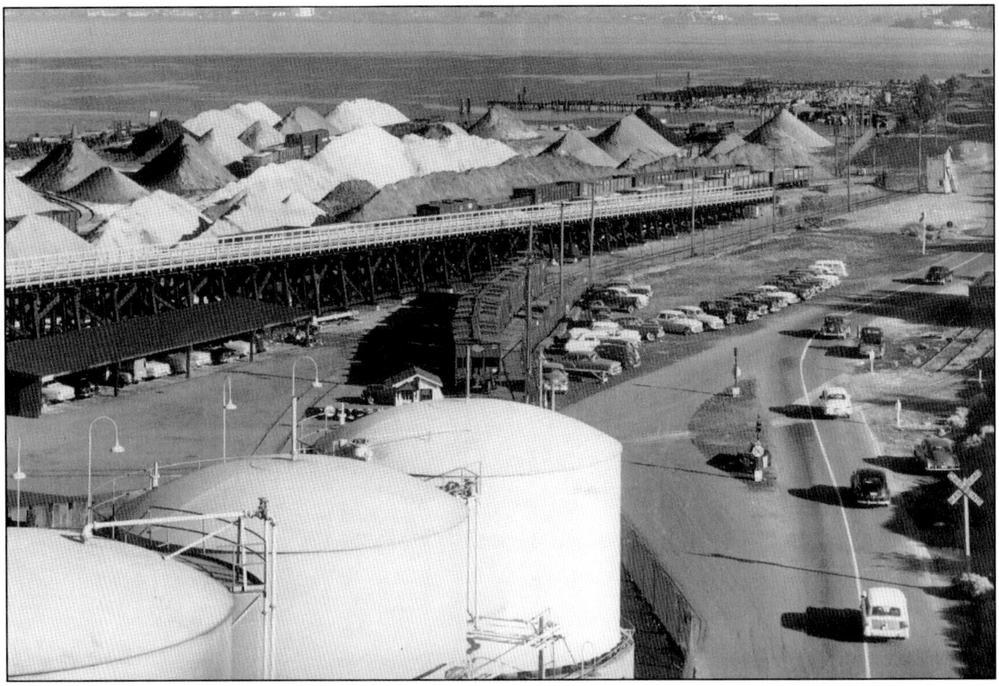

This 1957 view of the south end of the smelter site shows the mountains of different material used in the smelting process. Ruston Way is still used today, but a new road is scheduled for completion in 2012. (KP.)

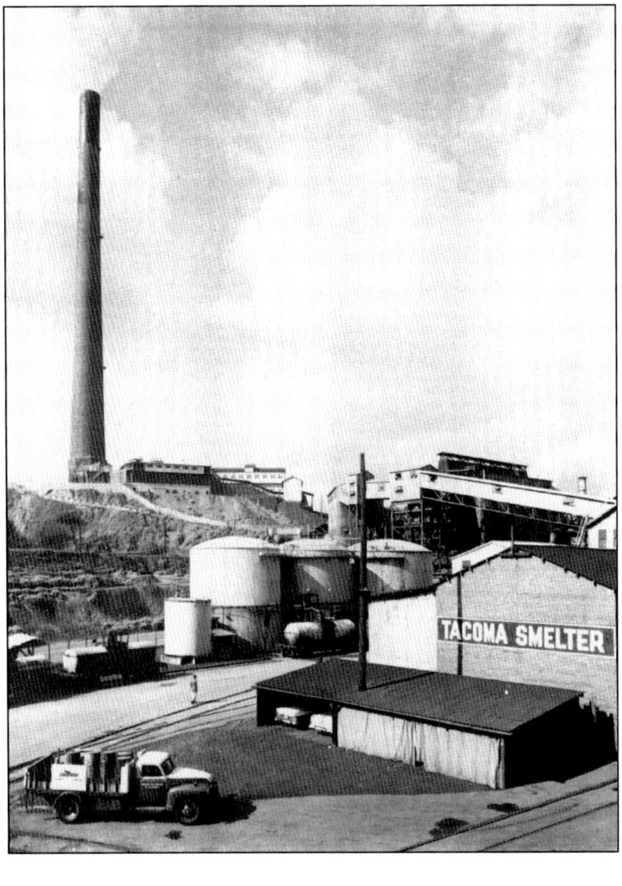

This view of the hillside where the tall smokestack stands, taken from the south end of the smelter complex, was probably captured in about 1949. The hillside is now known as Stack Hill. The large building at the south end features a sign heralding the name of the facility and visible to vehicles approaching along Ruston Way. (KP.)

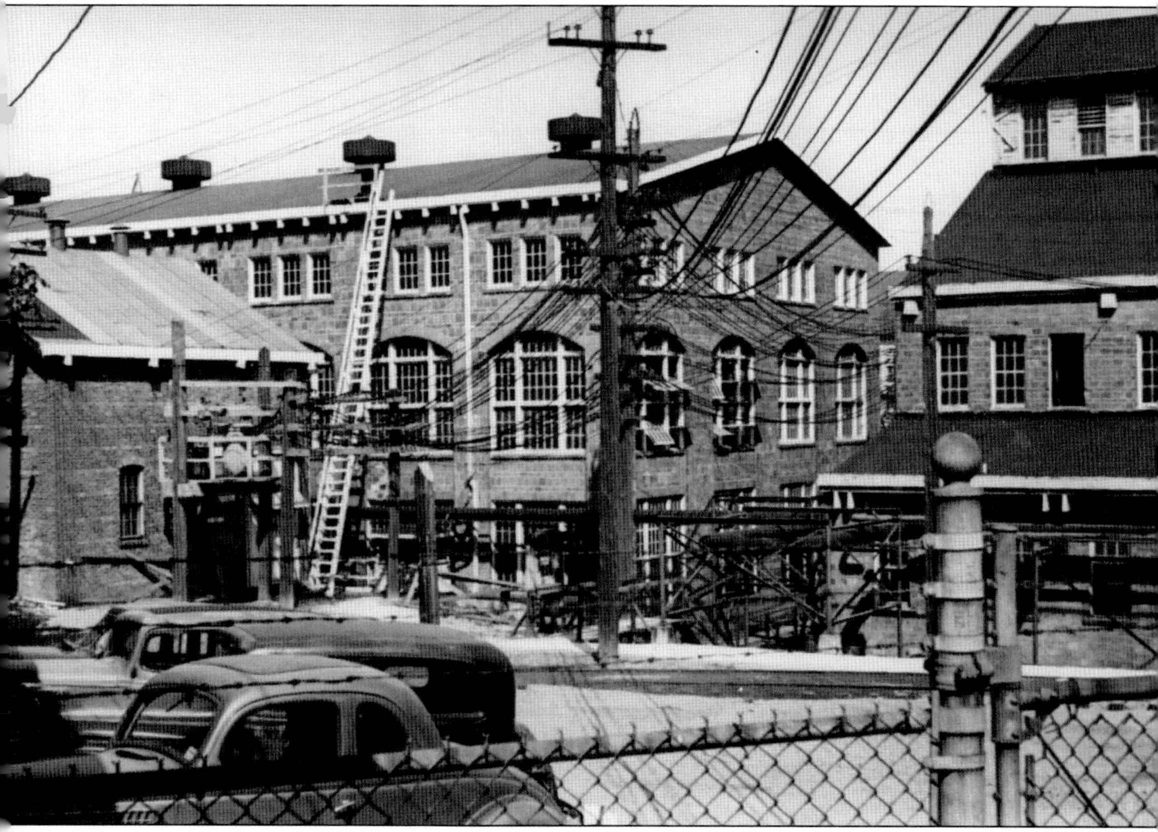

The area at the base of the hillside below Bennett Street was the location for the smelter powerhouse, well within the Ruston boundary. Operation of the furnaces required a huge volume of electricity. Having influence over the utility was likely an important reason Rust worked so hard to incorporate the town. Rust began the incorporation process when negotiations with Tacoma for suppling power were not going well. (KP.)

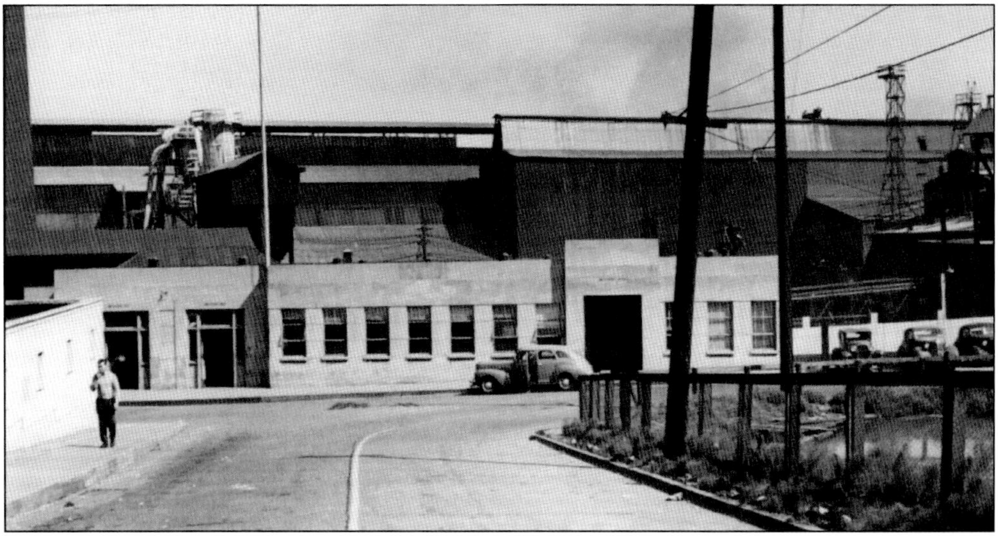

Administration offices and the company medical facilities were just inside the main entrance at the bottom of North Fifty-first Street. Everyone in a worker's family received medical care from company doctors and nurses. Dr. Pinto and nurse Johnny were well loved by employees and their children. This 1950 image looks directly at the medical offices. (KP.)

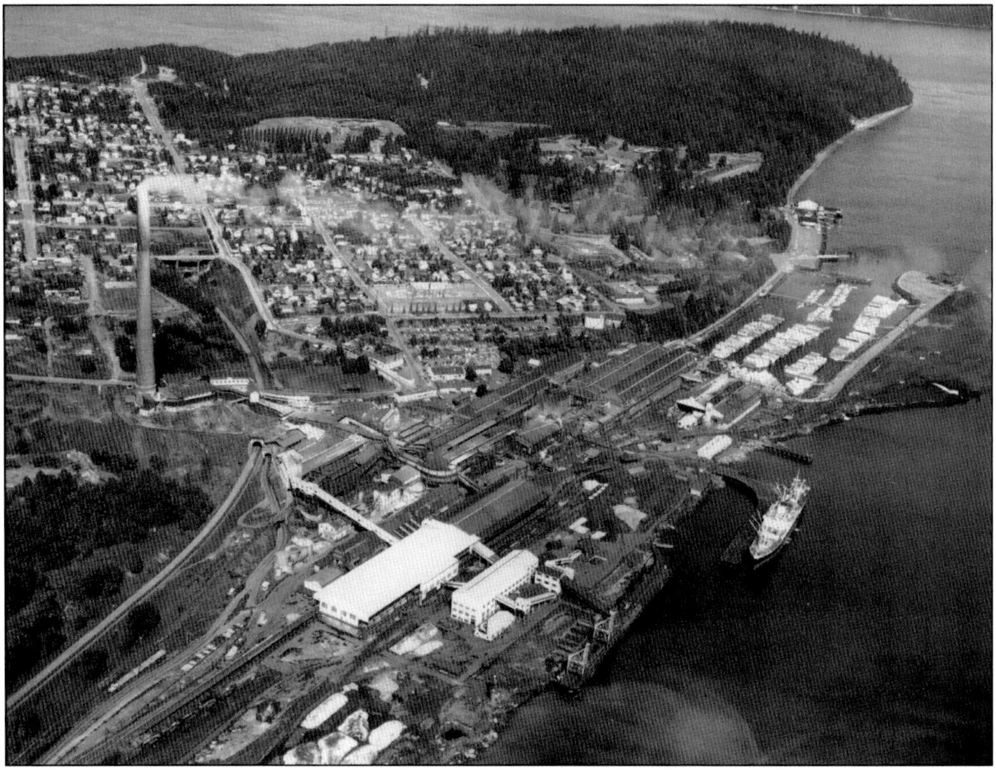

The majority of operations were not visible to the community, with the view blocked by 10-story buildings. The smelter began pouring slag to form the breakwater for the Tacoma Yacht Basin in the early 1920s, at the request of Metropolitan Park District of Tacoma. The landing for the Vashon Island ferry and the Point Defiance boathouse can also be seen just beyond the marina. (KP.)

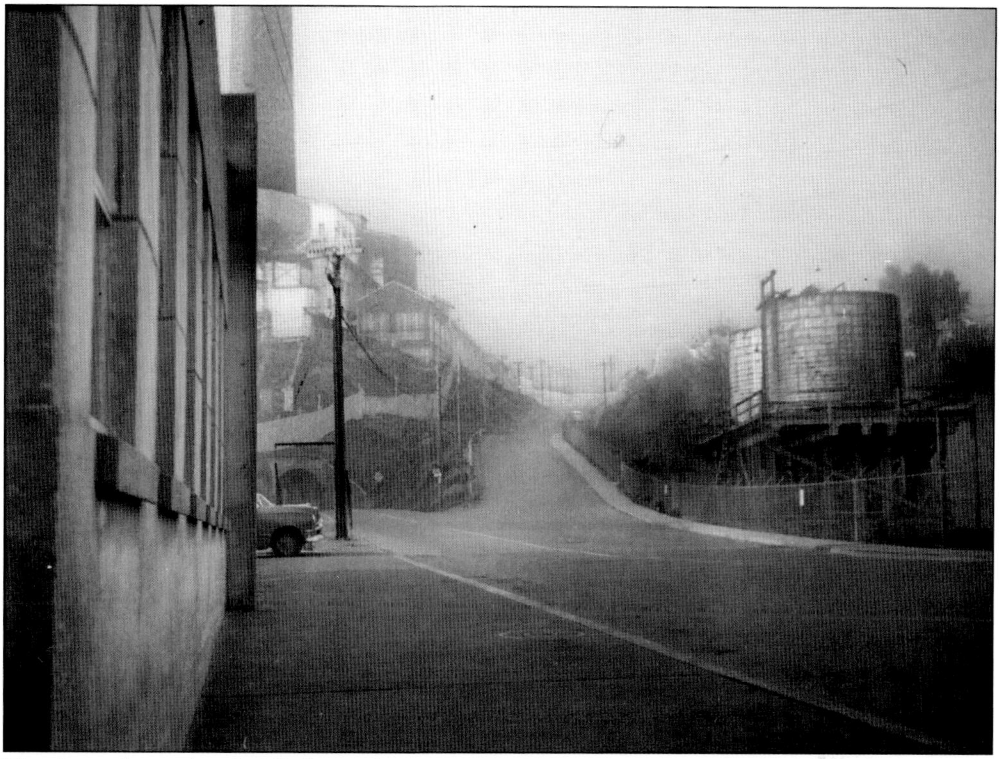

This foggy day in April 1959 shows the now nonexistent connection of Baltimore Street to North Fifty-first Street. This small section of road would later be named Gallagher Way in honor of longtime mayor Owen Gallagher. The medical offices are to the left, and the cooling pond and large tanks are to the right. (KP.)

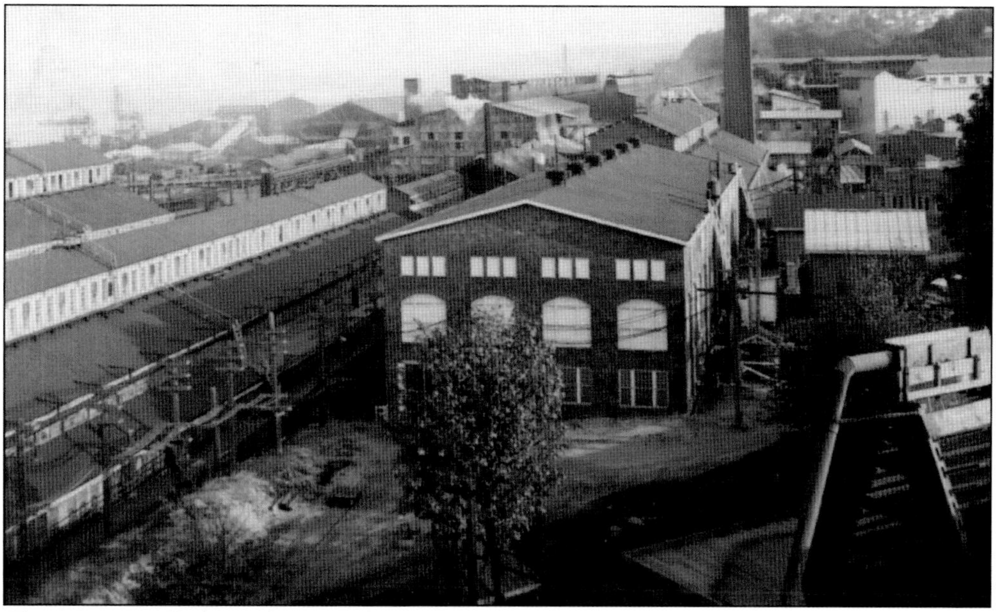

This view in 1953 shows the scene from Bennett Street, overlooking the powerhouse toward the Orchard Street hillside and beyond the Tacoma waterfront. (KP.)

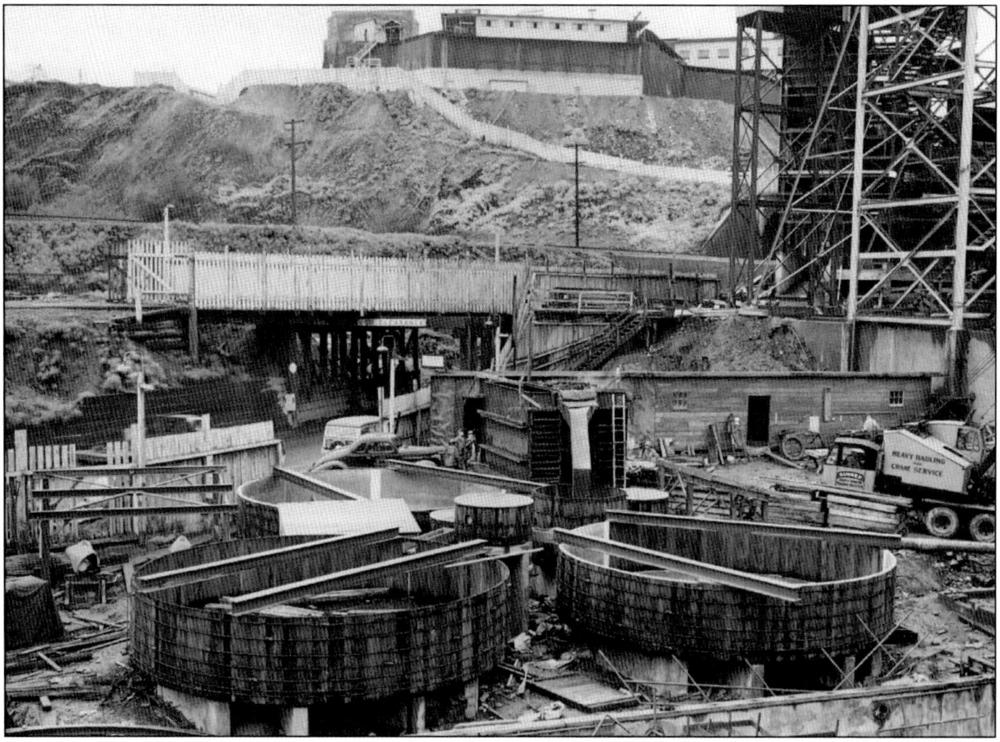

Construction photographs from 1949 offer a glimpse of what appears to be the old roadway out of the tunnel through the plant site, behind the white picket fence. The rail line is visible on the hillside above the roadway. (KP.)

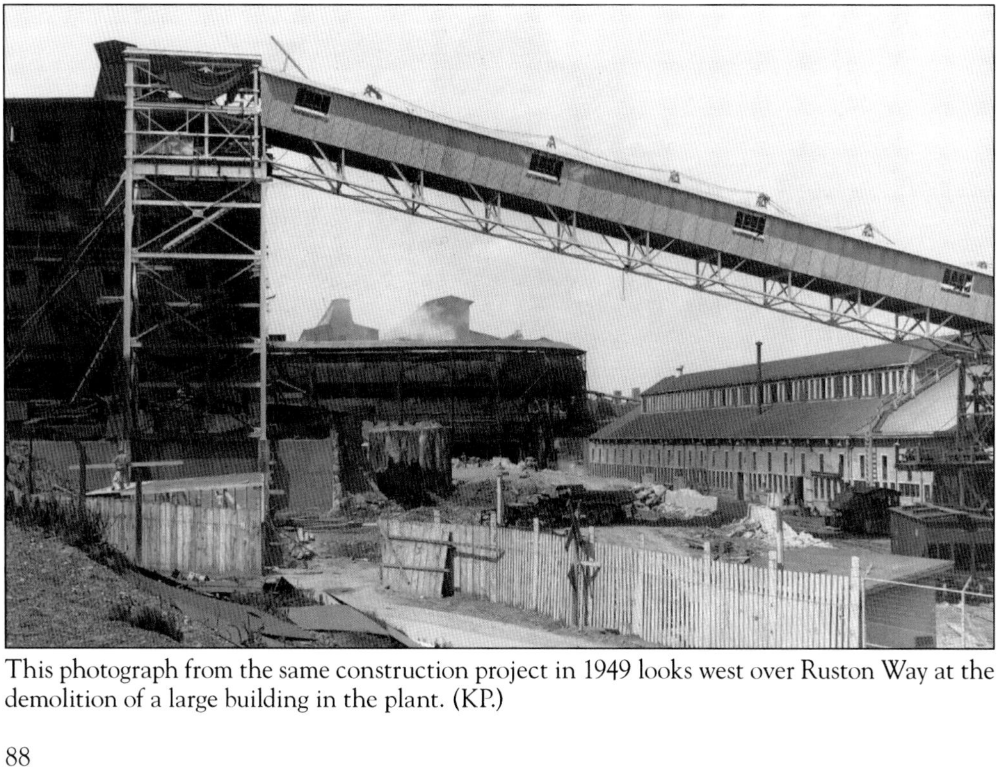

This photograph from the same construction project in 1949 looks west over Ruston Way at the demolition of a large building in the plant. (KP.)

The height of the stack can be felt in this 1970s image. The tall structure not only served as a marker on navigation charts, but it was a guide for the way home for generations of Ruston residents. (KP.)

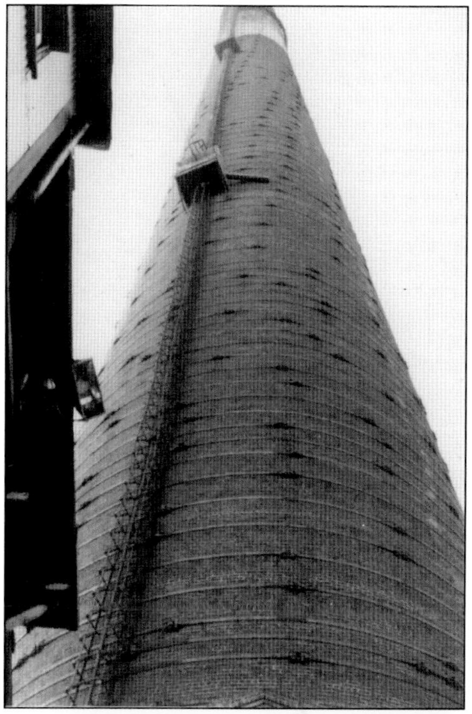

The new SO2 Plant, installed in 1949, captured more of the sulfur dioxide gases generated by smelting the copper ore. The gas was processed and sold. (KP.)

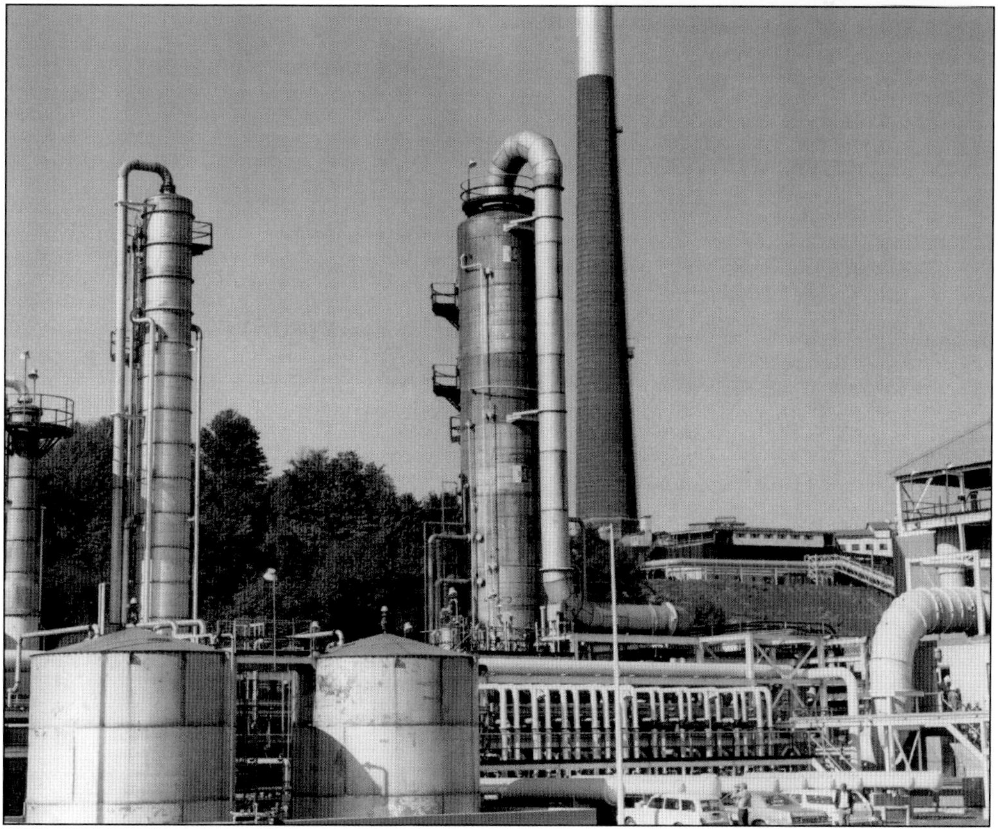

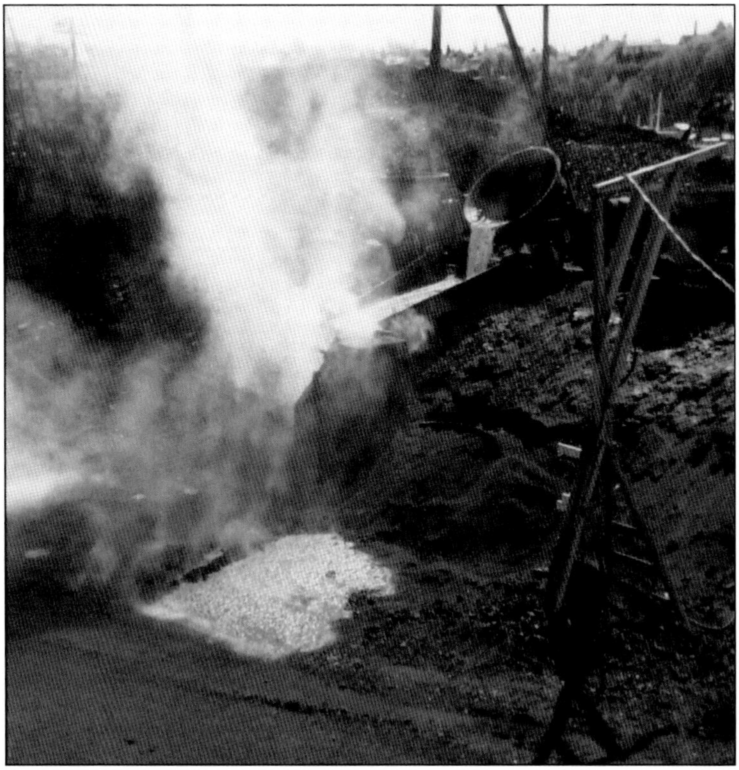

The majority of material sent to the furnaces became black slag rock, which contained discarded impurities. The red-hot melt was similar to the molten lava from a volcano and was poured in waste piles or into the bay to extend the shoreline. Neighbors reported hearing sonic booms regularly as the hot material hit the cold water, causing occasional explosions. (KP.)

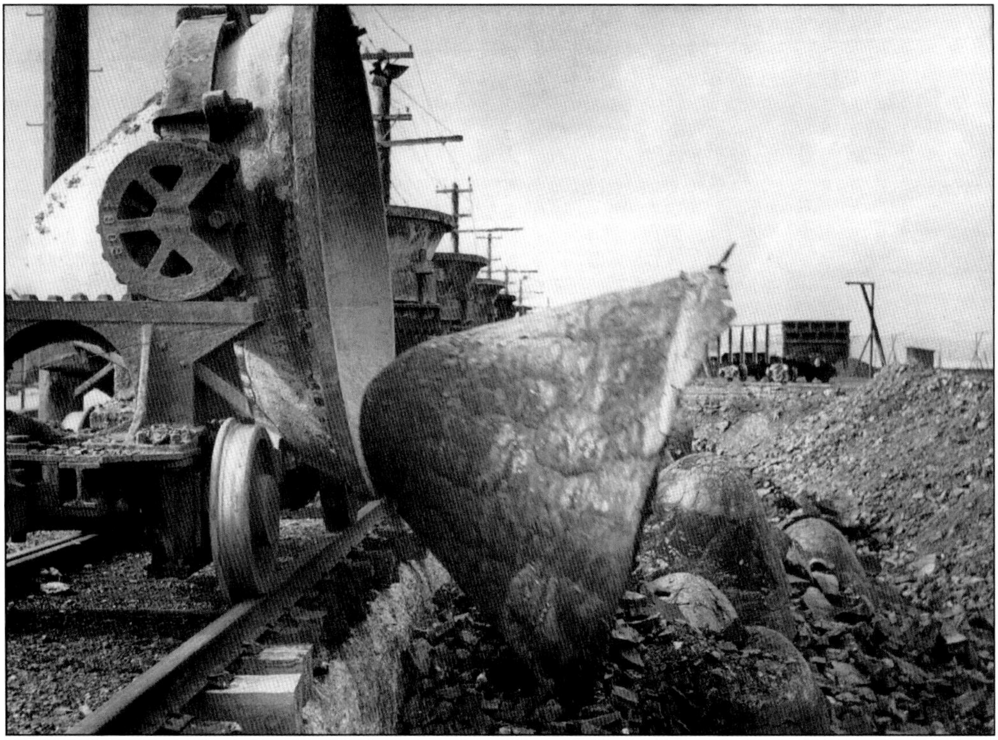

The giant 17-ton ladles would carry hot or cooled slag to various dumping areas. (KP.)

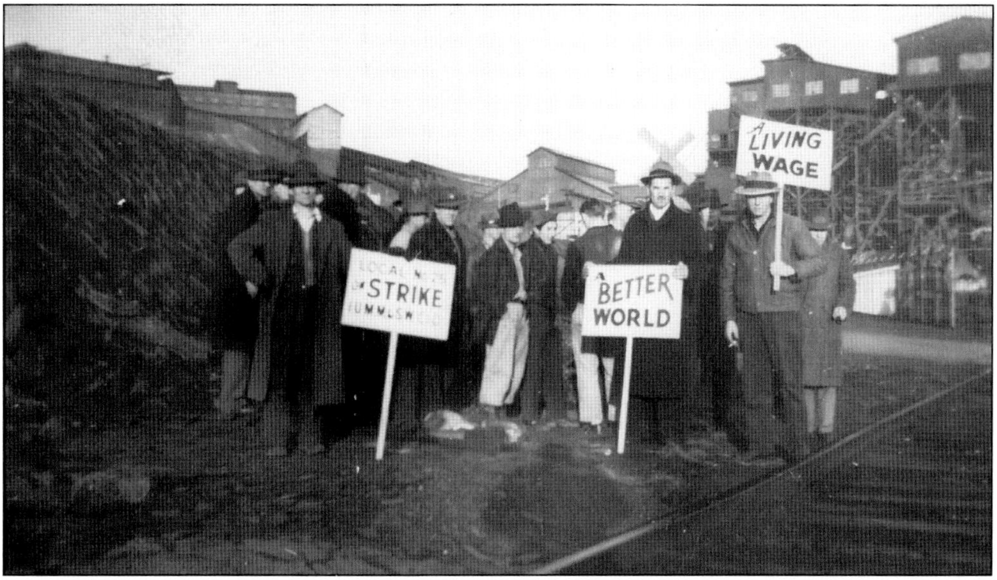

The birth of organized labor early in the 20th century had a big impact on smelter operations. Washington was home to some of the most intense battles, as unions struggled for the right to organize and bargain for better working conditions. The battle sometimes turned deadly, even in Ruston. Several nights of gunfire were exchanged during a strike in early 1914, with strikers stationed on the bluff south of the stack. On the night of January 7, Andrew Aronke, whose family home still stands at the end of Orchard Street, was killed at age 30. He left a grieving fiancée and angry coworkers, who blocked the smelter gates for days. Supplies and strikebreakers were smuggled in by boat. By 1946 (above), tensions still ran high, but without the threat of bloodshed. In 1959 (below), a strike brought billboards and protests to the front of the employment offices. Union members gave up their wages to walk the picket lines, hoping to put pressure on smelter management to concede on various contract issues. (KP.)

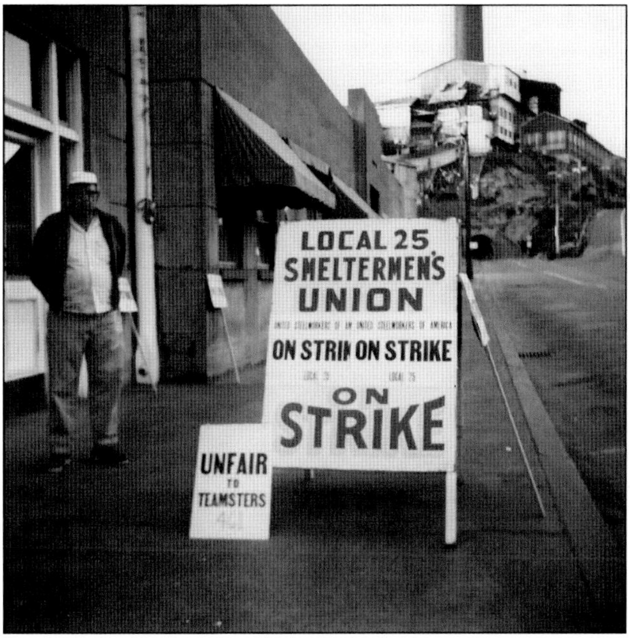

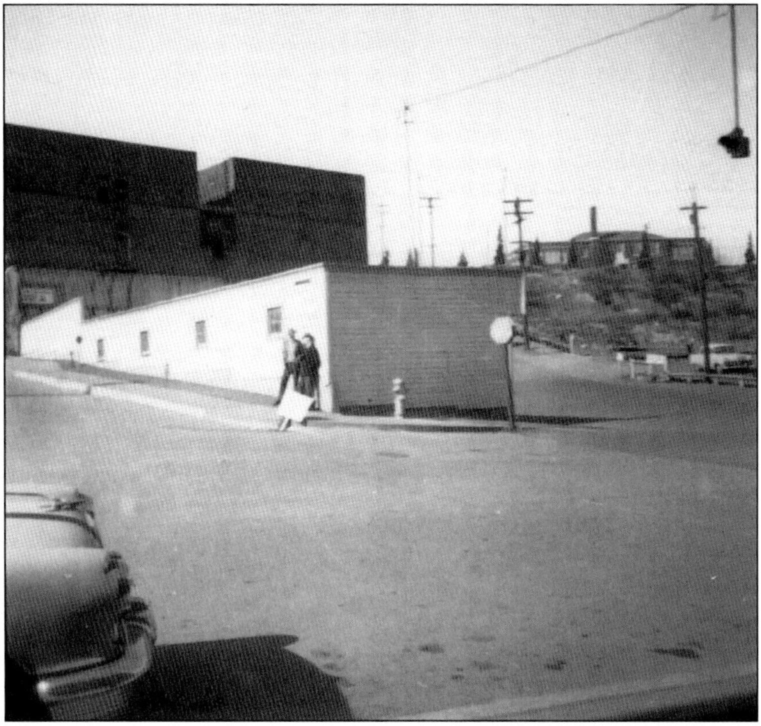

This photograph was probably taken during a strike, likely by management to monitor picketers. The view up Fifty-first Street shows the old Bayview Hotel was still standing, along with other buildings farther uphill. (KP.)

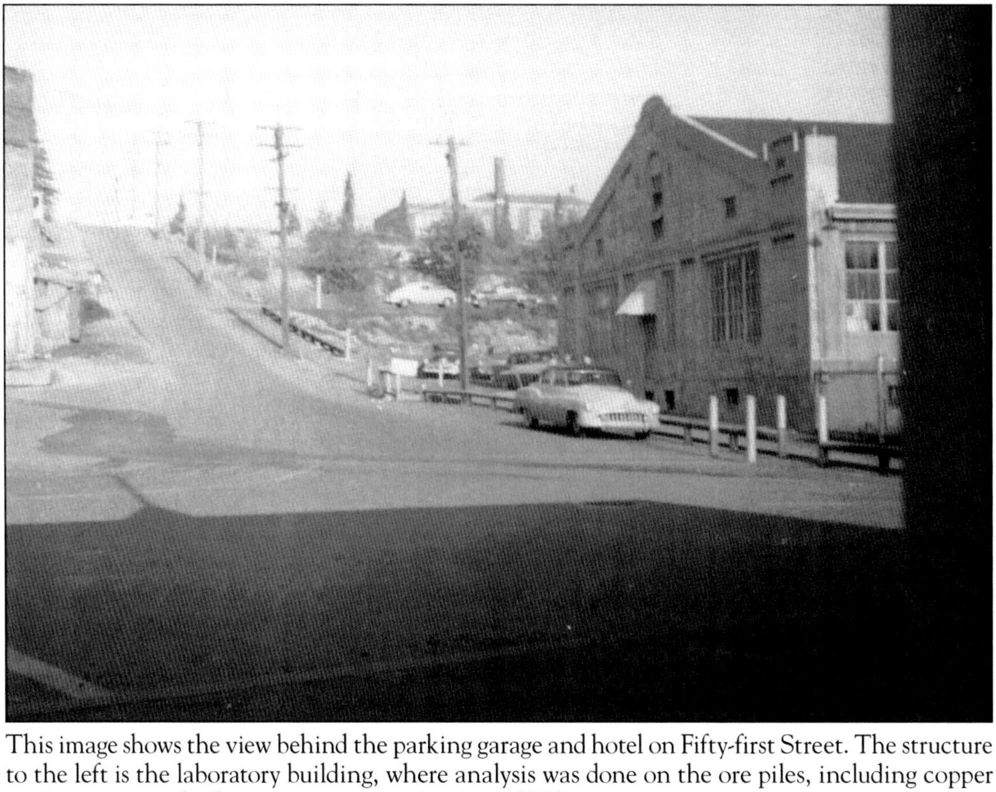

This image shows the view behind the parking garage and hotel on Fifty-first Street. The structure to the left is the laboratory building, where analysis was done on the ore piles, including copper purity testing and other necessary examinations. (KP.)

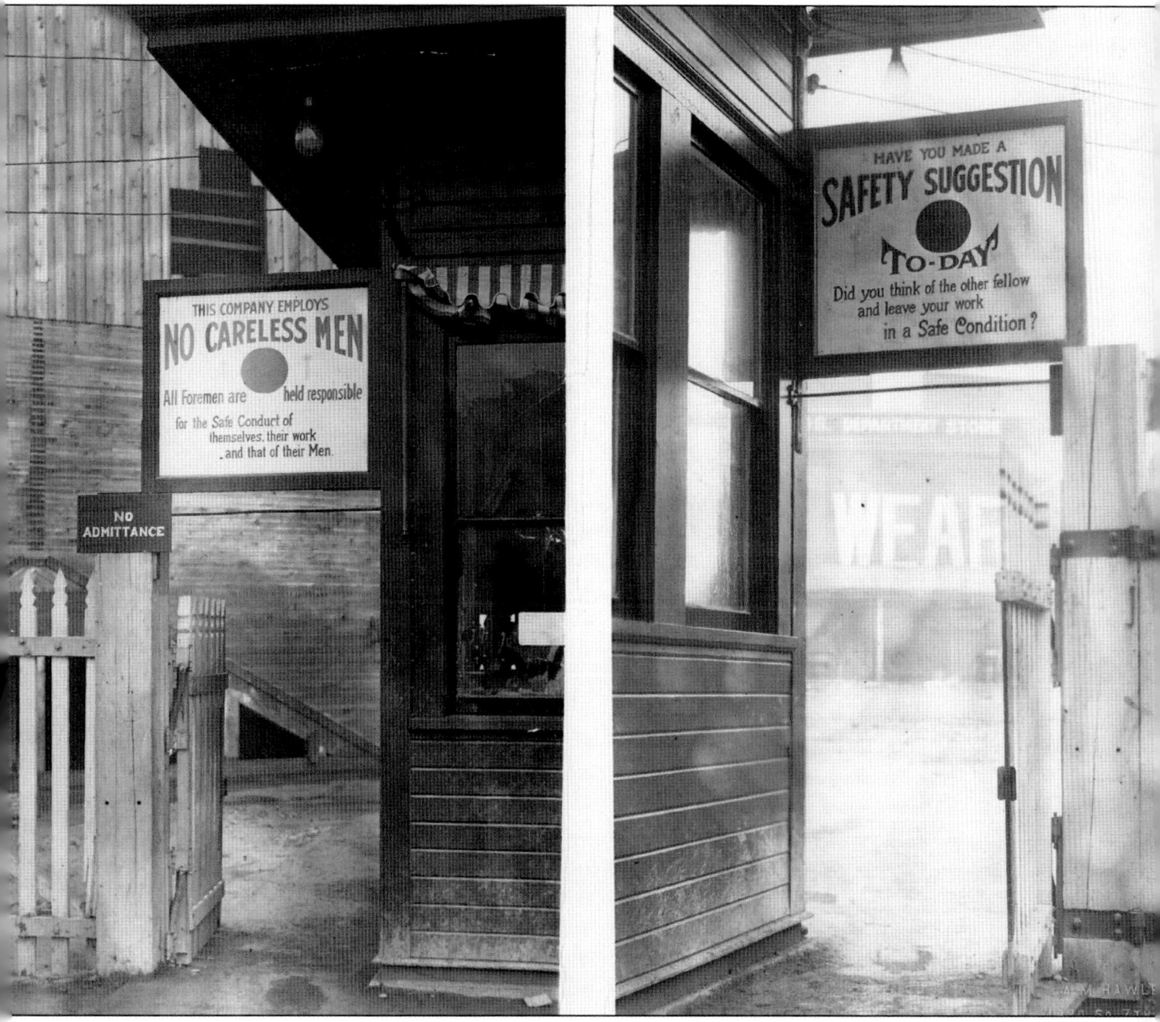

The increasing focus on workers' rights brought a shift in responsibility for employee safety. By the 1920s, new regulations placed the responsibility for safety on the company rather than the worker. This heralded a major change in policy and resources, as heavy industry focused more on making the workplace secure. In 1930, each day employees at the Tacoma Plant entered past the safety office, which had many signs reminding them to behave. By the 1980s, the safety of the surrounding community was also being debated. Emission of arsenic and the possibility of closing the smelter were hot topics for the Environmental Protection Agency. *News Tribune* headlines announced, "Tacoma will get a 'vote' on arsenic peril," and, "A Life-and-Death Choice." A local editorial declared, "Are we willing to tolerate any dangerous or unpleasant pollutants in our environment in exchange for employment and business opportunities and tax revenues? . . . We are, in a way, pioneers." The community divided. Many employees and families were fiercely loyal to the company. Environmentalists were equally passionate that no risk was acceptable and that ASARCO should be forced to close. (WSHS.)

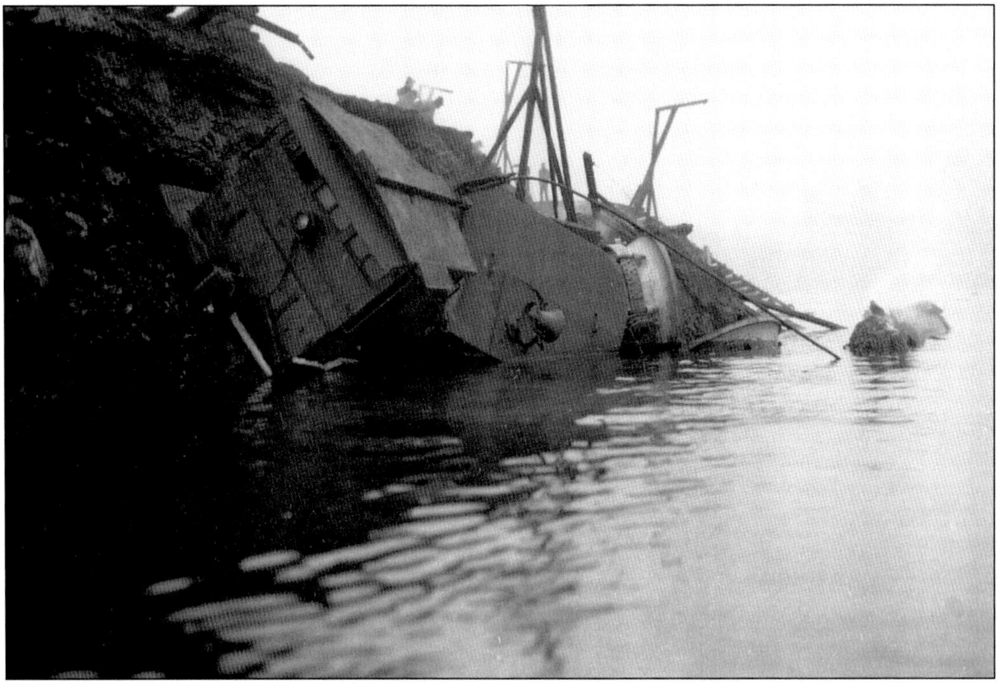

Not only was work around the heat of the furnaces dangerous, but other everyday jobs also held their dangers. Driving the slag train might have been routine, but the rail along the shoreline was susceptible to collapse if the slag was unstable. This wreck in 1938 was deadly. (TPL.)

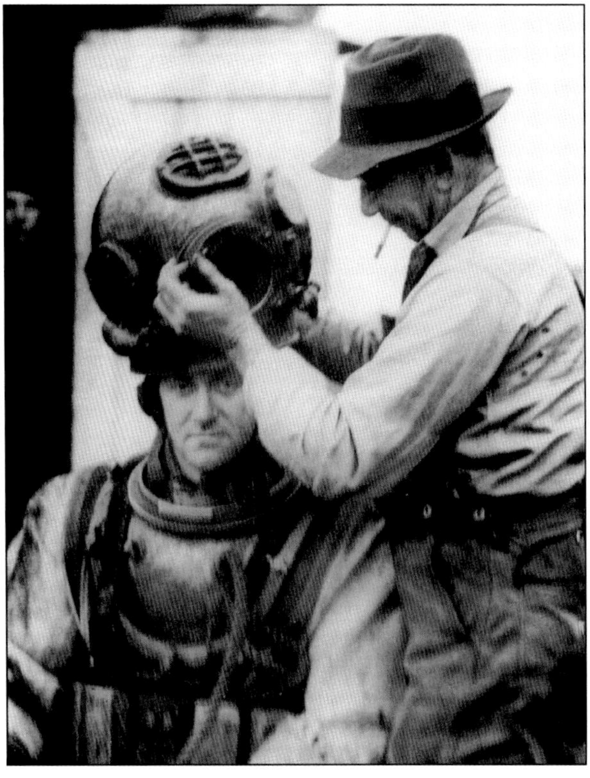

At age 25, Frank Birkby was killed by a blow to the head when the slag train he was conducting fell into the bay. A deep-sea diver had to be brought in to retrieve his body before the equipment was pulled from the bay and the rail line moved. (TPL.)

Collapse of the rail line appeared to be a constant problem, as seen in this 1960s-era photograph. (KP.)

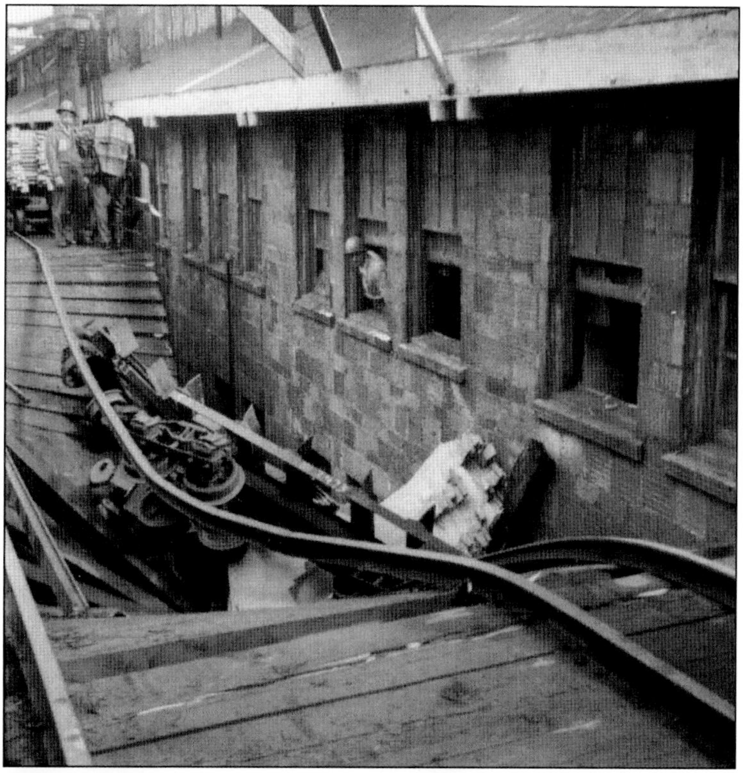

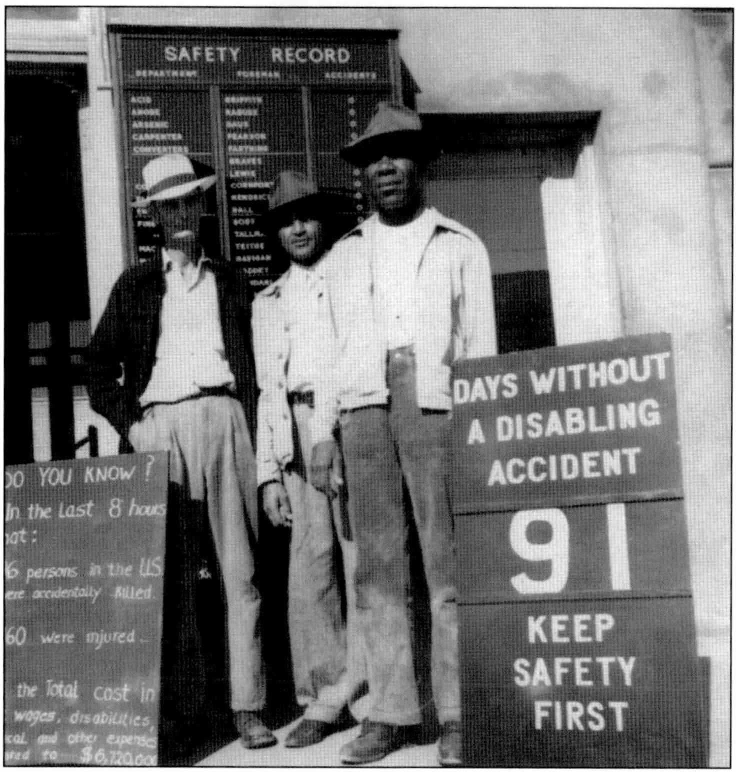

The practice of encouraging safe behaviors with a public display of how many days since the last accident is common in many companies today. This 1952 picture shows the front of the safety office at the bottom of North Fifty-first Street, near the employment and medical offices. These gentlemen were likely being recognized for safety performance. (KP.)

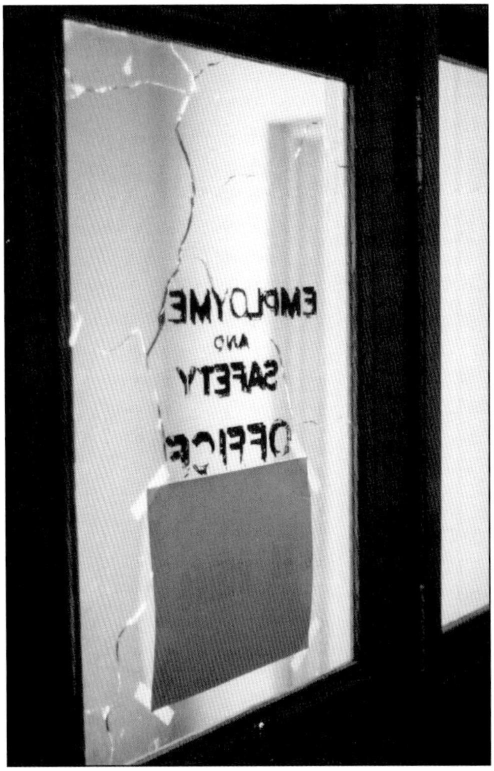

Although death threats were not as common during labor strikes by the mid-1950s, tension still ran high, as seen in this broken window at the administration offices. Employees could be trained for the day-to-day workplace, but it was difficult to prepare for this kind of hazard. (KP.)

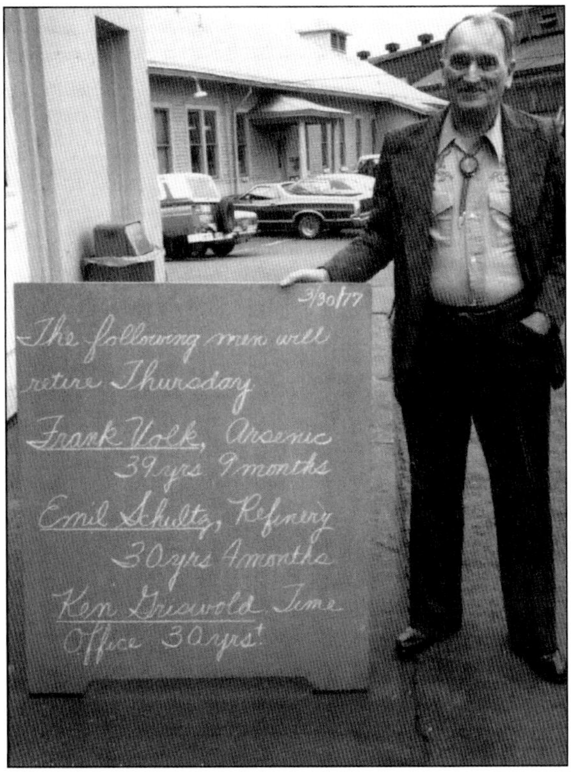

The goal of any good employee was to reach retirement in one piece, healthy enough to enjoy the fruits of his or her labor for many years. Longevity was common for employees at the Tacoma Plant, like those cited on the placard here. This photograph was taken just inside the main gate, looking northeast at the main administration building. (KP.)

This photograph was probably taken in 1946. Although World War II had ended the year before, there were still some women working, even in the heavy-labor jobs at the smelter. (KP.)

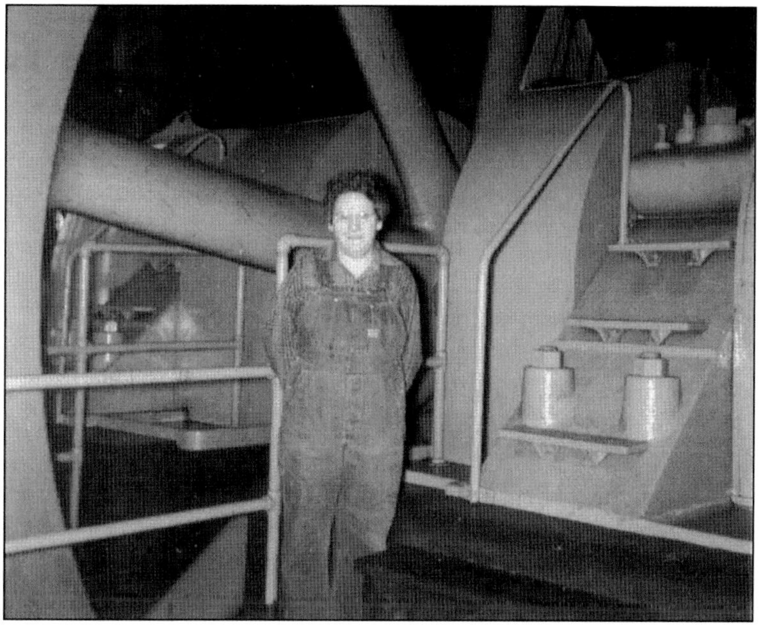

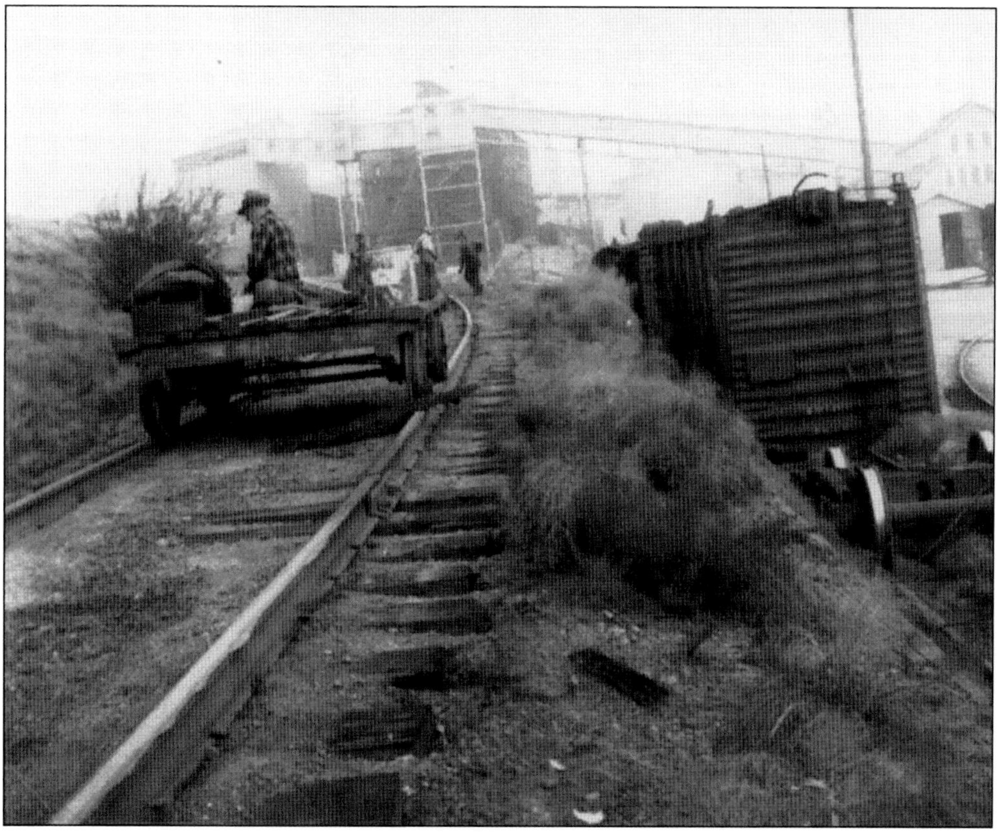

A major West Coast rail line runs through Ruston. It once had spurs leading to the smelter complex. One such track is seen in this 1953 photograph. This line led to a trestle over Ruston Way, the remnants of which are still visible today. (KP.)

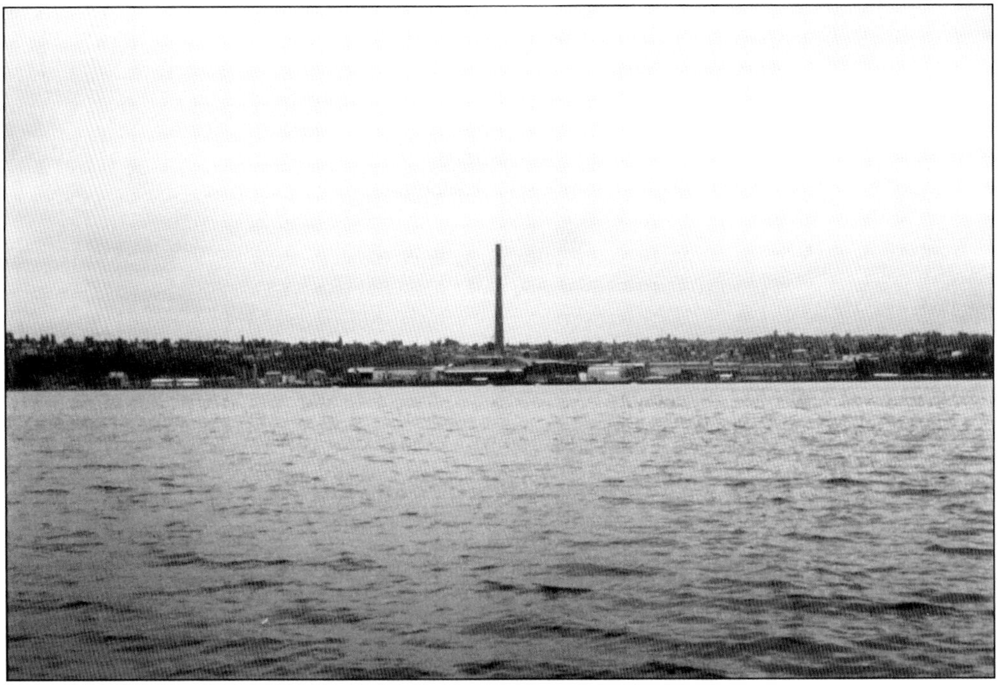

This 1960s image captures why the ASARCO smelter smokestack was used for navigation by boats and aircraft. The towering structure could be seen for miles in any direction. (KP.)

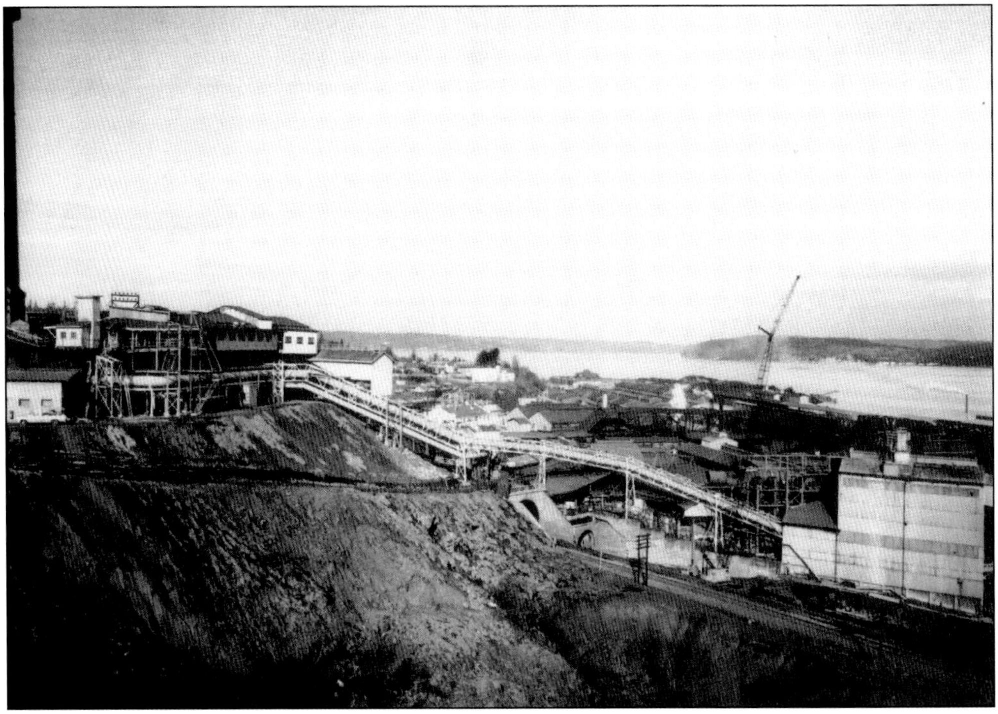

The arsenic kitchens processing area is seen in this c. 1978 image. The Tacoma Plant specialized in copper ores with high metallic arsenic content. Much of the metal was captured before going up the stack, was processed, and then sold. (TPL.)

Even western Washington is known for occasional long, hard freezes. This photograph captures one of those times, where it appears a pipe burst and water flowed unchecked onto one of the smelter docks during a cold spell. (KP.)

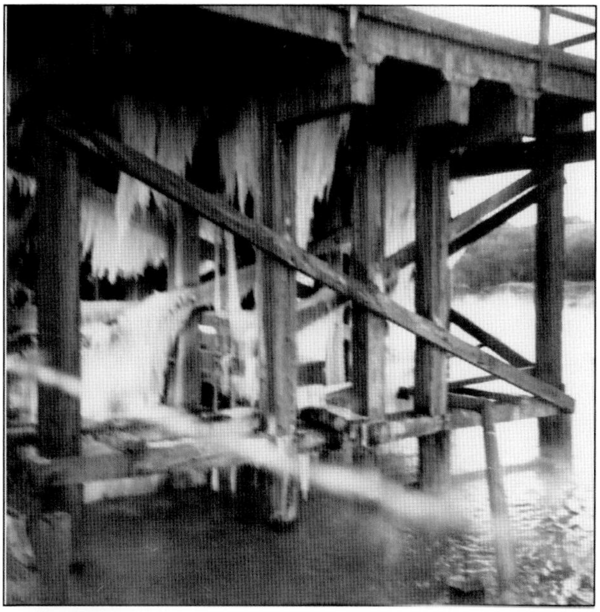

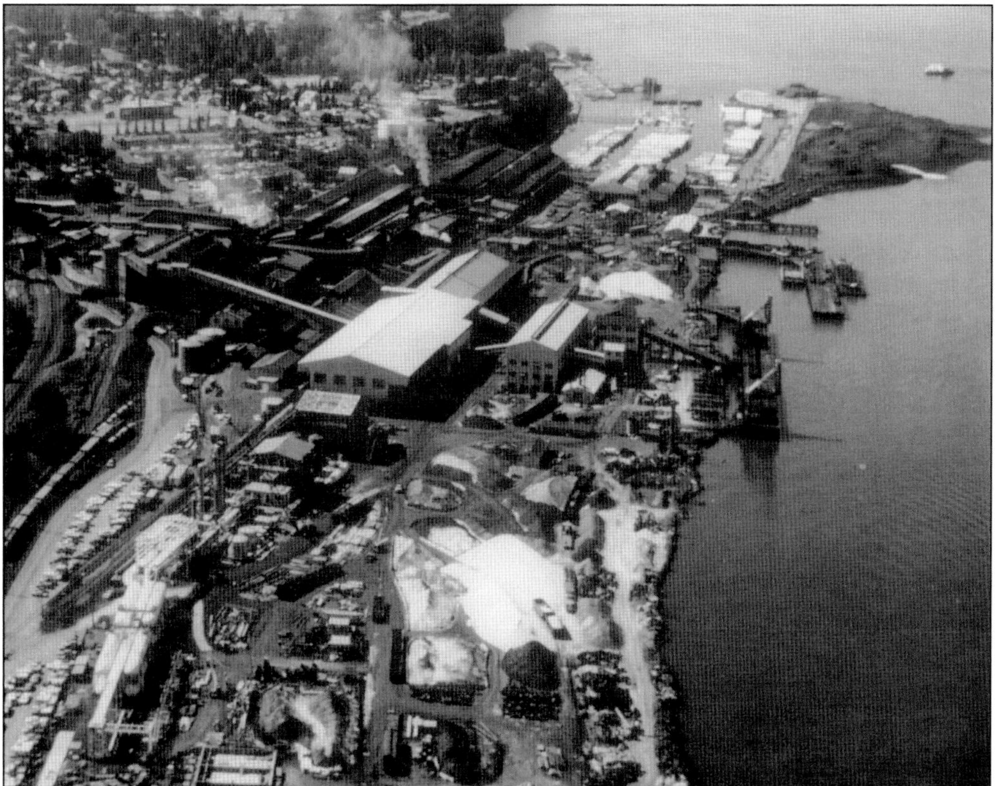

This 1973 aerial photograph shows the Tacoma Plant about 10 years before closure. The dark-roofed refinery buildings sit near the top of the picture. The Fine Ore Bins and Reverberating Furnace buildings are in the middle. Huge cranes line the main dock to load the heavy cargo on ships, to the right. A long train of cars sits on the spur off Ruston Way, to the left. (KP.)

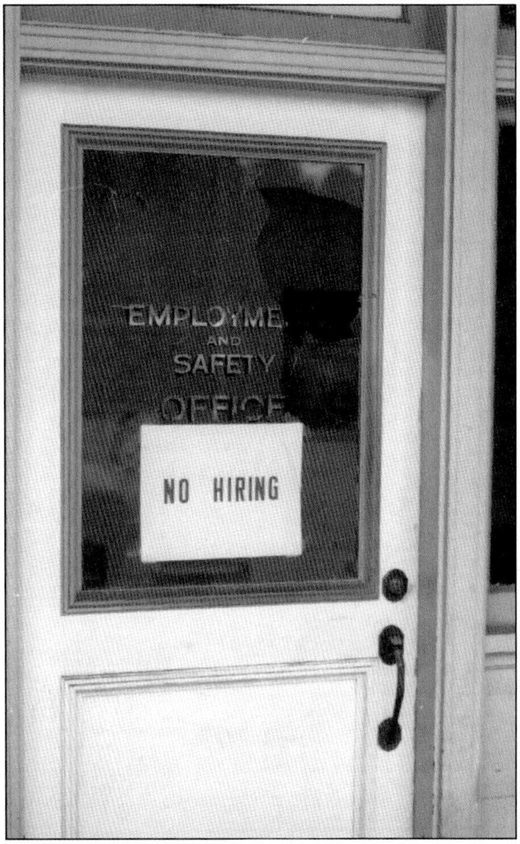

The refineries shut down in the late 1970s, with the smelter following suit in 1985. When the last 550 employees clocked out, many third-generation smelter workers were forced to find new jobs. (KP.)

The smokestack that once dominated the skyline of Point Defiance and Ruston has now been demolished along with the rest of the buildings. Remediation of the underlying soils is almost complete, and the site is ready for the next phase in Ruston history as the town moves forward. (KP.)

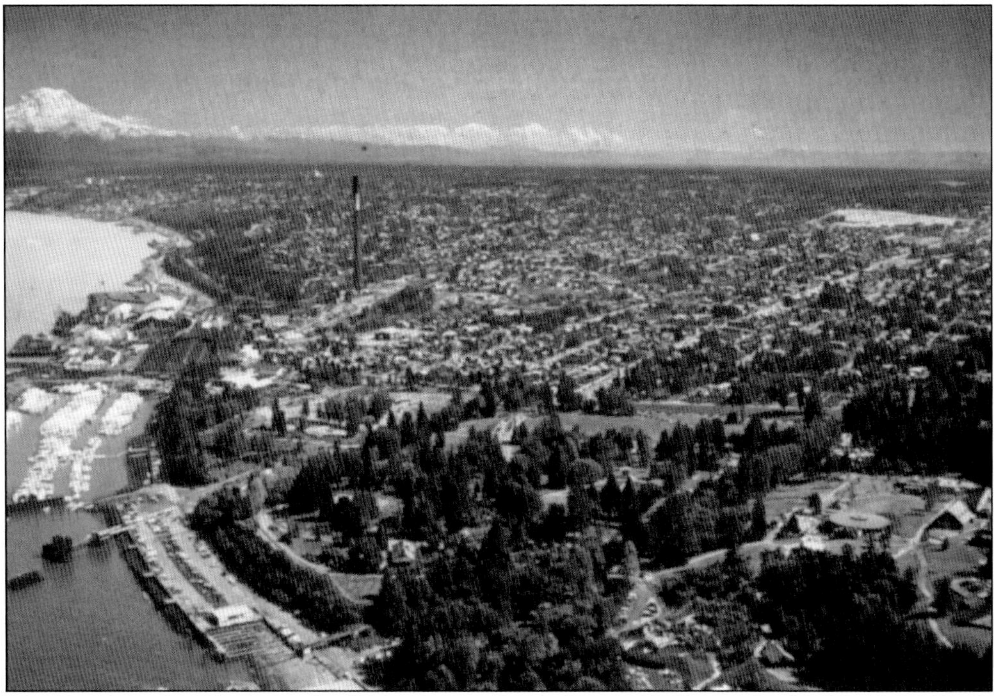

Six

Faces and Places

Ruston sits on the edge of one of the largest metropolitan parks in the nation. Despite being one of the smallest towns in the state, it is surrounded by the third largest city in Washington. This tiny enclave offers the best of small-town America, right next door to some great urban amenities. In addition to the allure of the big city and parks just outside Ruston's boundaries, the town has its share of color within as well. From "Chicken Ole" to Leo Wingard, the town's distinctive people have kept life interesting. On such a small stage, local politics are often heated and volatile, making for some lively election campaigns.

Public safety is important to any community. In Ruston, a small police force and volunteer fire department answer emergency calls. From 1939 to 1955, marshal Clarence Kerney patrolled Ruston's streets with only one arm. He lost the other in an accident during his day job at the smelter. It is rumored he quit as town marshal when Ruston bought its first patrol car. The vehicle had a manual transmission and required two hands to drive. Until that time, all patrolling had been on foot.

The fire department was once called to action by a special series of smelter whistle blasts, which could be heard throughout the town. The location of the emergency was written on a chalkboard before the fire engine left town hall so late-arriving firefighters would know where to go to help. Today, radio and pagers keep the department connected. Firefighting students occupy the house next to town hall to provide additional coverage. Both police and fire personnel are able to provide that small-town personal touch along with their excellent training and expertise.

This chapter offers a brief look at just some of the faces and places that make Ruston such an interesting town to live in.

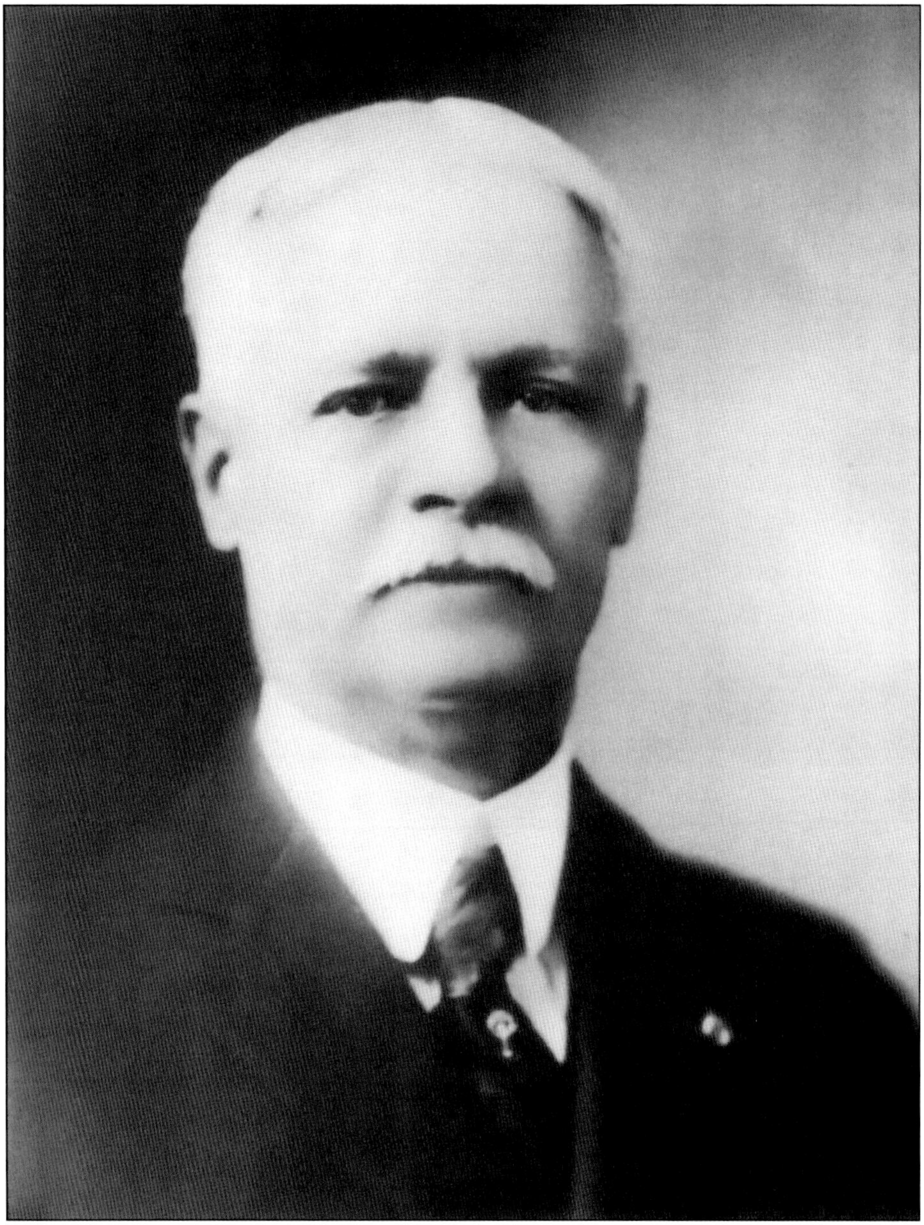

William Ross Rust was born in 1850 in Philadelphia, Pennsylvania. The family moved to Illinois, where the elder Rust ran a business that eventually failed in 1876. William then left, ending up in Colorado when he ran out of money. After building his own business in ore sampling, he sold it, moved to Tacoma, and bought the Ruston smelter to form the Tacoma Smelting and Refining Company. He began with 30 men who worked 50 tons of ore a day. Within 25 years, there were 1,600 employees handling 2,000 tons. In 1905, after the Guggenheims only offered $1 million for the operation, Rust broke off negotiations, saying he would not take less than $5 million. A year later, he received $5.5 million and remained as manager for five years. He later built the Rust Building in downtown Tacoma. Rust married wife Helen while in Colorado. He never lived in Ruston, instead building a mansion on Tacoma's North Slope. The family moved after his son Howard died unexpectedly. Rust was survived by one other son. (TPL.)

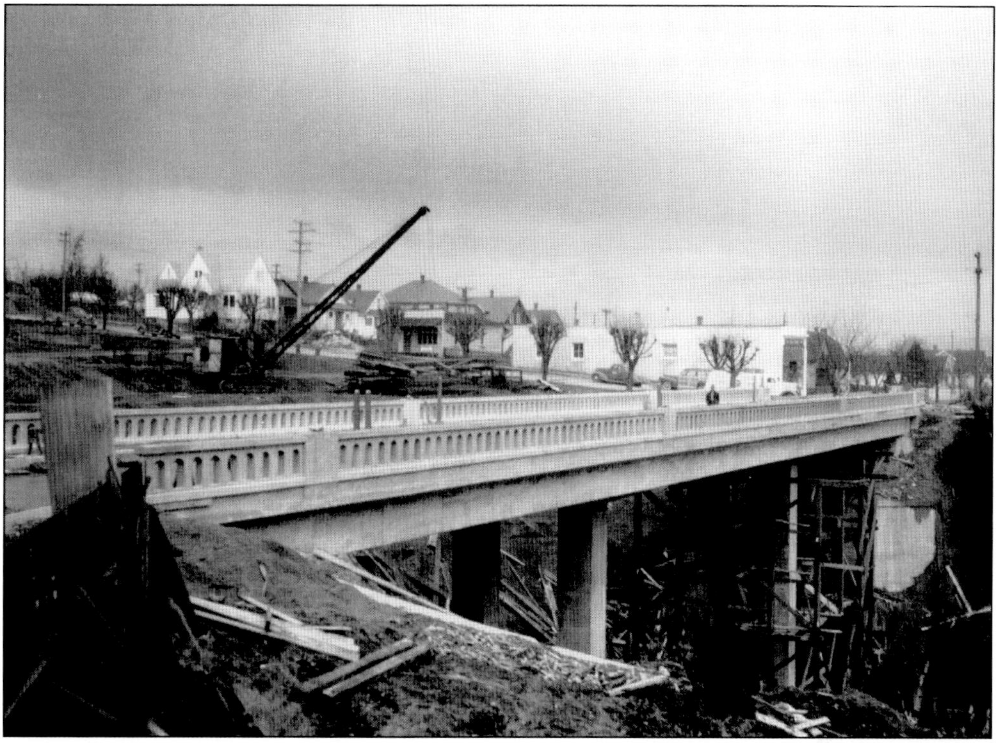

The new bridge over the Nelson-Bennett Train Tunnel replaced an aging wooden span in December 1941. The new bridge was 300 feet long and made of longer-lasting reinforced concrete. (TPL.)

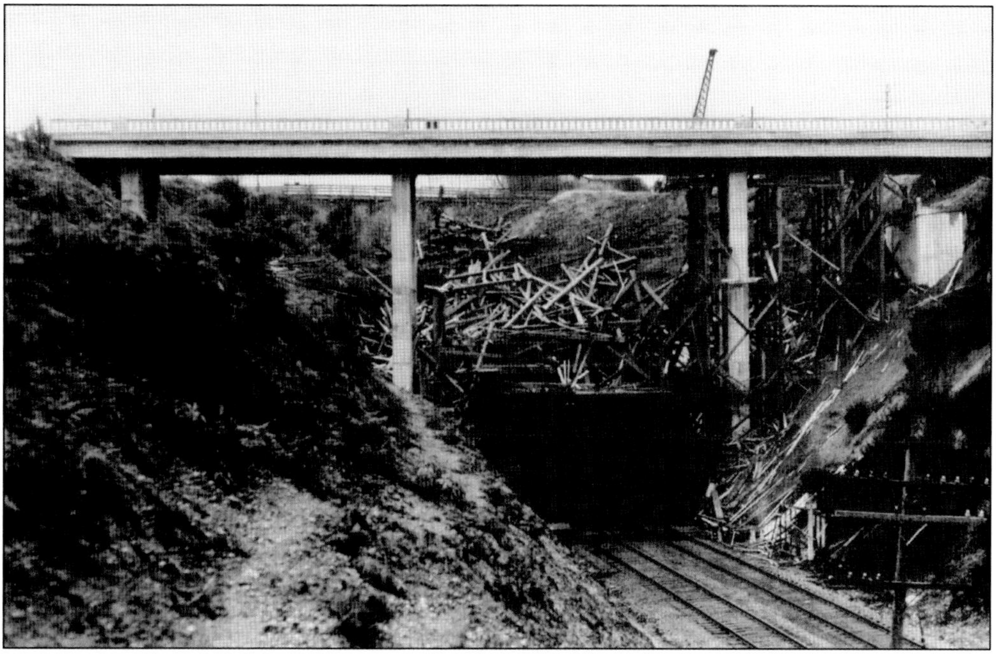

Remnants of the old bridge are seen on the hillside behind the new bridge, with the structure standing 125 feet above the rail lines below. The two rail lines were converted into one safer line in the 1990s. The total cost for the new bridge in 1941 was $31,000. (TPL.)

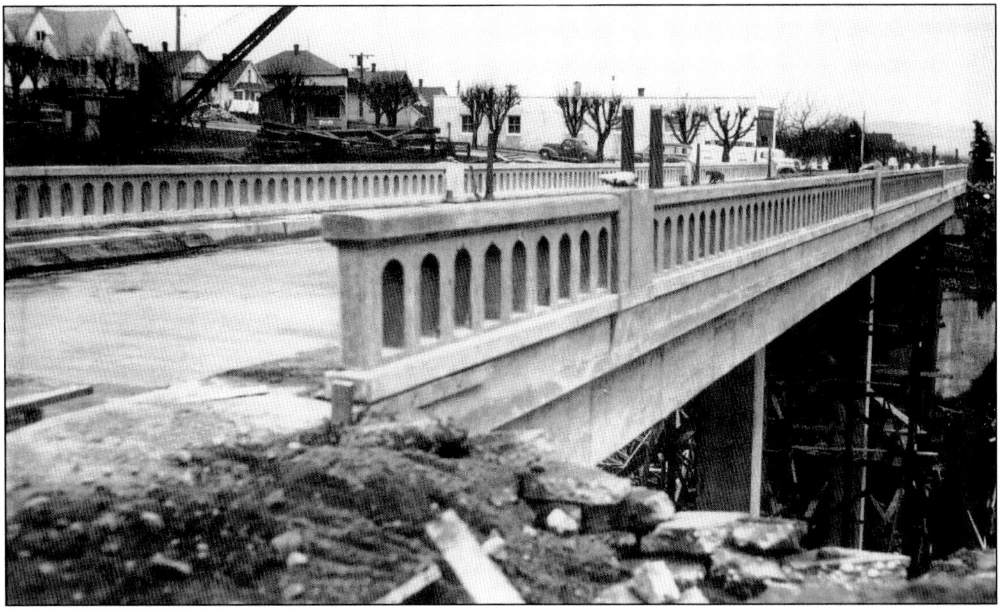

Both Tacoma and Ruston's mayors attended the official ribbon-cutting ceremony on December 13, 1941. A bridge jubilee was held afterwards, complete with dancing girls, a roller-hockey game, and a bowling competition between Ruston and Seattle teams. (TPL.)

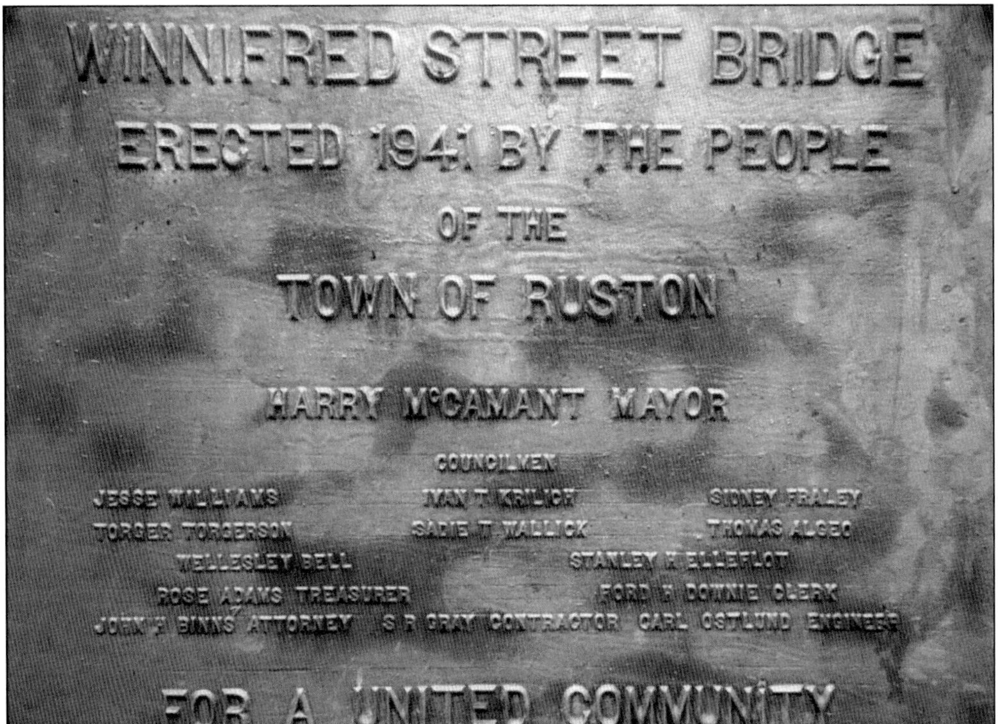

The plaque from the 1941 bridge commemorates longtime mayor Harry McCamant, council members, and town clerk Ford Downie and treasurer Rose Baily, both of whom served Ruston in those capacities for decades. (TR.)

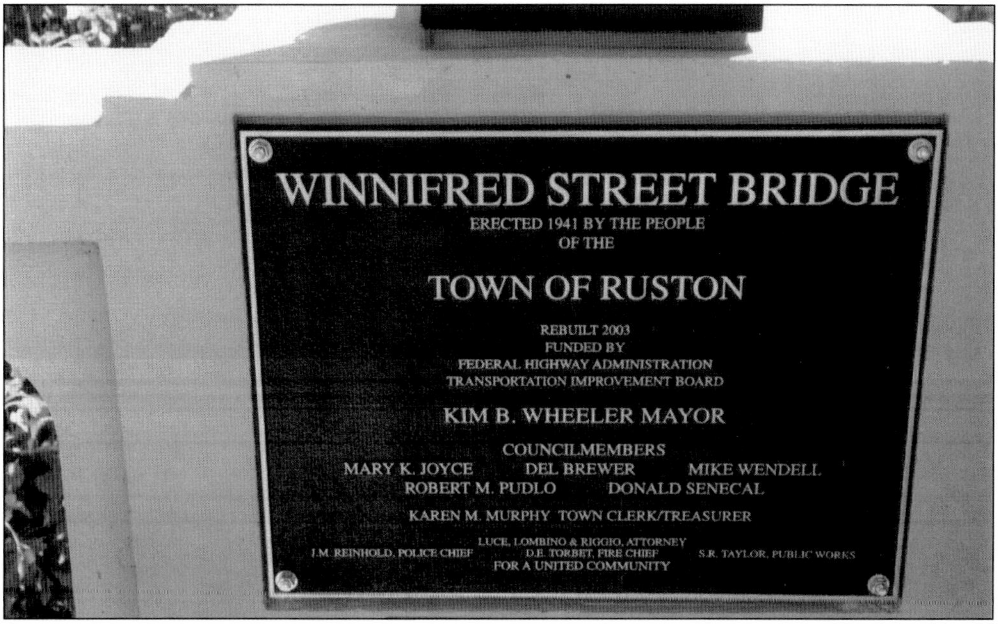

Even reinforced concrete will eventually fail. The bridge was finally closed for several years in the 1990s and rebuilt using federal dollars in 2003. Then mayor Kim Wheeler and the rest of the town officials are memorialized in a new plaque. The section of the bridge railing with the old plaque was moved to the median on Winnifred to serve as a permanent marker of Ruston's history. (TR.)

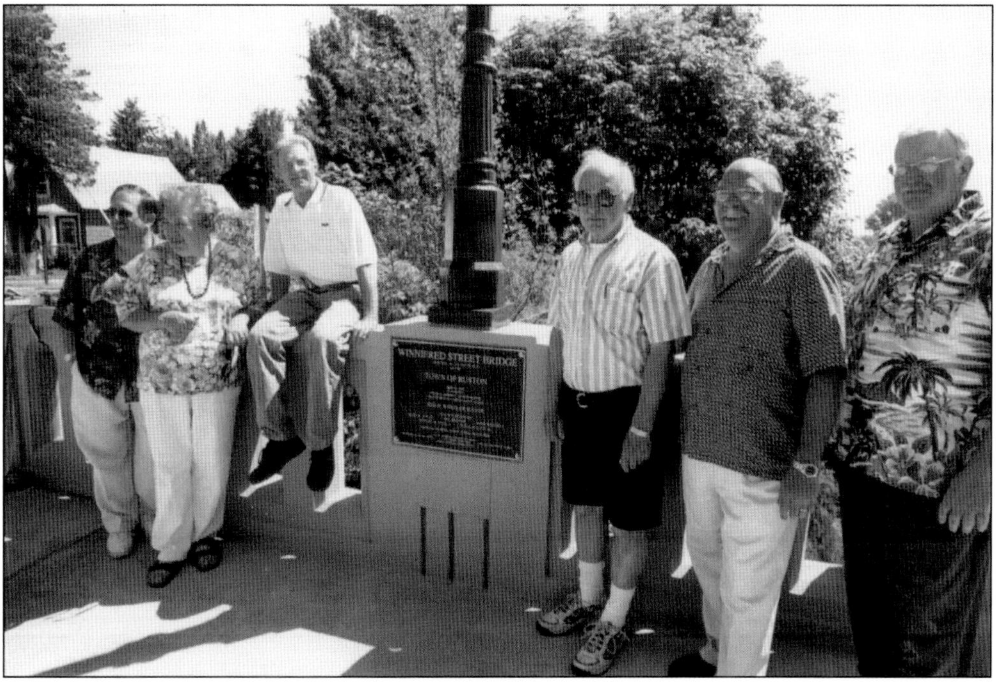

Town officials pose with the new plaque in 2003. From left to right are council members Don Senecal, Mary Joyce, Mike Wendel, and Bob Pudlo, mayor Kim Wheeler, and council member Del Brewer. (TR.)

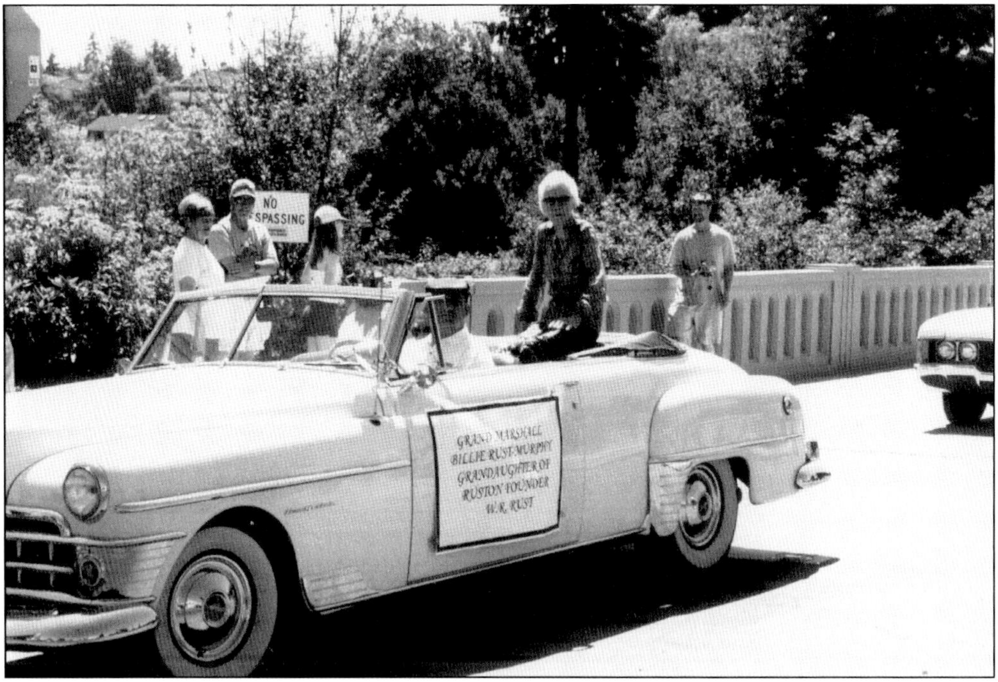

The 2003 bridge opening included a parade of antique cars and special guests. The grand marshal for the event was Billie Rust Murphy, granddaughter of William Rust. She was Rust's last living relative and had no children. She died the next year. (TR.)

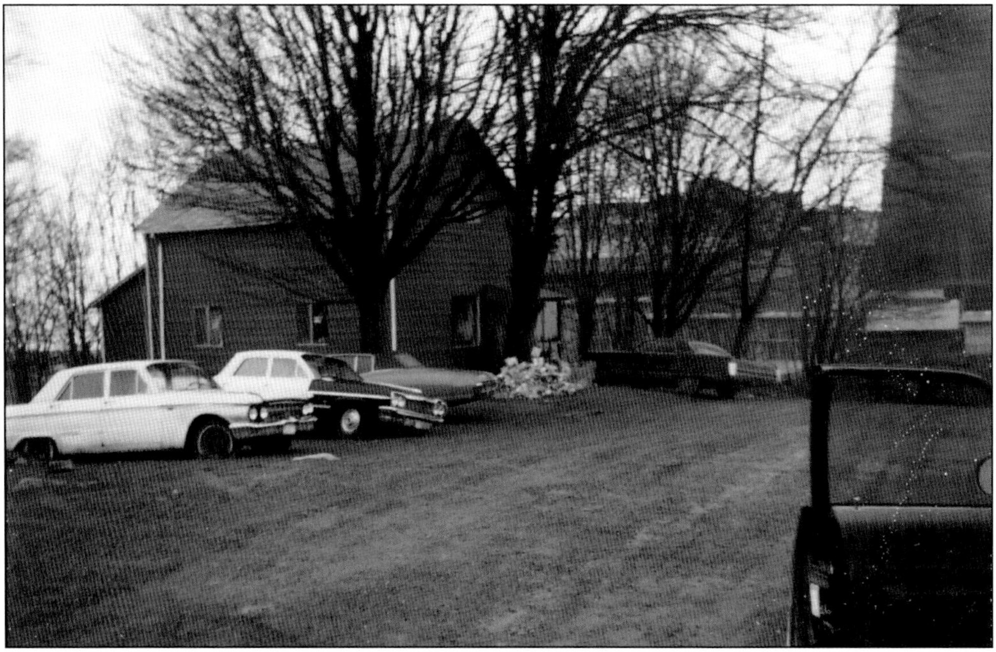

Over the years, some local eccentrics have taken on legendary status. "Sanitary Sam" lived on Commercial Street, near the base of the smelter stack. He was well known for his collection of garbage. The hillside behind his house was littered with appliances and junk. It is rumored that he died after he was forced to take a bath. (TR.)

With a similar reputation, "Chicken Ole" lived near North Fiftieth and Commercial Streets. At age 73 (right), he had chickens, goats, and rabbits living in the house. When some local schoolboys were caught shooting pigeons, the marshal made them help clean out Ole's house after it was condemned. Rather than wash dishes, Ole would eat off of newspapers, with each meal adding a new layer to his dining room table. One of the boys said, "I watched to see which poultry company came to take the chickens, and I swore I'd never buy one of their chickens again." Town officials moved Ole temporarily into a nursing home, burned his old house, and built him a new one. He set the new house on fire the day after moving in. This photograph (below) shows his house in 1944 prior to demolition. (TPL.)

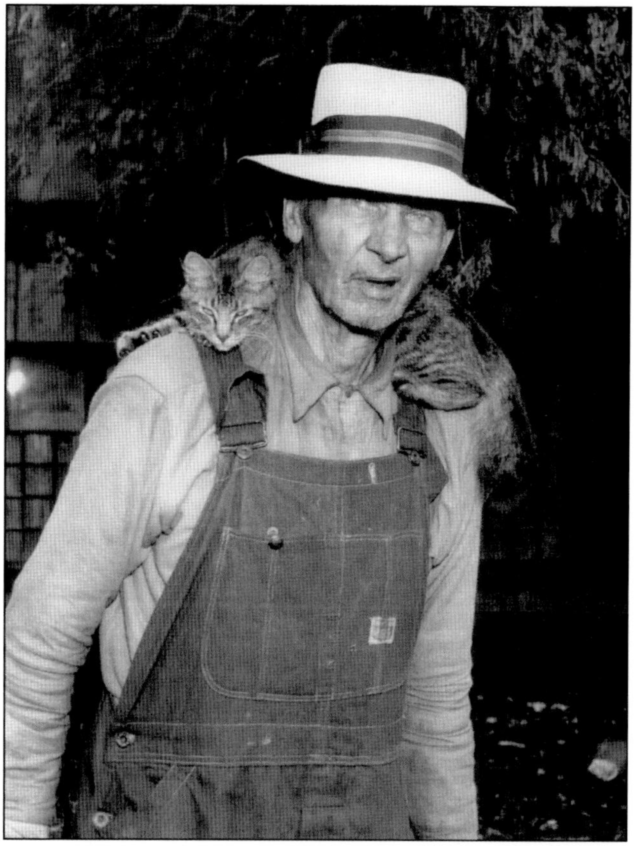

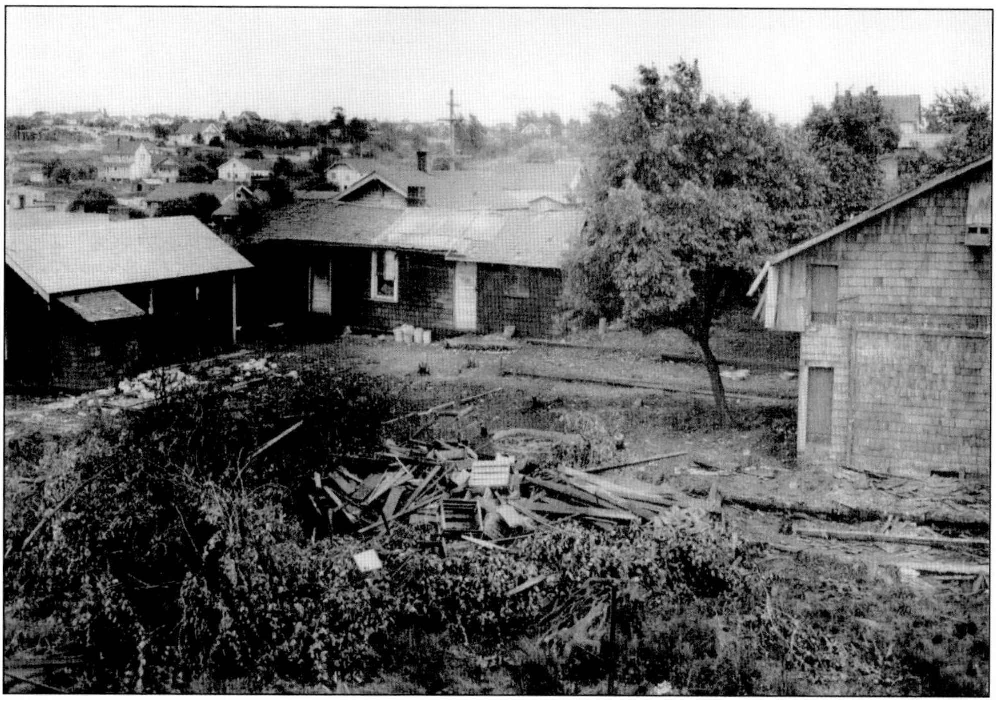

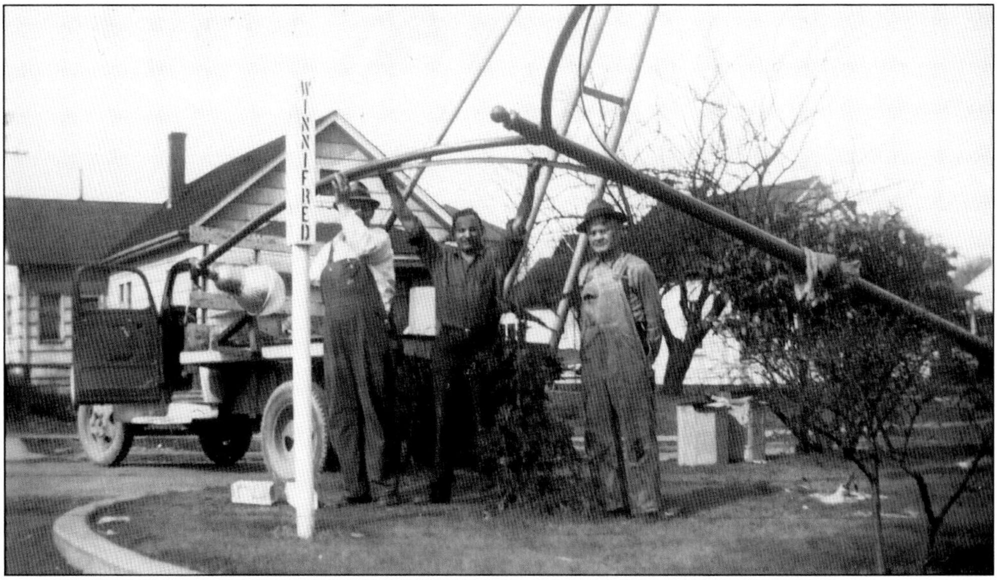

New streetlights were an important community event. Town employees helped set up new lights along the median on Winnifred Street. Shown on March 18, 1949, are, from left to right, Mr. Kerney, Joe Ferri, and Sig Elleflow, who also read electrical meters for the town. These lights stood tall for decades and were replaced in 2010. (TR.)

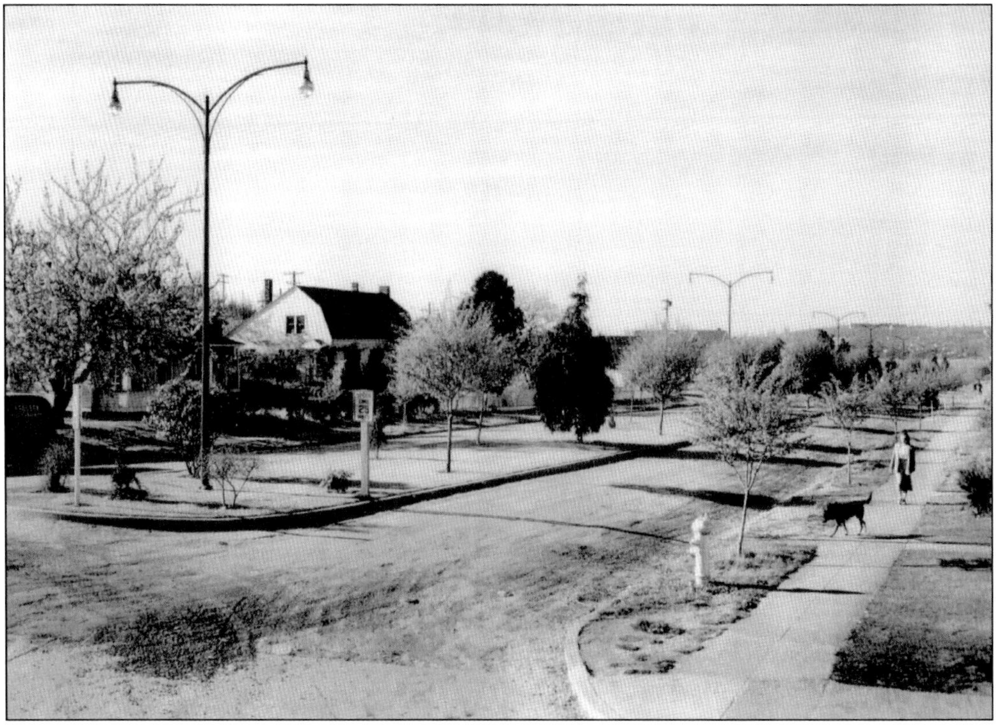
The new lights towered above the trees along Winnifred Street. This view looking north from North Fifty-first Street shows the road was still unpaved. One of the oldest homes in Ruston stands in the middle of the picture; it belonged to J.P. Garrison, former mayor and council member. His family remained active in local politics until his daughter-in-law Etta died in 1994. (TPL.)

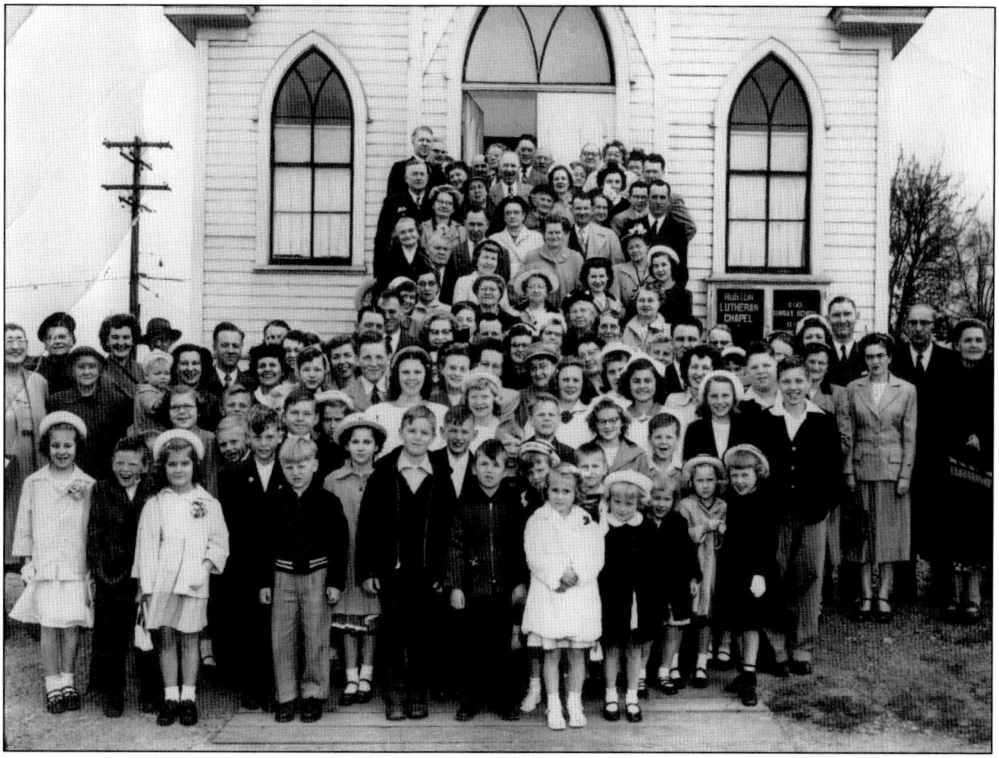

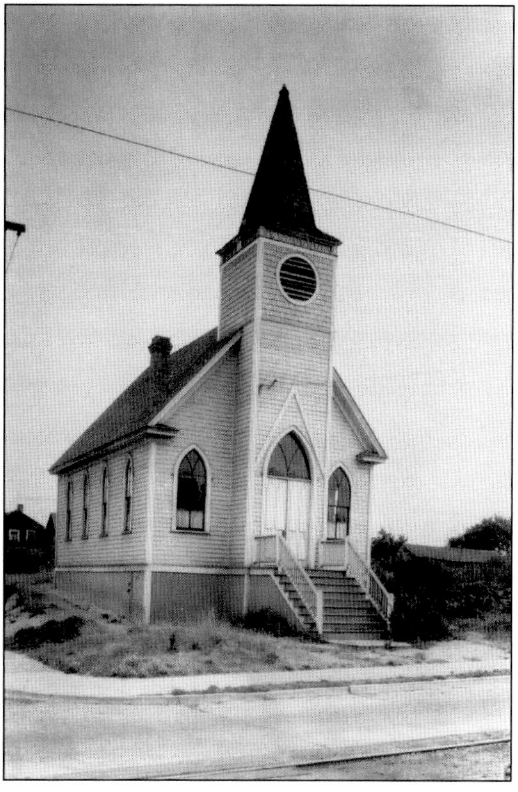

The Ruston Lutheran Chapel and congregation (above) are seen here in April 1953. As a typical industrial town, Ruston only had two church buildings but many more taverns at any given time. First called St. James English Evangelical Lutheran Church, the chapel on the corner of North Fifty-second and Pearl Streets (right) was known by many names over the last century: the Smelter Church, Ruston Chapel, Ruston Lutheran Church, and First Swedish Lutheran Church. There is no longer any congregation that meets inside the small space. The building housed antique shops in the 1970s until 2005 and is now available as a wedding chapel. (TPL.)

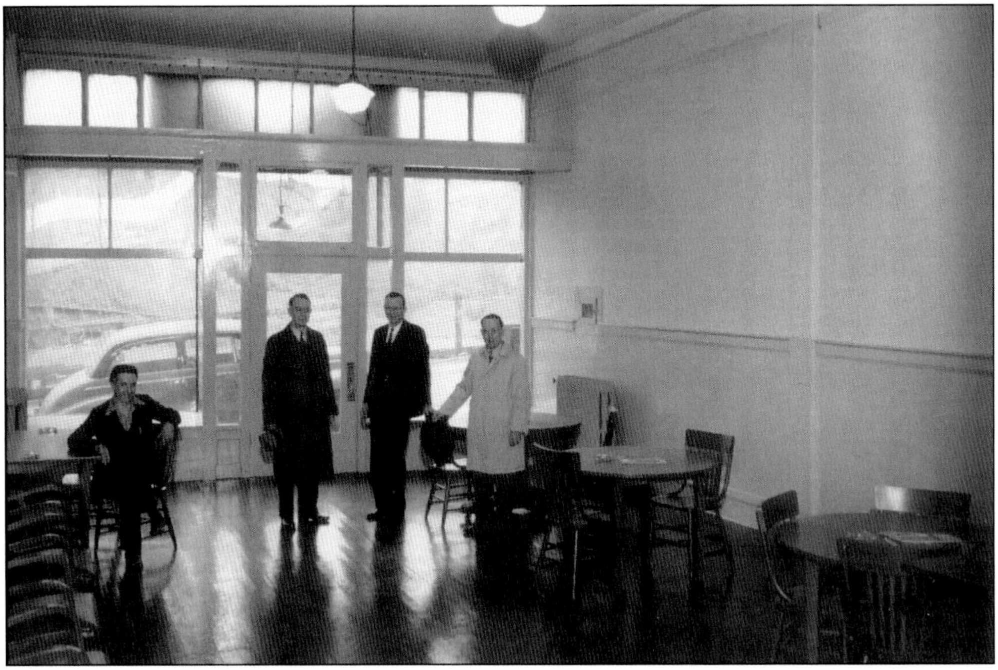

When World War II increased demand for copper, smelter operations ramped up. The Tacoma Housing Authority built the Ruston Terrace Dormitory on Commercial Street to house 60 men to work at the smelter. A second building was later added. Pictured above are chairman of the housing authority Fred Shoemaker, W.C. Tapling, Harold Bergerson, and facility manager Leo Wingard (seated and the only man specifically identified). Wingard bought the property, and the area eventually became a junkyard. The deserted barracks were full of childhood legends. There are stories about a murder there during the war, and children would sneak in and roller-skate in the old cafeteria. Wingard ran for election often and almost won a seat in 1977, when he tied with Doris Sage. The tie was broken by a coin toss, with Wingard losing. He later claimed the election was rigged and sued the county elections department. (TPL.)

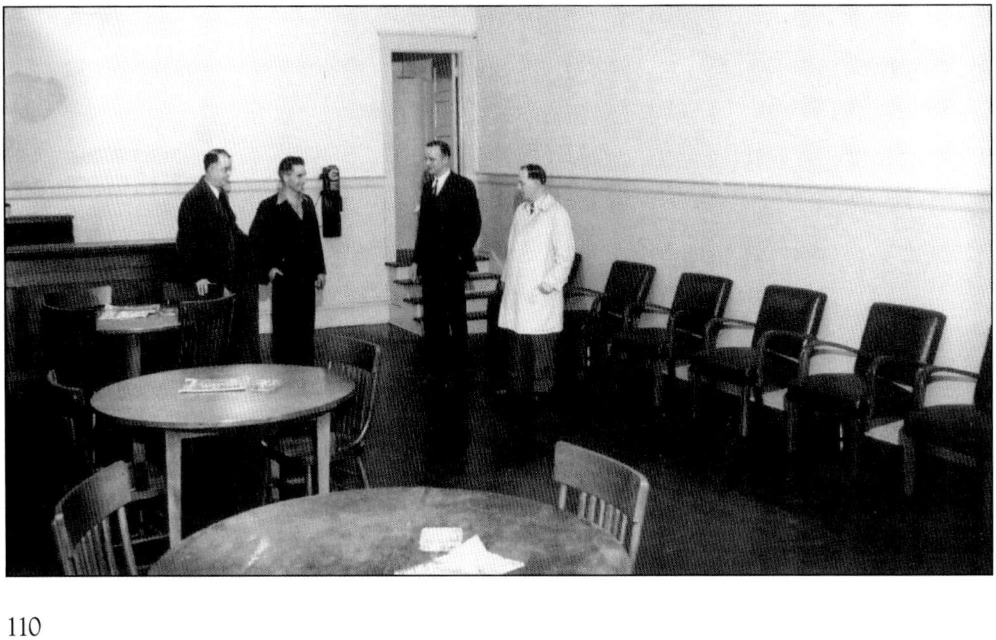

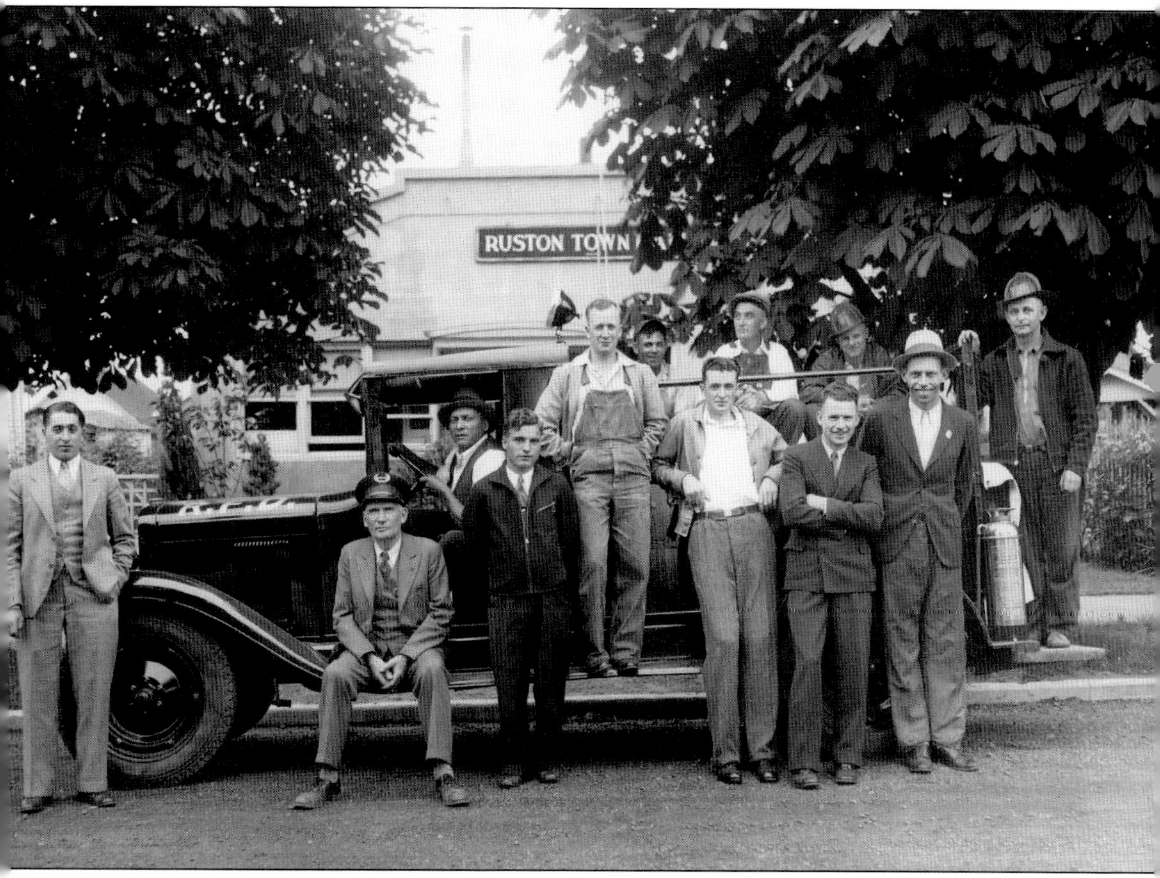

This 1935 photograph shows the new Ruston fire engine and, presumably, the volunteer firemen at the time. A young Owen Gallagher is standing in the white shirt in front (third from right), but most of the rest of the men are unnamed. Owen grew up in Ruston in the home his father built on the southeast corner of North Fifty-second and Winnifred Streets. Owen served on the town council and as mayor for over 30 years. His son Daniel lived in the same house until the early 2000s. Owen built the house on the corner of Fifty-third and Winnifred Streets, mostly by hand, even digging out the basement using shovels and wheelbarrows. Jeff Tallman is pictured here in the overalls (fourth from right). Tallman, who served as a janitor for the Ruston School after retiring from the smelter, was from a second-generation Ruston family. His son Pete also lived in town and was one of the last ASARCO employees to retire from the plant. Victor DiLoreto stands on the far left in the suit. DiLoreto also worked for the town. (TR.)

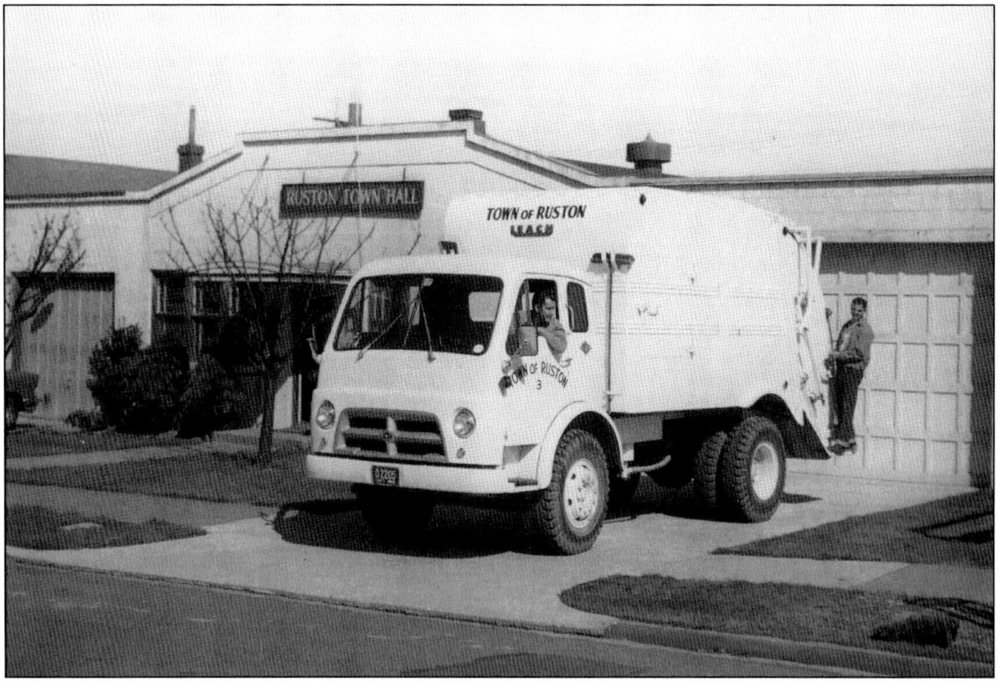

The town's new garbage truck was a source of pride in March 1958. Shown are driver Leroy Linke and laborer Victor DiLoreto. Linke and DiLoreto made their homes in town for decades after this photograph was made. (TR.)

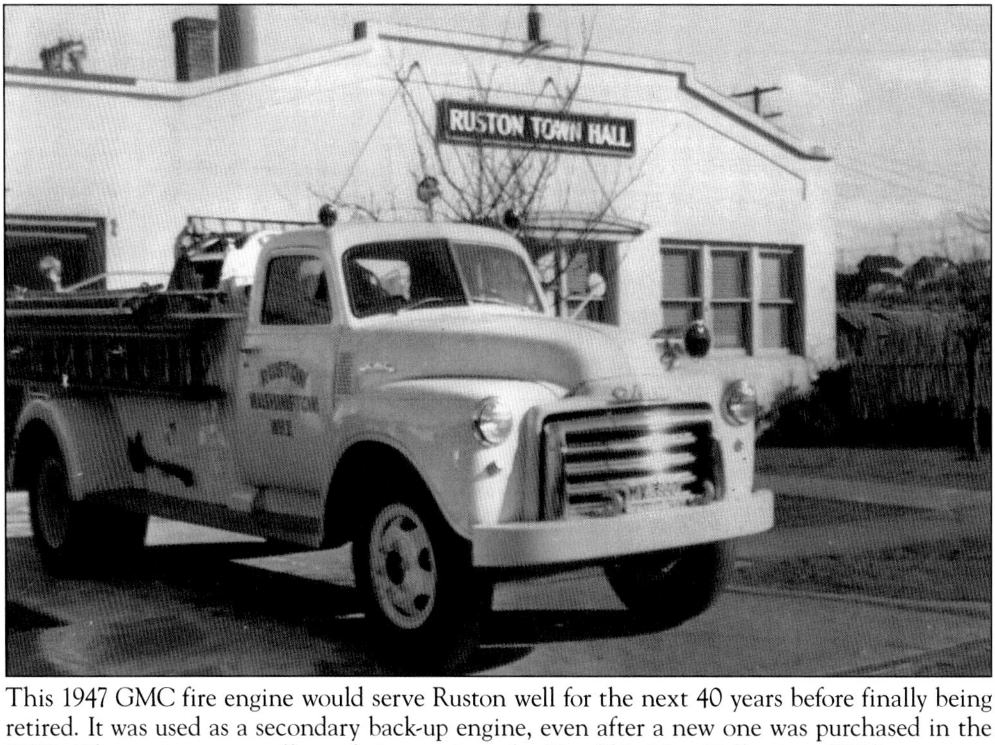

This 1947 GMC fire engine would serve Ruston well for the next 40 years before finally being retired. It was used as a secondary back-up engine, even after a new one was purchased in the 1980s. The engine eventually made its way into the Harold LeMay Collection. (TR.)

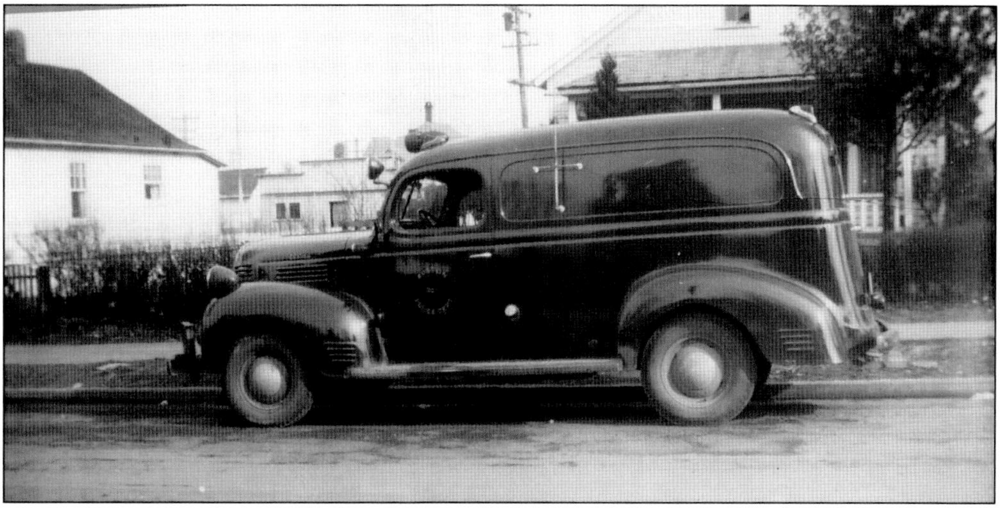

The Ruston Police Department logo can be seen on the door of the new police vehicle in this undated photograph. Note the radio antenna on the side and room for prisoners in the back. This may have been the vehicle that led to Marshal Kerney's decision to quit. (TR.)

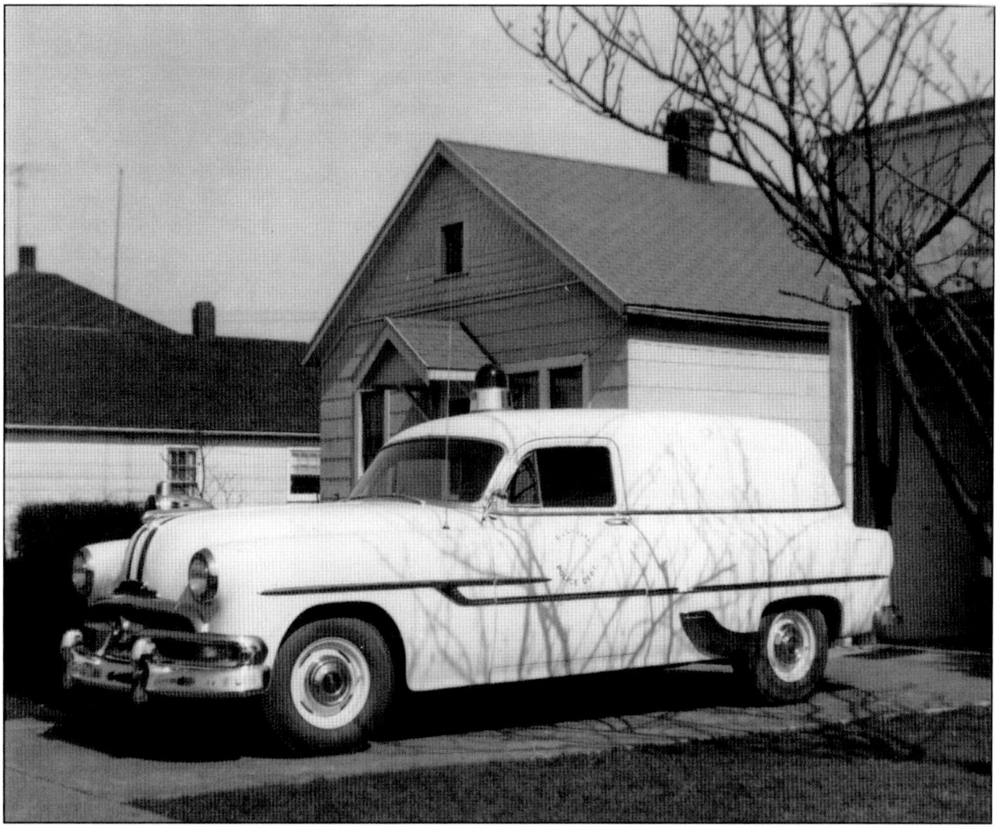

Medical aid has been available to Ruston residents for a long time. This 1953 ambulance was stationed in a garage on one side of town hall, with the fire engine on the other side. The house pictured behind the ambulance belonged to Myrtle Johnson, who sold it to the town in 2005; it now serves as a bunkhouse for firefighters. (TR.)

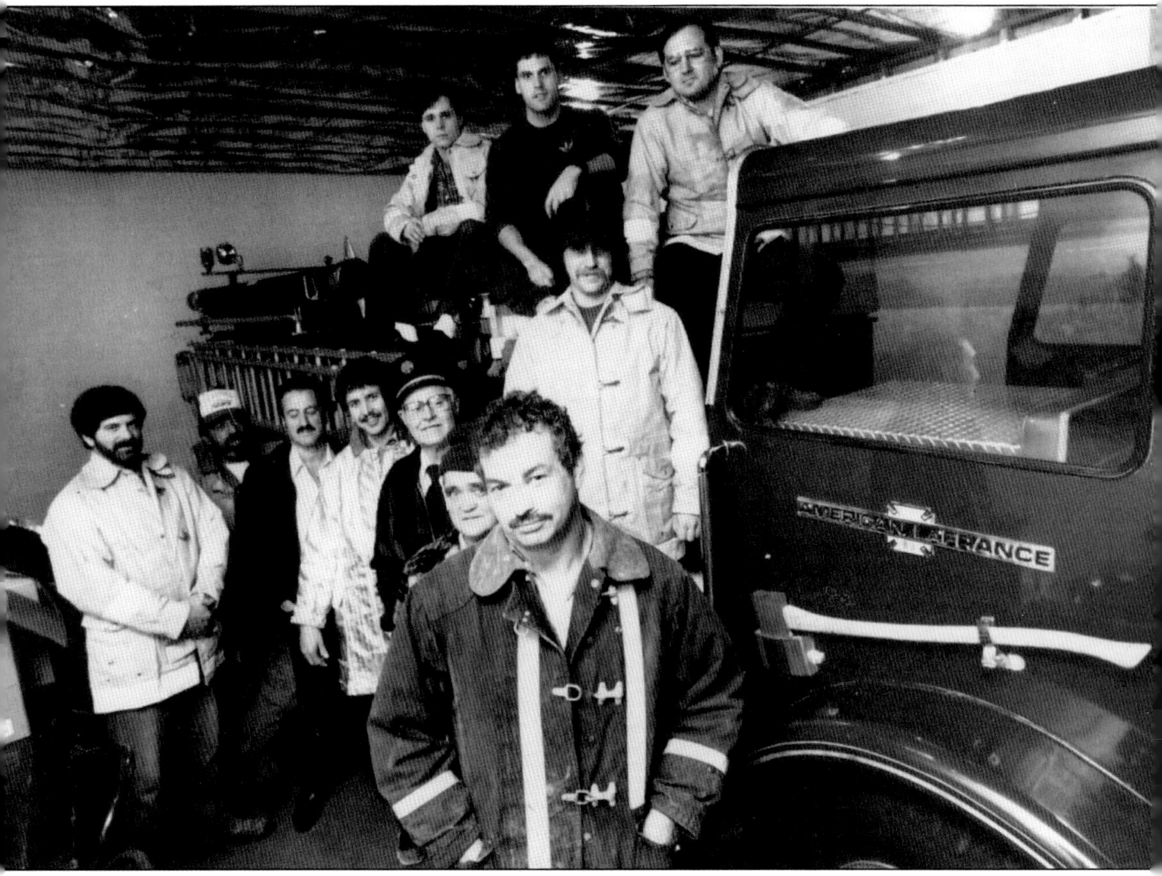

After the smelter closure in 1985, the town contracted with Tacoma for fire services for a brief time. The high cost soon brought Ruston back to a volunteer department. Another political storm had ensued in 1978, when the mayor took the unusual step of appointing the police chief as head of the volunteer fire department. The fire chief and five firemen resigned. The change did not last long, and the department returned to a separate operation. Pictured are some members of the 1980s department, with chief Gerald Tritt in front. Behind him are, from left to right, Don Torbet, unidentified, Frank Ross (owner of Ruston Inn Restaurant), unidentified, former chief Elmer Schoenecker, and assistant chief Tommy Brosseau. On top the truck are unidentified, Joe Mondeau, and Jim Pickett. Standing behind Chief Tritt is Steve Taylor. (Carol Tritt.)

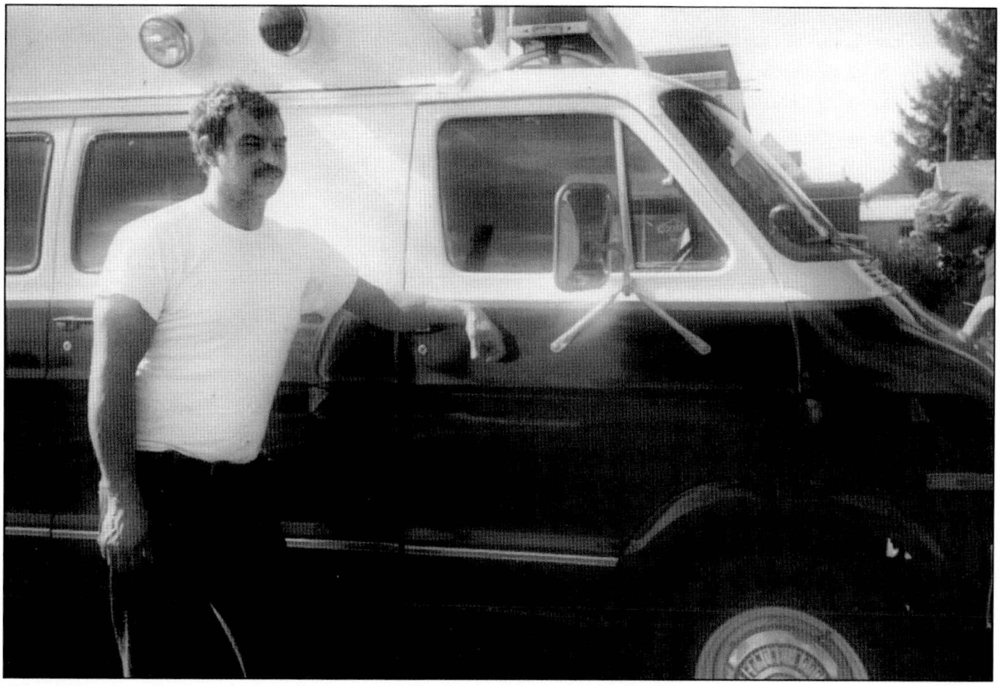

Chief Tritt's wife, Carol, founded a Firefighters Auxiliary branch. The group raised funds to purchase this medical aid van and equipment in the 1990s. Although no longer available to transport residents, it brought the necessary medical equipment to the doorsteps of those in need. (Carol Tritt.)

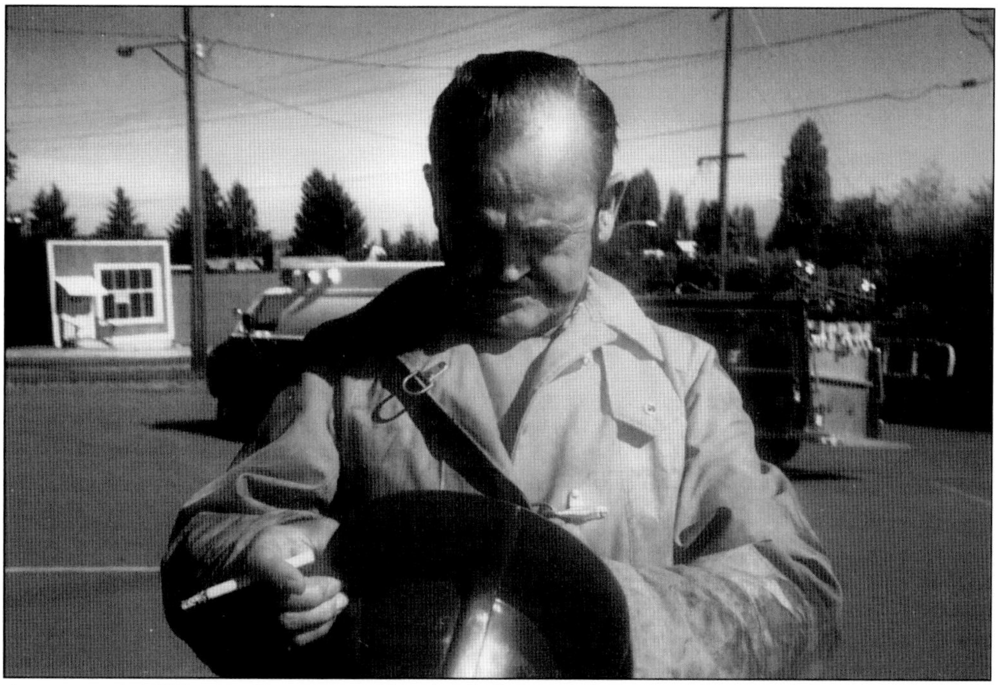

Assistant chief Tommy Brosseau studies his helmet in this 1987 photograph. Brosseau worked as the town maintenance chief for many years in addition to volunteering with the local fire department. (Carol Tritt.)

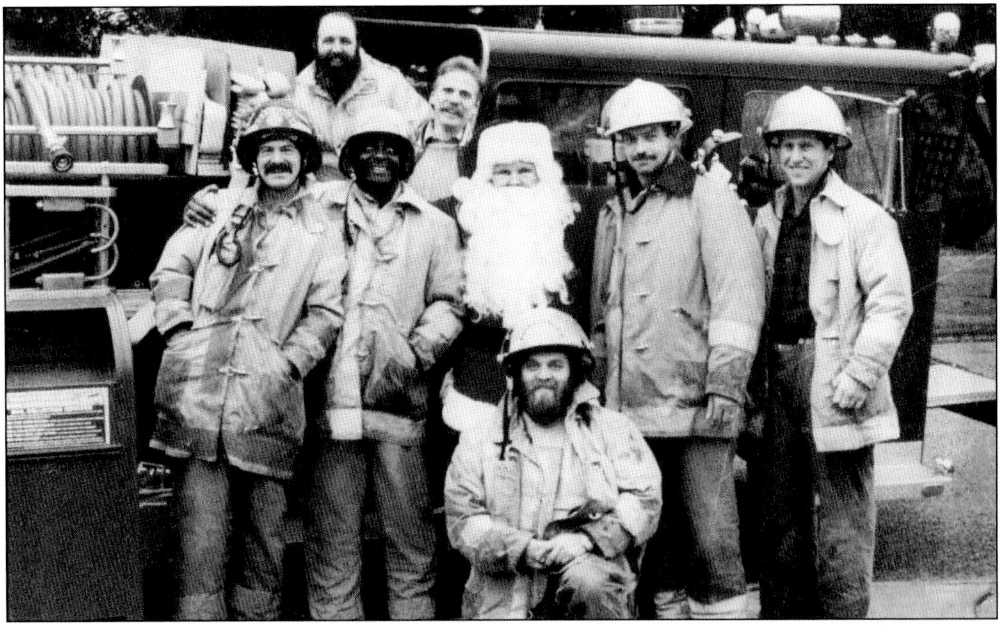

The fire department brings Santa to town each Christmas. Pictured from left to right are Don Torbet, Phil Parker, Steve Hanna, Craig Fletcher, Santa (Mike Hagen), Steve Tucker, Gerald Tritt, and Steve Taylor. Tucker and Taylor are the town maintenance men. Parker was a longtime council member. Because the air mask would not seal over the beard, he was later asked to shave or leave the department. He chose to keep his signature beard. (TR.)

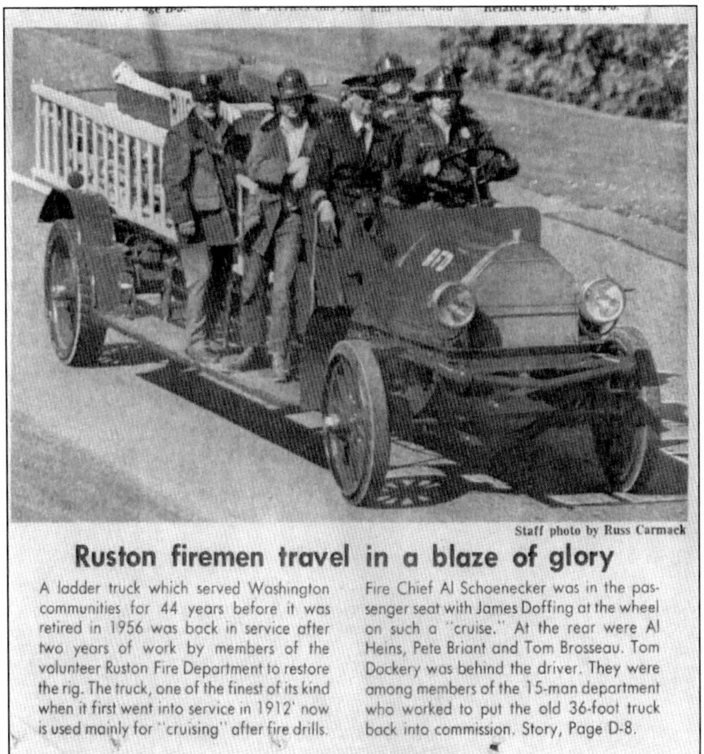

Staff photo by Russ Carmack

Ruston firemen travel in a blaze of glory

A ladder truck which served Washington communities for 44 years before it was retired in 1956 was back in service after two years of work by members of the volunteer Ruston Fire Department to restore the rig. The truck, one of the finest of its kind when it first went into service in 1912' now is used mainly for "cruising" after fire drills. Fire Chief Al Schoenecker was in the passenger seat with James Doffing at the wheel on such a "cruise." At the rear were Al Heins, Pete Briant and Tom Brosseau. Tom Dockery was behind the driver. They were among members of the 15-man department who worked to put the old 36-foot truck back into commission. Story, Page D-8.

Former Ruston fire chief Elmer Schoenecker purchased this antique fire engine for personal use. Other Ruston volunteer firefighters helped restore the old engine to full capacity. Schoenecker often gave local children rides and showcased the rig in local parades. (TR.)

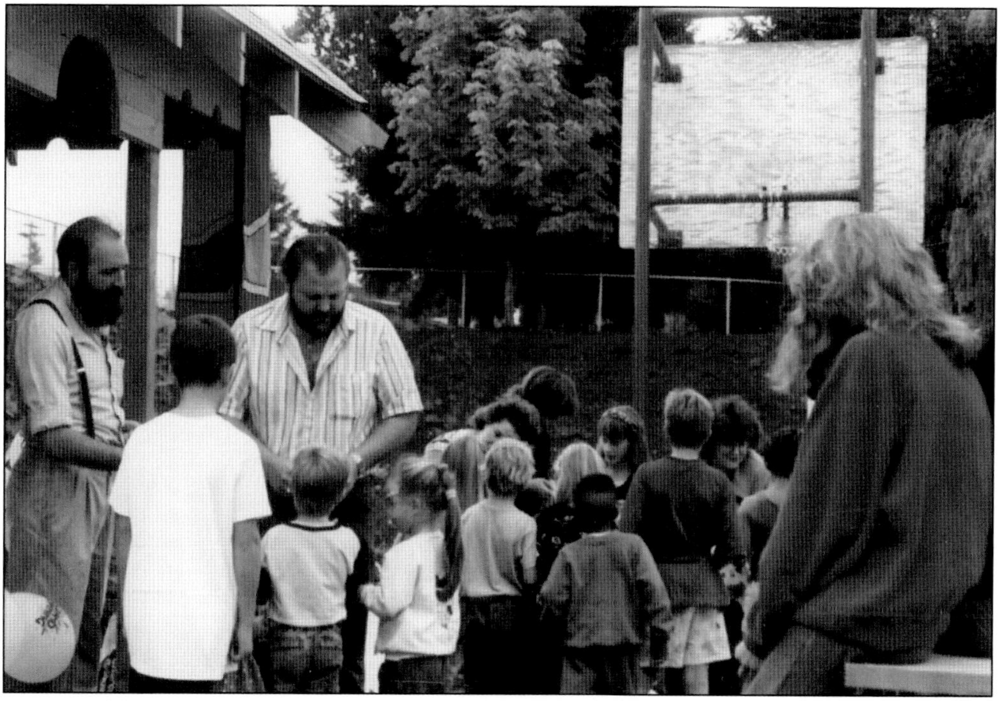

Ruston celebrated Washington State's centennial with the dedication of a new gazebo in Rust Playfield. Play, basketball, and baseball areas were already in use by the time of this 1989 photograph. Shown at the far left are mayor Phil Parker (left) and Mike Hagen. (TR.)

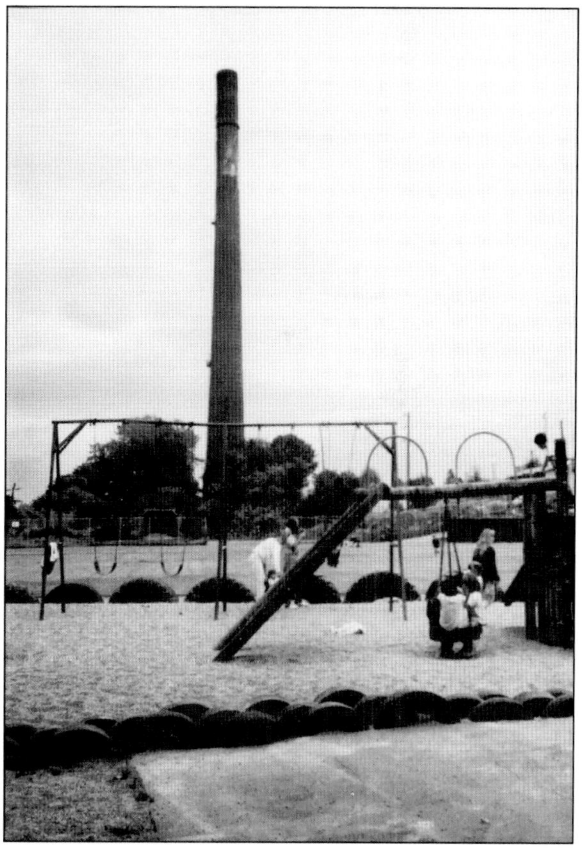

The shuttered smelter stack still dominated the Ruston skyline until its demolition in 1993. Once a sign of prosperity and high-wage jobs to many in the local community, it was a source of pride. Mayor Parker had once dreamed of putting a restaurant on top. It began to tilt in its final years of disuse. (TR.)

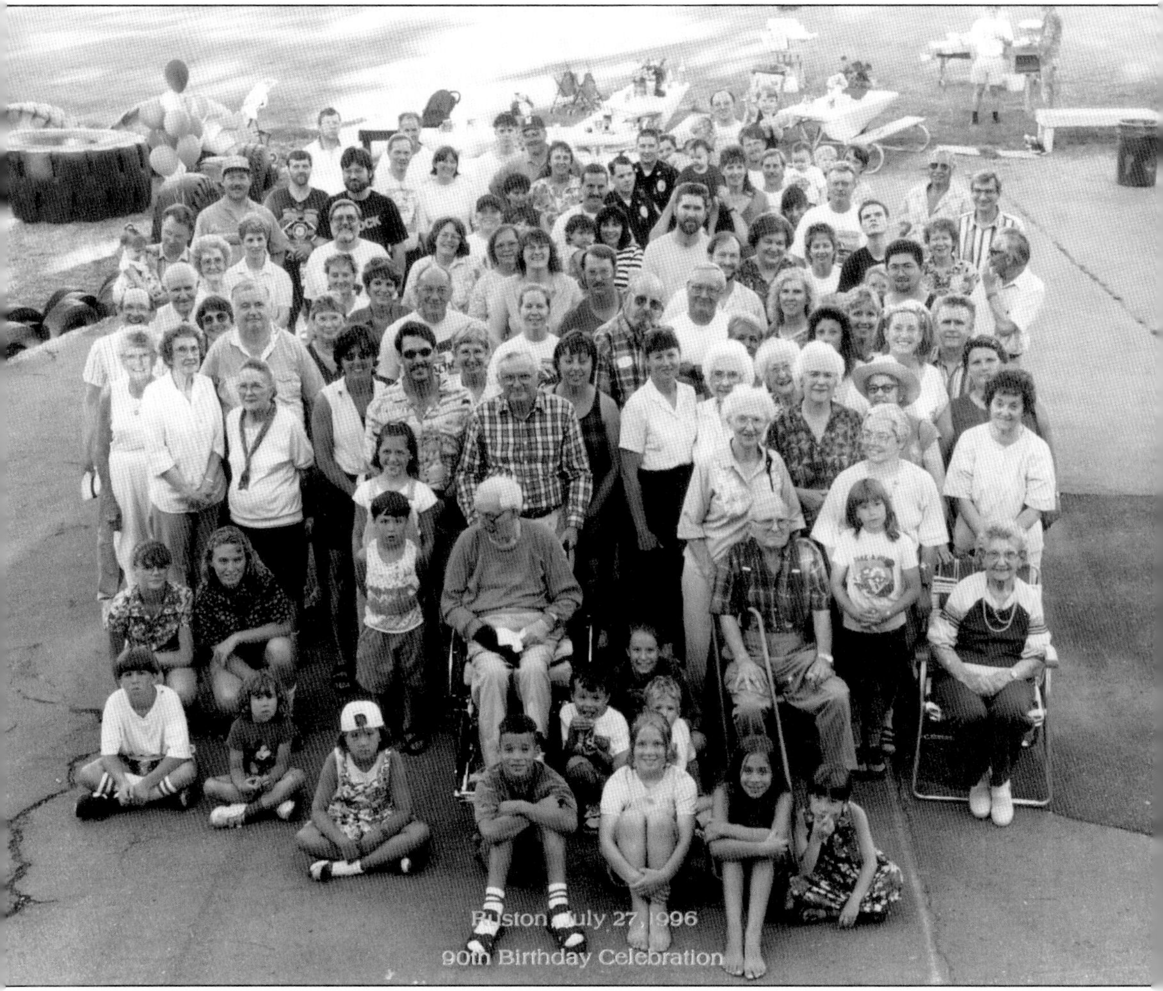

Ruston celebrated its 90th birthday in 1996 with a picnic at the Rust Playfield. There are too many people pictured here to mention by name, but sitting in the wheelchair in front is Leo Wingard. In the second row of people standing, Myrtle Johnson is third from the right, three people to the right of Leo's son Jim (standing behind his father). Loretta Prettyman, who took over for Ford Downie as town clerk, is second from right, next to Johnson. Prettyman served almost 30 years and Downie, over 40. Many residents pictured here reported that Ruston's world once revolved around the smelter whistle. The sound at each shift change brought an instant flood of workers. The whistle was a signal for children to hurry home, the call for firemen to respond to help, and it even blew to welcome in the New Year. Even though her husband walked down the hill to work each morning, Myrtle Johnson talked about how the blast was her signal to take the car to pick him up each afternoon. John Krillich described the rush after the whistle: "The sidewalks were just black with men. It was a veritable parade up and down Pearl Street." (TR.)

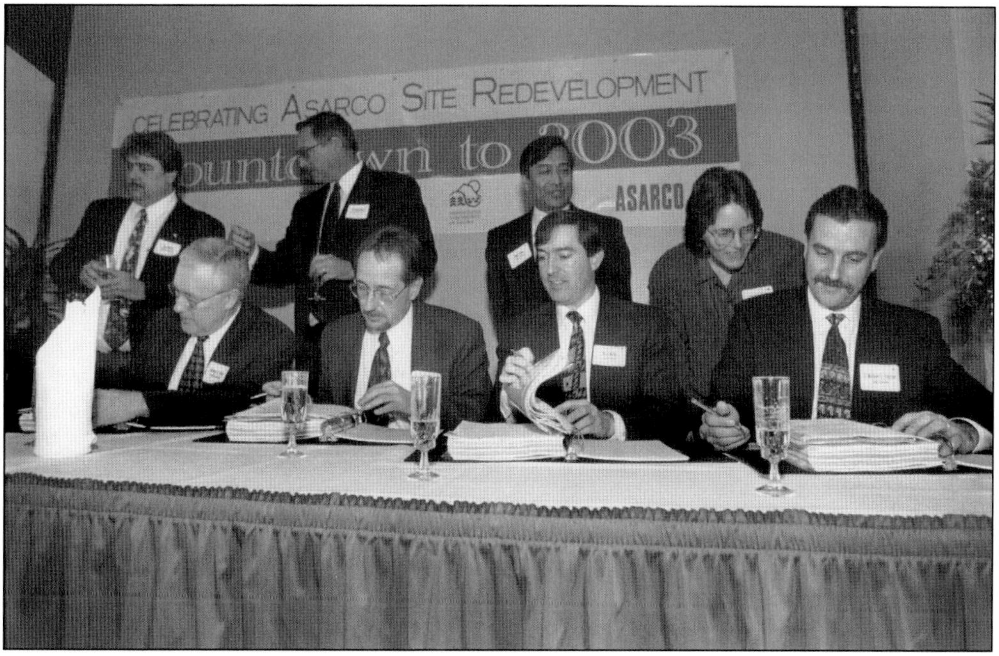

Ruston joined Tacoma, Metropolitan Park District, and ASARCO in signing what was called the Definitive Agreement. The agreement culminated years of planning and negotiating on the redevelopment plans for the ASARCO smelter property and adjacent breakwater peninsula owned by Metro Parks. ASARCO went bankrupt before all the terms of the agreement could be realized, and the property sold in 2006. (KP.)

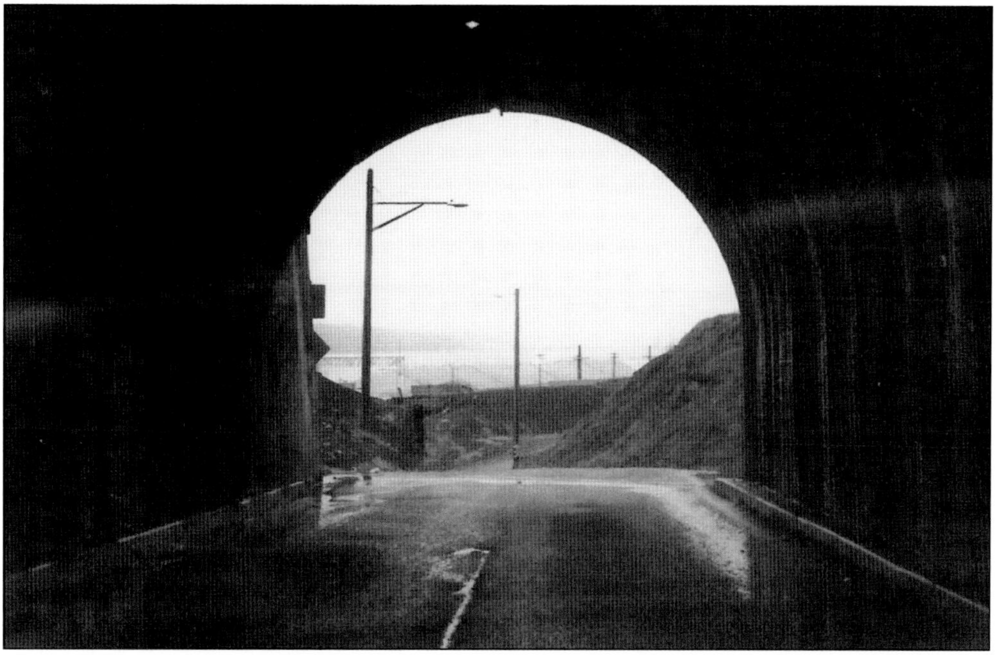

One of the more distinctive features in town was the car tunnel under the hillside where the stack once stood. Icicles formed in winter, cars honked, and bicyclists braved the narrow road. It is slated to be filled with dirt and a new road completed by early 2012. (Courtesy of Beth Torbet.)

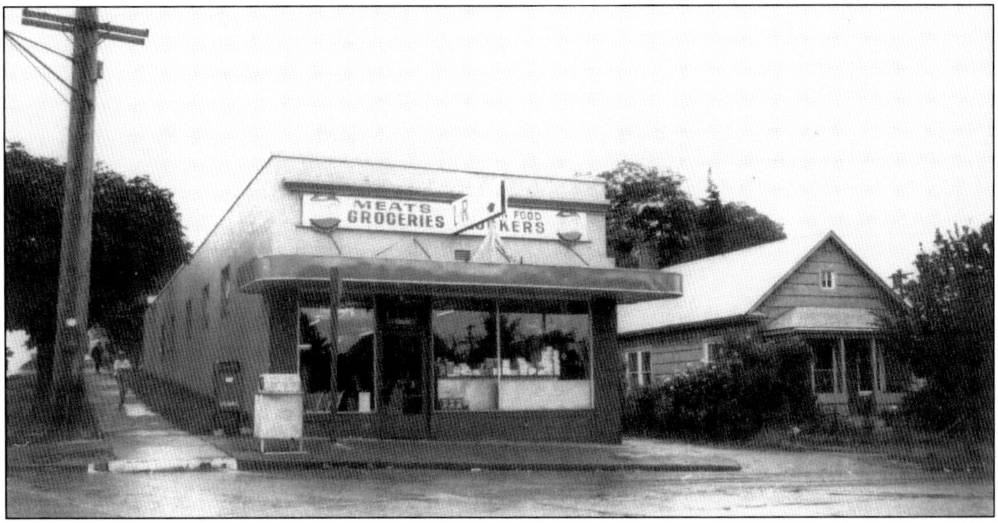

Commercial buildings have come and gone from many locations in Ruston over the years. After the 1917 fire burned his business on North Shirley Street, Ed Olson moved his general store to this location at North Fifty-first and Winnifred Streets by 1919. The store went through several renditions; the one shown here is from 1968. Don's Ruston Market now occupies the building, operated by Don and Beth Torbet. (TPL.)

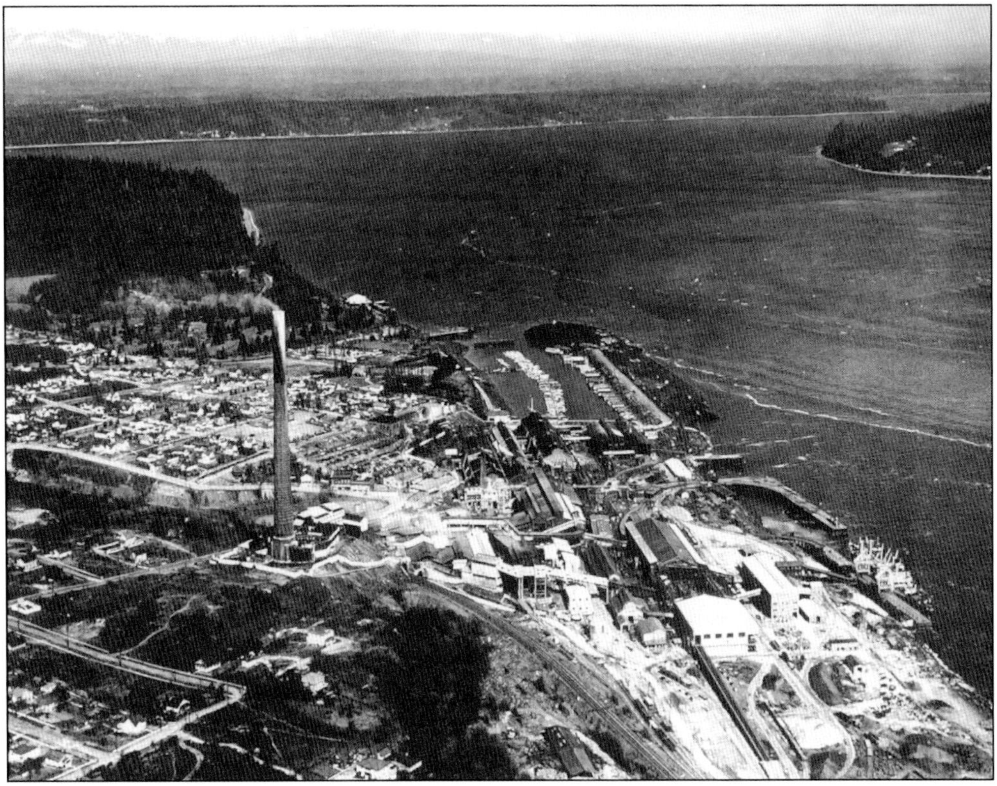

Always the center of any discussion of Ruston, the giant industrial smelter complex is shown in this view, looking west towards the Narrows and Gig Harbor. The Funland amusement area is visible in the distance, on the east side of the end of Pearl Street. (KP.)

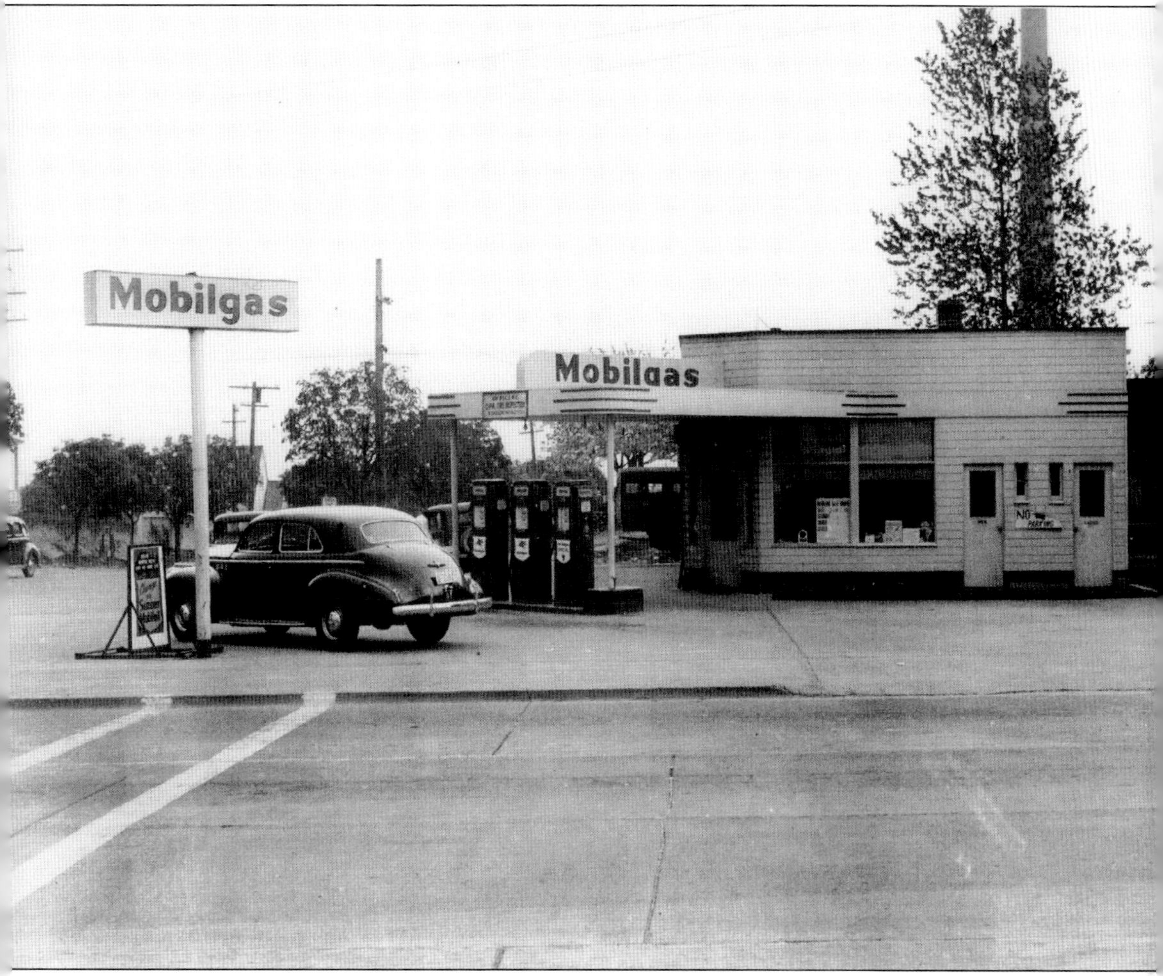

There are few photographs of Ruston's signature commercial corner at North Fifty-first and Pearl Streets. The southwest quadrant has held a gas station for over 70 years, as evidenced in this 1945 image. The ever-present stack can be seen behind the tree. Local banker Richard VanDeMark locked himself in the bathroom of the service station and committed suicide five years before this picture was taken. The 29-year-old man lived with his parents on North Ninth Street. He left a note at the scene, but no motive could be determined. Most residents lived, worked, and played within the town limits. With the many taverns in town, drunkenness was often a problem. In 1912, a man was sentenced to 33 days for "giving intoxicating liquor to a habitual drunkard." In April that same year, the Ruston judge suspended five days of jail time for two men charged with disorderly conduct when they volunteered to leave town. Someone was even given a $1 fine for "insulting and using profane language in public." (TPL.)

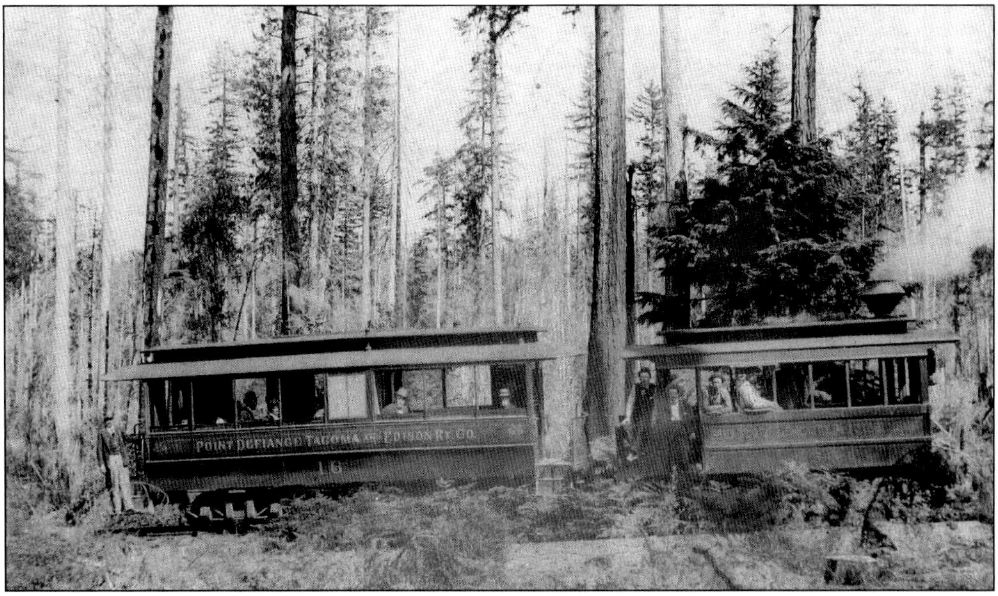

Ruston's neighboring Point Defiance Park is a popular recreational destination, second only to Mount Rainier in Washington State. Before automobiles, people traveled by streetcars, like this 1890 Edison Railway car that would have traveled through Ruston. Passengers had to pay an extra nickel at North Forty-fifth and Orchard Streets for the rest of the ride to the park. The stop was dubbed "Poor Man's Corner" for those who chose to forego the extra nickel fee by walking from there. (TPL.)

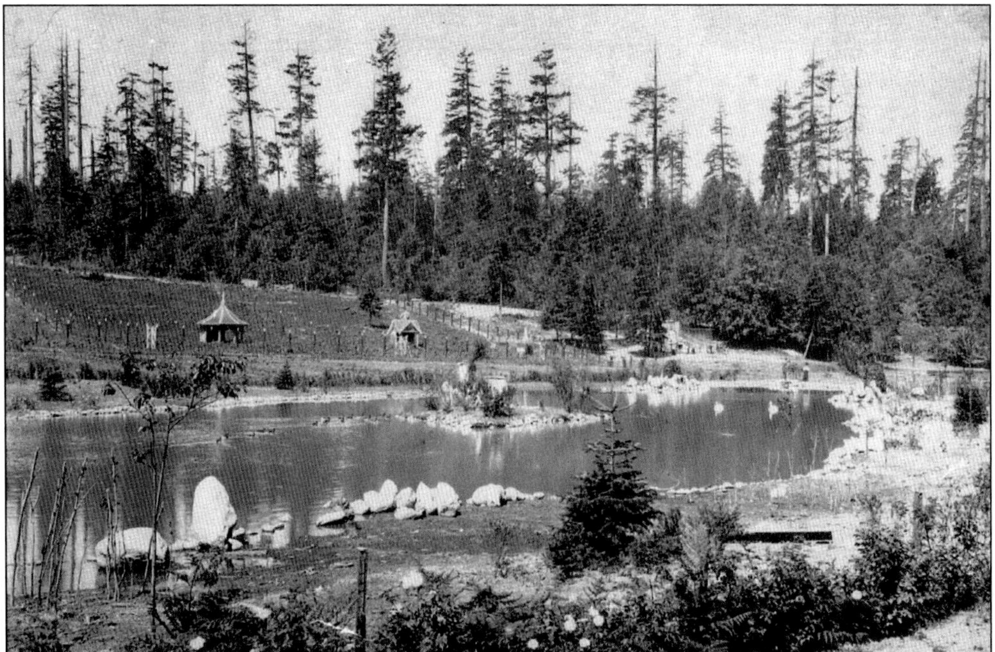

The 1903 lake at Point Defiance was designed by landscape architect and park superintendent Ebenezer Roberts. He was a driving force in helping Tacoma secure ownership of the park in 1905. Animal pens are laid out on the far side of the lake for buffalo and deer. (TPL.)

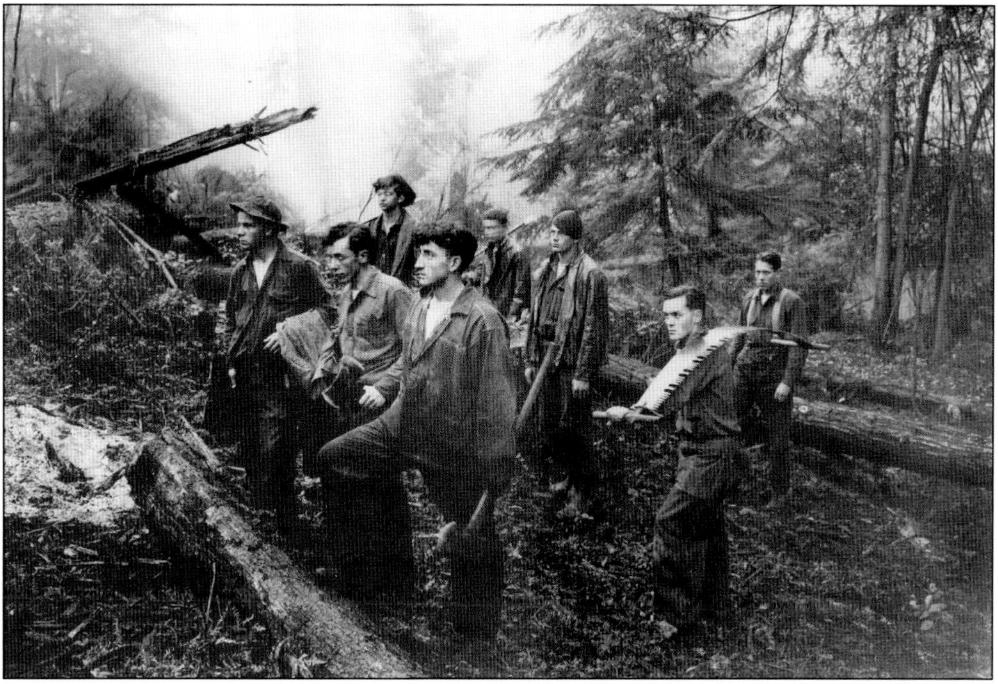

Roosevelt's Civilian Conservation Corps (CCC) had a hand in developing Point Defiance Park. Most of the men stationed here were from the Northwest. George Newman is pictured front and center with a crew working to clear brush to reduce fire danger. (TPL.)

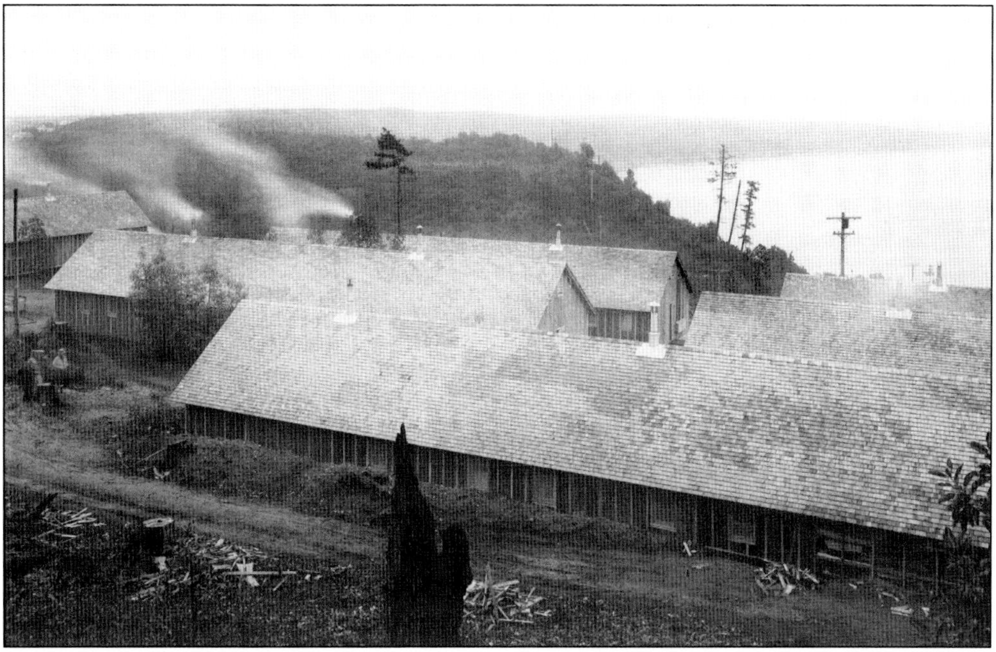

The men lived at Point Defiance in a camp with 15 buildings, which included a hospital and a barbershop. They worked seven hours a day, Monday through Friday, and were paid $30 per month, $25 of which was sent home to their families. Free schooling was offered in the evening. The camp was located just south of Fort Nisqually. (TPL.)

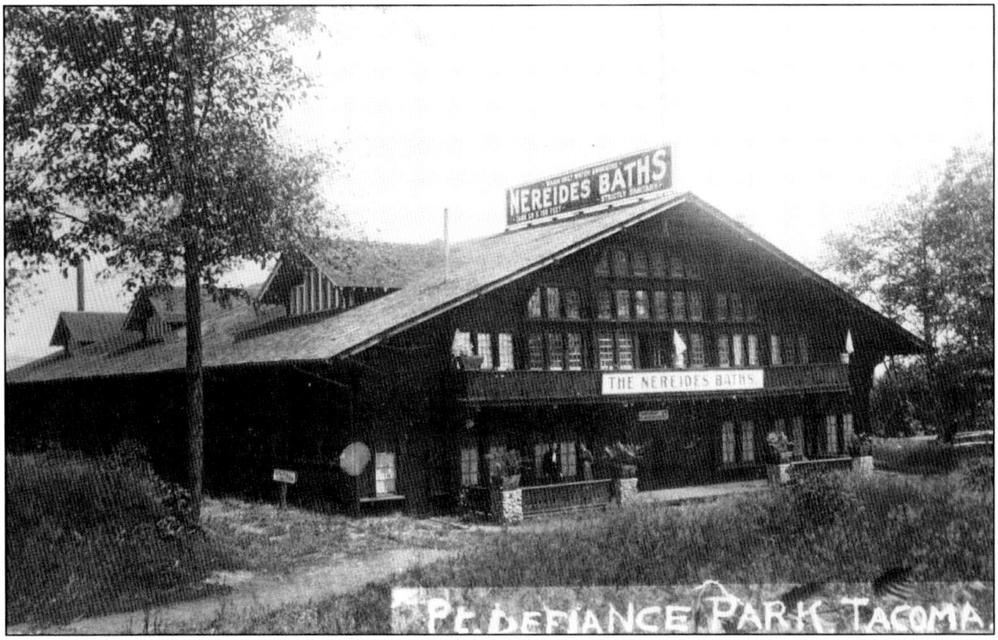

One of the unique uses of the park was Nereides Baths. The building on the bluff pumped up water from Puget Sound, which was heated for patrons. The sign atop promises the baths to be "strictly sanitary." This was the first indoor swimming facility in Tacoma. (TR.)

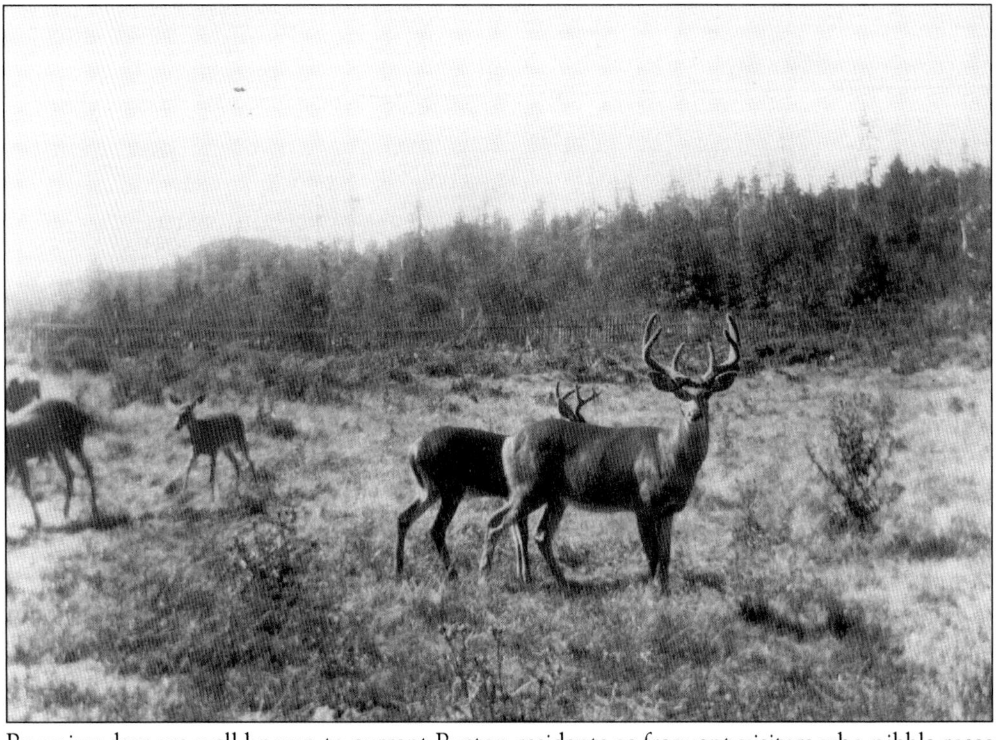
Roaming deer are well-known to current Ruston residents as frequent visitors who nibble roses and other local delicacies. In 1899, deer were penned near the lake in Point Defiance Park for the public to view. (TPL.)

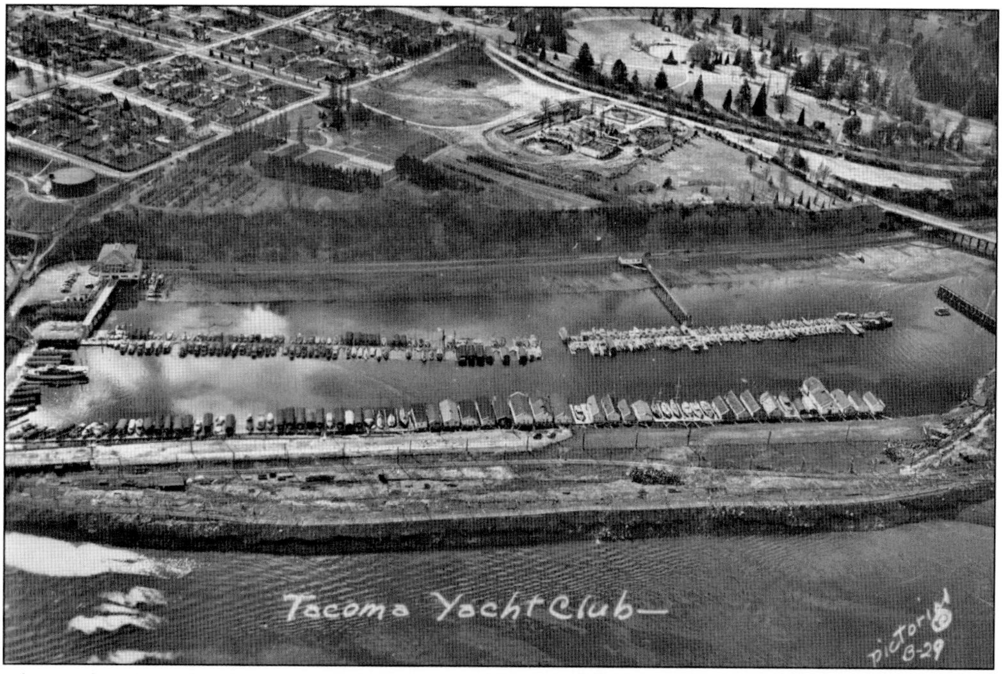

This undated aerial image of the breakwater and marina shows the slag peninsula in its early stages. More land was formed over decades of pouring molten slag onto this shoreline. (Robin Paterson.)

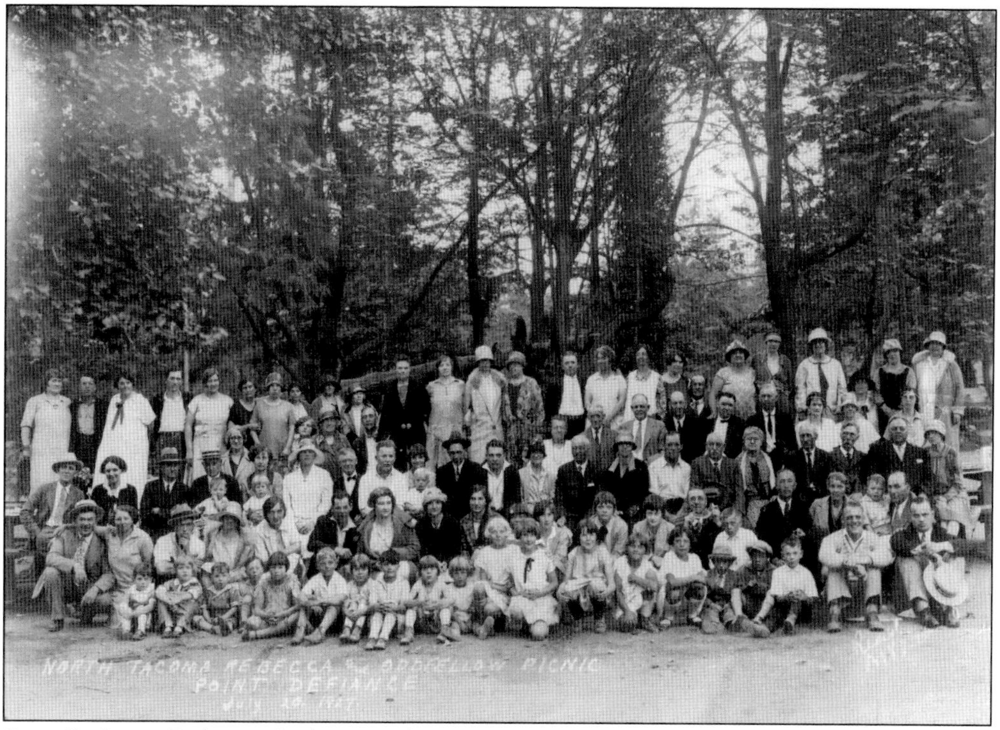

Point Defiance Park was the location for many a large picnic a century ago, just as it is today. This July 1927 photograph captures the North Tacoma Rebekah and Odd Fellows picnic. (Don and Beth Torbet.)

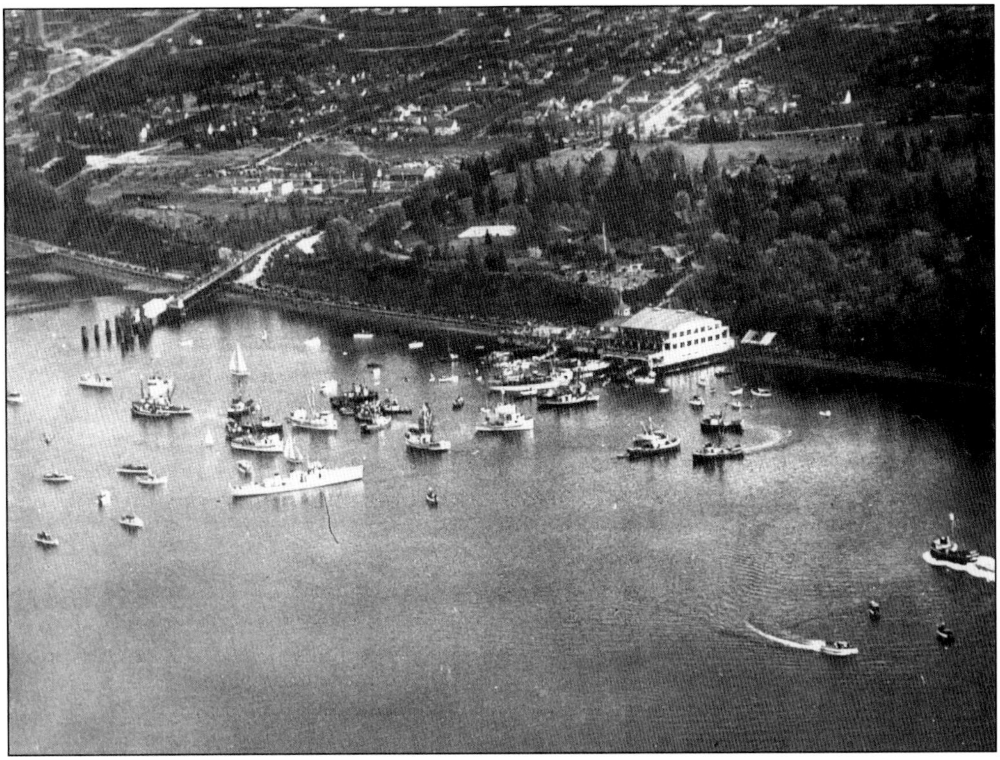

This undated photograph of the original boathouse at Point Defiance Park shows the developing town of Ruston in the upper left. It also outlines how close Ruston is to this regional treasure. (KP.)

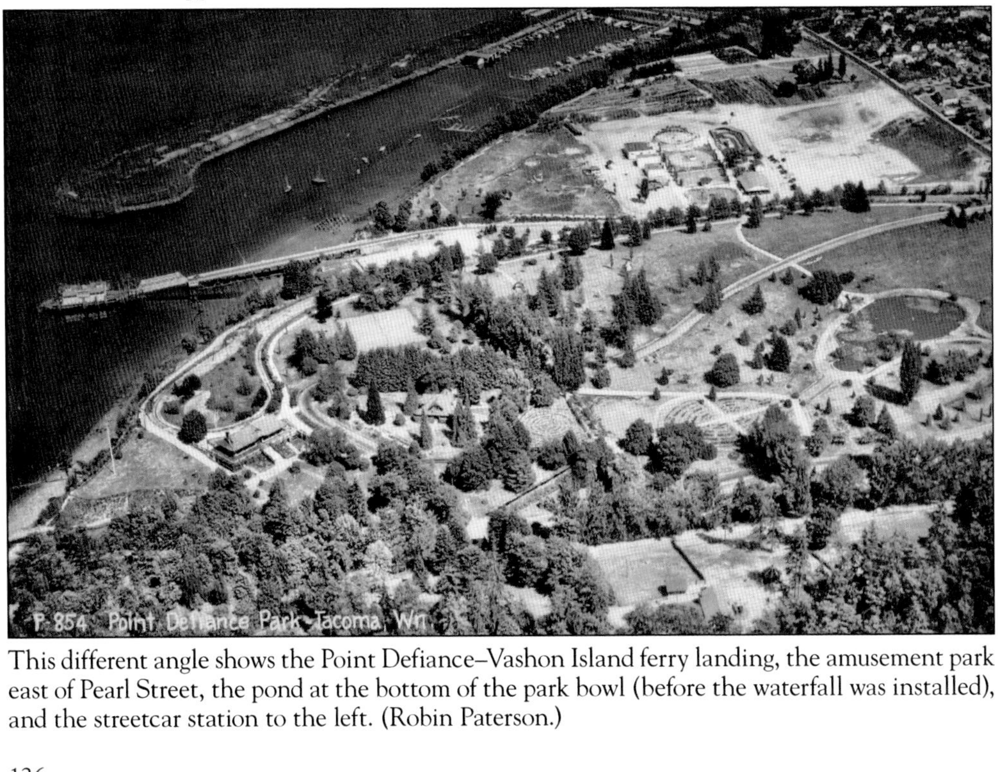

This different angle shows the Point Defiance–Vashon Island ferry landing, the amusement park east of Pearl Street, the pond at the bottom of the park bowl (before the waterfall was installed), and the streetcar station to the left. (Robin Paterson.)

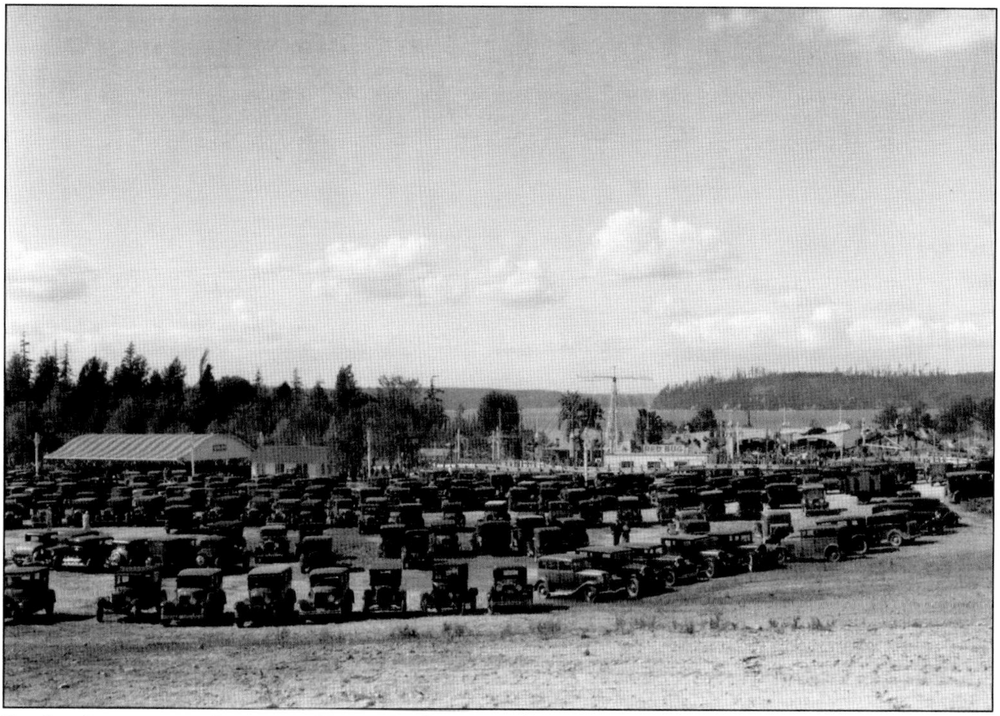

Funland was a popular part of Point Defiance Park in the 1930s and 1940s. The carnival rides are visible behind the full parking lot in this 1933 photograph, looking north from Fifty-fourth Street along the east side of Pearl Street. The carnival-type rides drew many soldiers from Fort Lewis during World War II, as well as generations of Ruston children. (TPL.)

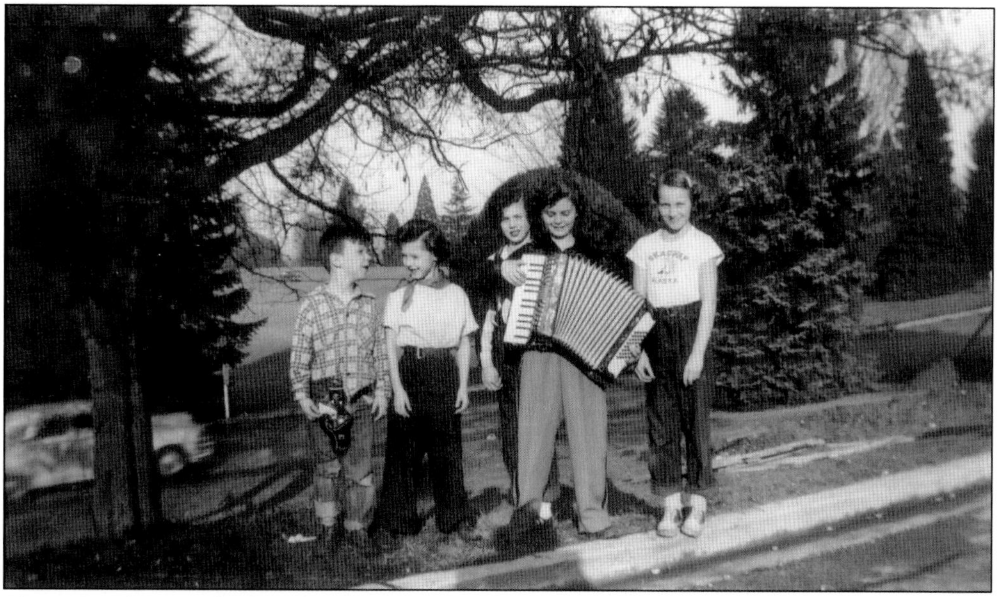

This 1950s photograph of Ruston schoolchildren at Point Defiance Park captures the joy of childhood during a simpler time. Having this spectacular park on its doorstep is one of the many reasons Ruston is such a wonderful community in which to raise a family and build robust connections, which keep the town strong for many more generations to come. (Carol Gore.)